D1126156

JESUS IN THE MEMORY OF THE EARLY CHURCH

JESUS IN THE MEMORY OF THE EARLY CHURCH

Library of Congress Catalog Card No. 76-27072
International Standard Book No. 0-8066-1561-3

Manufactured in the United States of America

CONTENTS

ACKNOWLEDGEMENTS

These essays originally appeared in the following publications:

ANAMNESIS in *Norsk Teologisk Tidsskrift* 47 (1946) and in *Studia Theologica* 1 (1948).

THE PASSION NARRATIVE IN MATTHEW was translated from *New Testament Studies* 1, (1955).

THE PURPOSE OF MARK'S GOSPEL was translated from the *Svensk Exegetisk Arsbok* 22/23 (1958).

ABRAHAM IN LUKE-ACTS appeared originally in *Studies in Luke-Acts: Essays Presented in Honor of Paul Schubert*, ed. by L. Keck and J.L. Martyn, (c) 1966 by Abingdon Press.

THE JOHANNINE CHURCH AND HISTORY is reprinted from *Current Issues in New Testament Interpretation: Essays in Honor of Otto Piper*, ed. by W. Klassen and G.F. Snyder, (c) 1962 by Harper and Row.

CHRIST, CREATION, AND THE CHURCH was originally published in *The Background of the New Testament and its Eschatology: In Honor of Charles Harold Dodd*, (c) 1956 by Cambridge University Press.

THE PARABLES OF GROWTH is from *Studia Theologica* 5 (1951).

Abbreviations

ASNU	Acta seminarii neotestamentici upsaliensis
Bill	H. Strack and P. Billerbeck, *Kommentar zum Neuen Testament*
BO	*Bibliotheca orientalis*
BZNW	Beihefte zur ZNW
CTM	*Concordia Theological Monthly*
DTT	*Dansk teologisk tidsskrift*
EvT	*Evangelische Theologie*
HNT	Handbuch zum Neuen Testament
HUCA	*Hebrew Union College Annual*
JBL	*Journal of Biblical Literature*
JTS	*Journal of Theological Studies*
LCL	Loeb Classical Library
Meyer	H.A.W. Meyer, Kritisch-exegetischer Kommentar über das Neue Testament
NedTT	*Nederlands Theologisch Tijdschrift*
NovT	*Novum Testamentum*
NTS	*New Testament Studies*
NTT	*Norsk Teologisk Tidsskrift*
RHPR	*Revue d'histoire et de philosophie religieuses*
SBT	Studies in Biblical Theology
SBU	*Symbolae biblicae upsalienses*
SEA	*Svensk exegetisk årsbok*
SJT	*Scottish Journal of Theology*
SPB	Studia postbiblica
STK	*Svensk teologisk kvartalskrift*
ST	*Studia theologica*
TDNT	G. Kittel and G. Friedrich (eds.), *Theological Dictionary of the New Testament*
TLZ	*Theologische Literaturzeitung*
TQ	*Theologische Quartalschrift*
TU	Texte und Unterschungen
TZ	*Theologische Zeitschrift*
UUA	Uppsala universitets årsskrift
WMANT	Wissenschaftliche Monographien zum Alten und Neuen Testament
WZKM	*Wiener Zeitschrift für die kunde des Morgenlandes*
ZNW	*Zeitschrift für die neutestamentliche Wissenschaft*
ZRGG	*Zeitschrfit für Religions und Geistesgeschichte*
ZSTh	*Zeitschrift für Systematische Theologie*

To BIRGIT

in memory of many happy years

PREFACE

The title of this volume is derived from the subtitle of the first, programmatic paper, my inaugural address as professor of New Testament at the University of Oslo in 1946. The second essay, on preaching Christ to people who were already Christians, is almost an appendix to the first one. The other essays are, in some way or another, related to the theme of "Anamnesis" as well as to my book *Das Volk Gottes* (Oslo, 1941).

Four of the essays, one on each evangelist, grew out of an attempt, made in the fall of 1957, to prepare a manuscript for a revised English edition of the book. It turned out that I would have had to re-write it completely, and I was not able to do so. When these essays are published together, the reader may detect that in spite of differences of approach, they all deal with the interrelations between Jesus, the church, and Israel, as understood by each of the evangelists. "The Purpose of Luke-Acts" is an expanded version of a paper presented to the New England section of the Society of Biblical Literature in April, 1976; the paper was included as a supplement to the earlier essay on Luke-Acts.

"Christ, Creation, and the Church" elaborates another aspect of the title-essay and broadens the perspective by including other writings as well as the Gospels and Acts. The last essay makes an attempt to recover the meaning of some of Jesus' parables within their original setting and thus to trace the relationship between the message of Jesus himself and the preaching of the church that remembered him. After some hesitation, I decided to include the article in its original form, without any attempt to engage in a discussion with more recent parable research. I have, however, omitted the last pages of the original publication (*StT* 5 [1951] 159-166), which were only loosely related to the specific theme. Some parts of my reflections on Jesus and the church have, in an altered and abbreviated form, been incorporated in the Conclusion to this collection.

Apart from this, I have only made minor, mostly stylistic, changes. Some footnotes have been omitted or abbreviated. No systematic attempt has been made to include recent literature, but some sporadic references have been added. Three appendices to "The Passion Narrative in Matthew" have been omitted; students interested in detailed synoptic comparisons can still find them in *NTS* 1 (1955).

The publication of this volume would not have been possible without the encouragement and help of several former students. Fred O. Francis, Hiram Lester, J. Paul Sampley, and Robert D. Webber first took the initiative and translated the essays from German and French. Joseph D. Shaw translated the essay on Mark from Norwegian. Donald Juel and Paul Donahue helped me to revise the translations and check the notes. My thanks to all of them.

Nils Alstrup Dahl
The Divinity School
Yale University

CHAPTER 1

ANAMNESIS

Memory and Commemoration in Early Christianity[1]

In times past history was considered one of the fine arts. It had its muse, Clio, and the muses were called daughters of Mnemosyne. According to this mythological allegory, history was born from memory. This allegorical language is outdated. History has now become a liberated young woman who looks quite critically upon her maternal ancestors, memory and tradition. However, it is impossible for her to disown them completely. The historical enterprise makes sense only on the presupposition that there is something in the past that deserves to be preserved in memory or to be rescued from oblivion. Historical research must always take into consideration that persons or past events have produced such an impression that the memory of them has been perpetuated.

New Testament studies is the scientific investigation of a collection of writings whose size does not exceed that of the average novel of our time. It is true that the study of these writings offers so many problems that the New Testament scholar ought to be a specialist in a whole series of disciplines. But chairs are especially set aside for the study of these writings because they contain something that is particularly worthy of being retained. They include everything essential that has been preserved for us concerning Jesus and the first Christians. A

---

[1]Inaugural lecture given at the University of Oslo in November, 1946. The lecture was published in French with more complete annotation than has been included here in *ST* 1 (1948), 69-95.

consideration of the place that memory and commemoration occupy in these writings may be of considerable interest for the understanding of the New Testament as a whole.

In itself the New Testament use of the terms designated "memory" and "to remember" does not offer particular lexicographical or semantic difficulties.[2] When Christians adopted these terms they did not give them an essentially new meaning. This is easily explained. In a world that had the cult of memory and endeavored to model itself on the classical ideals, Christianity appeared as a completely new message and introduced a new element into the life of the Greco-Roman world. A Jesuit scholar has given to one of his works a strikingly apt title, *Christentum als Neuheitserlebnis*.[3] If one passes from the Greek or Jewish literature of this time to the writings of the New Testament, one is particularly struck by the freshness and spontaneity of the latter.

Nowhere in the New Testament do we find reflections on the nature or functions of memory. For the Greeks, Aristotle had already elaborated a psychological theory of memory. In comparison, the unsophisticated terminology of the New Testament might be judged imprecise. According to Aristotle, the word *mnēmoneuein* "to remember," could be applied only to something past but not to anything present or future.[4] In the New Testament, it can just as well have for its object something present or future.[5] *Mnēmoneuein* and other analogous terms signify not only to recollect but also to think of something or someone.[6] And "to think of" could include to make mention[7] of something and frequently to mention someone in prayer.[8] Or indeed it could

---

[2]Most New Testament authors use *mnēmoneuō* in the present tense but *emnēsthē* in the aorist and *memnēmai* in the perfect (2 Cor. 11:2; 2 Tim. 1:4). In Revelation only *mnēmoneuō* is used, in the aorist (18:5) as well as in the present. The author of Hebrews uses a variety of forms, including the present and the aorist of both verbs, *mnēmoneuō* and *mimnēskomai*. Cf. the article of O. Michel in *TDNT*, IV, 675-682.

[3]K. Prümm, *Christentum als Neuheitserlebnis: Durchblick durch die christlich-antike Begegnung* (Freiburg i. B.: Herder, 1939).

[4]De Memoria 449b.

[5]A future object occurs in Heb. 11:22; cf. Barn. 19:10.

[6]Cf. Col. 4:18, "Remember my fetters." The meaning is either: "Pray for me, I who am imprisoned" or "Consider that I write as a prisoner for the sake of the gospel and heed my words."

[7]Cf. Heb. 11:22; Ign. Eph. 12:2; Smyrn. 4:3; Barn. 13:7.

[8]Cf. the idiom *mneian poioumai* in Rom. 1:2 and other Pauline thanksgivings. Passages like 1 Thess. 1:2ff.; Phil. 1:3ff.; and 2 Tim. 1:3ff. show how memory and intercession are integrated in this type of commemoration. Cf. also the use of *mnēmoneuein* in Ign. Trall. 13:1; Magn. 14:1; Rom. 9:1; Mart. Pol. 8:1; and possibly Col. 4:18.

signify to keep someone in mind with the sense of "to come to his aid," as is the case when Paul speaks of the collection as "remembering the poor of Jerusalem."[9] But likewise when the object pertains to the past the main concern is not simply the recollection of past events. When we read, for example, that the woman who has given birth to a child "no longer remembers the anguish," this does not mean that the mental impression of the anguish has been obliterated, but that she is no longer conscious of it in her joy at having brought a child into the world.[10] "To remember," in the New Testament, signifies almost always to recall something or to think about it in such a way that it is expressed in speech or is formative for attitude and action.[11]

This usage is in itself neither particularly remarkable nor peculiar to the New Testament. We find analogous usage in ordinary Greek as well as in modern languages. But the predominance of this usage in the New Testament is certainly due to the influence of the corresponding semitic concepts and of the *Septuagint*. The Hebrew word *zakār*, "to remember," signifies in effect that a thing or event "is called forth in the soul and assists in determining its direction, its action."[12] The influence of the Old Testament is most evident in statements where God is the subject. When God "remembers the covenant" he intervenes and acts in conformity with it,[13] and when he "no longer remembers their inequities," he has pardoned them.[14]

The God of Israel was a God who acted and manifested himself in history. That is why the memory of his work of salvation and of his commandments[15] had a fundamental importance in the religion of Israel. Two essential points should be noted here.

---

[9]Gal. 2:10. Cf. Heb. 13:3 and the litotes "Do not forget" in Heb. 13:2, 6.

[10]John 16:21. In Phil. 3:13, "forgetting what lies behind" means that Paul no longer lets his past shape his life even though he still remembers it.

[11]Hermas, however, finds it difficult to remember what was revealed to him (Vis. I, 3, 3; II, 1, 3).

[12]J. Pedersen, *Israel, its Life and Culture* (tr. Mrs. Aslaug Møller; London: Oxford Press, 1926), I-II 106, cf. 233ff. Cf. B.S. Childs, *Memory and Tradition in Israel* (London: SCM Press, 1962); W. Schottroff, *"Gedenken" im Alten Orient und im Alten Testament: die Wurzel zākar im semitischen Sprachkreis* (WMANT, 15; Neukirchen: Neukirchener Verlag, 1964).

[13]Luke 1:72; cf. Exod. 2:24; 6:5; Lev. 26:42; Ps. 105:8, etc. Cf. also Luke 1:54 and Ps. 98:3.

[14]Heb. 8:12; 10:17; cf. Jer. 31:34. On the phrase *eis mnemosynon*, Matt. 26:13; Mark 14:9; Acts 10:4 (cf. 10:31) cf. W.C. van Unnik,"De Achtergrond en Betekenis van Handelingen 10:4 en 35", *NedTT* 3 (1949), 260-283 and 336-354.

[15]E.g. Deut. 7:18; 32:7ff.; Ps. 105:5.

The first concerns the cultus: by various mnemonic signs[16] and particularly by the great festivals with their ritual actions and accompanying words, psalms, and hymns, Israel "remembered" YHWH.[17] At the same time the religious ceremonies with their prayers, sacrifices, blowing of trumpets, etc., were supposed to recall to YHWH his great deeds of former times, and to cause him "to remember" his people anew.[18] By this cultic "commemoration," past salvation became once again an actual and present reality. We read in the ordinances of the Mishnah relative to the celebration of the Passover that "in every generation a man must regard himself as if he came forth himself out of Egypt."[19] Like Passover, the first day of the year was a festival remembrance in the synagogue as well as in the old temple.[20] But new commemorations like Purim and Hanukkah were later added. According to the synagogue liturgy, the Exodus from Egypt was commemorated in the daily prayers as well as on the sabbath and other festival days, including the Kiddush-ceremony that marked the beginning of a solemn festival.[21]

The second point to be mentioned is the tradition, especially as it had taken form in the rabbinic schools of New Testament times. Rabbinic teaching, in effect, consisted of a vast system of scriptural interpretations, juridical rules and precedents not to be forgotten. When doubts arose concerning judicial or ritual questions, the task was to recover the adequate

---

[16]*E.g.* Num. 15:37-41; Deut. 6:5-9; 11:18-21; Ps. 103:18; Mal. 4:4.

[17]Cf. the epoch-making work of S.Mowinckel, *Psalmenstudien II: Das Thronbesteigungsfest Jahwäs* (Kristiania, 1922). Further, J. Pedersen, *Israel*, III-IV, esp. 401ff.

[18]Commemorative sacrifice: Lev. 2:2; Num. 5:26; showbread: Lev. 24:7; trumpets: Num. 10:9f.; other cultic objects: Exod. 28:12, 29; 30:16; 39:7; Num. 31:4. "Remember!" is a habitual formula of prayer (Ps. 74:2; 106:4, etc.).

[19]Mishnah, *Pesahim*, 10:4. Cf. the rules for the passover meal, with the father's explanation of the various usages (passover haggadah), *ibid.* 10:4-6.

[20]In the synagogue liturgy, New Year's Day is the "Day of Remembrance" above all. It is celebrated in commemoration of the first day of creation (cf. bRosh Ha-Shanah 27a). The *zikronoth*, prayers and biblical citations, deal at length with God's remembrance in past and present. Cf. *The Authorized Daily Prayer Book* (ed. J.H. Hertz; New York: Bloch, 1965), 876-883.

[21]Cf. the Shema' with accompanying benedictions, esp. the prayers "From Egypt thou didst redeem us," and "True and trustworthy" (Hertz, *Daily Prayer Book*, 128f. and 310f.). Cf. also the prayers "May our remembrance ascend" and "And thou hast given us" (148ff. and 460ff.; 802ff. and 808ff., etc.). The Kiddush for Sabbath evening includes, to give one example, the phrases "a memorial of the creation" and "in remembrance of the departure from Egypt" (408f.). In Mishnah, *Berakoth* 1:5; Deut. 16:3 is interpreted as a reference to the daily commemoration of the Exodus in worship.

biblical citation in order to apply it and recall what Rabbi X or Y had said on the case in question or on other similar cases.[22] In this way the law of God was kept alive in Israel. Efficacious "memory" is involved here, even if we have to recognize a certain intellectualization of the notion of memory in the school traditions. The early church did not transmit tradition in such an institutionalized, scholarly form.

The church's memory grew spontaneously out of its missionary experience. This is clear, for example, in what is probably the oldest writing in the New Testament, 1 Thessalonians. Paul mentions that he constantly remembers their congregation, and has been comforted to hear that the Thessalonians have fond memories of him.[23] But Paul's essential concern is that the Thessalonians also remember what he had said to them. Throughout the epistle, we find the formula: "just as you know...." *kathōs oidate*.[24] When he exhorts the Thessalonians he not only says that they should live in conformity with the precepts he has given them and with the traditions he has transmitted to them, but he also adds "just as you are doing." It is only a question of doing still more perfectly.[25] Here we have a polite, ingratiating phrase. But there is more to it than that: the initial acceptance of the gospel puts the whole of life under obligation. A community of baptized Christians which has come to share in the gospel and which has received basic catechetical instructions already knows what must be done. They have received the Holy Spirit and are on the right road. They need to preserve what they have received and to remind themselves of it in order to live out the reality into which they have been introduced. The first obligation of the apostle vis-a-vis a community is to make the faithful remember what they have received and already know - or should know.

The other Pauline epistles could also serve to illustrate the same outlook.[26] A similar point of view is also present

---

[22]Already in Tob. 2:6 a quotation is introduced by the formula "I remembered the prophecy of Amos." In rabbinic terminology *zāker* and cognate words are frequently used in connection with memorization, recollection, and citation of scriptural passages. Cf. *e.g.* Mishnah *Yebamoth* 16:7, *Gittin* 1:5, *Eduyoth* 1:4-6, *Kelim* 17:5, *bPesahim* 66a, *Sanhedrin* 82a; W. Bacher, *Die exegetische Terminologie der jüdischen Traditionsliteratur* (Leipzig: Hinrichs, 1905), I, 51-55 and II, 63; B. Gerhardsson, *Memory and Manuscript* (Lund: Gleerup, 1961), 152, etc.

[23]1 Thess. 1:3ff.; 4:6.

[24]1:5; 2:1, 4, 11; 3:3, 4; 4:2; 5:1ff.

[25]4:1ff.; cf. 4:9ff.; 5:11.

[26]Cf. *e.g.* 2 Thess. 2:5, 15; 3:4, 6, 7, 10; Gal. 1:6-9; 3:1ff.; 4:8ff.; 1 Cor. 11:2; 15:1ff.; Rom. 6:17, 15:14ff.; 16:17ff.; Col. 2:6ff.; Eph. 2:11ff.

elsewhere in early Christianity. The epistle of Jude offers us its most characteristic expression when it speaks of the "faith which was once for all delivered to the saints." Here the author makes it clear that, although Christians were "once for all fully informed," he is eager to remind them of certain things."[27] We find the same idea in a slightly different form in the first epistle of John when the author says that what he writes is an "old commandment which you had from the beginning."[28] It can also be found outside the New Testament. For example, the martyr-bishop Ignatius freely interpolates in his exhortations the words: "just as you are already doing."[29]

These examples suffice to show that such is the common view among the leaders of the early Christian communities.[30] Those who have been led to faith and who have received baptism know already what is necessary for salvation. From that moment, they need only recall their initiation and permit this memory to shape their conduct. This knowledge is not an anamnesis in the platonic sense of the term, namely a reminiscence of the Ideas which the soul had contemplated in its preexistence. But, to state the matter somewhat boldly, I would say that for the early Christians, knowledge was an anamnesis, a recollection of the *gnōsis* given to all those who have believed in the gospel, received baptism, and been incorporated into the church. In effect, in Christ "are hid all the treasures of wisdom and knowledge" (Col. 2:3). Clearly, there always remains a possibility of growing in knowledge; but this essentially signifies an ever growing assimilation and an ever more perfect application of what has been once for all received.[31]

It was of primary importance for the faithful to conserve the original gospel and the memory of the heritage of the apostles in the struggle against nascent heresies. This stands out particularly in the later writings of the New Testament. But the basis

---

[27]Jude 3 and 5, cf. 17; 2 Peter 1:12ff.; 3:1ff.; cf. 1:9. In James this outlook appears in the exhortation "Receive with meekness the implanted word" (1:21).

[28]1 John 2:7; cf. 2:24 and 3:11. There are numerous references to prior knowledge.

[29]Ign. Eph. 4:1; Trall. 2:2; 3:2; Rom. 2:1; Smyrn. 4:10; Pol. 1:2; 4:1. Cf. Pol. Phil. 10:3; 7:2; 12:1.

[30]Cf. also 1 Clem. 53:1: "For you know the sacred scriptures, dear friends, you know them well, and you have studied the oracles of God. So I write these things to remind you of them (*pros anamnēsin*)." Compare 62:2 and, with some variation, Barn. 1:2-9; 4:9; 9:9.

[31]To this need to recall corresponds the Pauline tension between the indicative and the imperative.

for this development was present from the very beginning. In fact, the rudiments of church tradition arose out of the experience of newness. In view of this decisive newness that characterizes the gospel and incorporation into the church, all that could be added later would have only secondary importance. In Christ, God had spoken his last word and had given ultimate salvation to people living in the last days, in the fullness of time. Christians must be sustained in the grace in which they were once called to participate while they await Christ's return. Today we see more clearly than did Protestant scholarship at the turn of the century the bond that exists between the Christianity of the first century and the Catholic church of the second.[32]

In no way do I intend to claim that everything in the New Testament is tradition and recollection. It is sufficient to mention the practical ordinances of 1 Corinthians, the scriptural interpretations of the Epistle to the Hebrews, or the visions of the Apocalypse. But these writings also refer to the foundations that have been laid once and for all.[33] Paul himself says to the Roman church that he has written his letter to revive memories *hos epanamimnēskōn hymas* (15:15). Such letters as Colossians, Ephesians, and 1 Peter can accurately be called reminders. In large measure, scholarship has succeeded in demonstrating that the epistles bear the mark of the ideas and formulas of kerygmatic, catechetical or liturgical tradition.[34] All of this casts some light on what inspired the pseudonymous writers from the earliest times of Christianity. They wrote in the names of the apostles in order that the churches, through the written word, might remember the teaching of the apostles when the latter had disappeared. Indeed 2 Peter states this explicitly (1:12-15, 3:1).

---

[32]A reaction against the liberal concensus was sharply expressed in Karl Holl's essay "Der Kirchenbegriff des Paulus in seinem Verhältnis zu dem der Urgemeinde," *Sitzb.Akad.Berlin* (1921), 920-947 (the essay later appeared in his *Gesammelte Aufsätze: II, Der Osten* [Tübingen: Mohr, 1928], 44-67). In his book *Orthodoxy and Heresy in Earliest Christianity* (tr. R.A. Kraft *et al.*; Philadelphia: Fortress, 1971 [first German edition in 1934]), Walter Bauer tended to reverse the traditional opinion that "orthodoxy" preceded "heresy". At least for some areas, like Egypt and Syria, he made a good case. Nevertheless, the dogmatic assumption that the first preaching was also the true one goes back to a very early date; cf. esp. Gal 1:9.

[33]Cf. *e.g.* 1 Cor. 3:10ff.; 15:1ff.; Heb. 1:1-2; 2:3f., etc.; Rev. 1:3-5.

[34]The pioneer was A. Seeberg, with such works as *Der Katechismus der Urchristenheit* (Leipzig: Deichert, 1903). For a survey of more recent literature, cf. E. Krentz, "The Early Dark Ages of the Church - Some Reflections," *CTM* 41 (1970), 67-85.

This same desire to keep the word of the apostles present in the memory of the communities led to the transmission and collection of occasional writings such as the letters of Paul, and thus contributed to the development of the New Testament canon.[35]

In the epistles of the New Testament, the writers call to memory the life, words, and deeds of the apostles,[36] and possibly also the religious fervor of the communities at the time of their foundation - their "first love."[37] More often they stress their very initiation into Christianity: "Remember then what you received and heard; keep that, and repent," we read in the letter to Sardis in the Apocalypse (3:3). And in Ephesians it is said: "Remember that at one time you Gentiles...were at that time separated from Christ...having no hope and without God in the world. But now in Jesus Christ you who were once far off have been brought near in the blood of Christ" (Eph. 2:11ff.).[38] As Paul puts it in a famous passage, it is the very content of the gospel of salvation that is recalled: "I would remind you, brethren, in what terms I preached to you the gospel, which you received." Then he continues with this lapidary formula that summarizes the essentials of the gospel message: "that Christ died for our sins in accordance with the scriptures...and that he appeared to Cephas, then to the twelve."[39]

By these and other similar citations we see that for Paul, as well as for the first apostles, the gospel, the preaching of salvation, was the message of a past event: the act of God in Christ. This is one of the traits that characterizes New Testament studies in our time; it puts the accent precisely on this aspect of the question. For example, one might cite a work of great importance such as that of C.H. Dodd, *The Apostolic Preaching and its Developments*.[40] In order to indicate the origins of this viewpoint, one could say - very summarily - that New Testament studies of the last century were often theological-intellectualistic and sought to determine the "doctrinal conception" (*Lehrbegriff*)

---

[35]Cf. *e.g.* 1 Clem. 47:1; Pol.Phil. 3:2; 11:2ff. We find the same themes toward the end of the development of the canon. In Athanasius' famous thirty-ninth Festal Letter, in which he outlines the New Testament canon as we have it, his stated purpose is not to innovate but to recall ancient tradition. Phraseology and outlook remind us of Paul, Luke, and Ignatius.

[36]*E.g.* 1 Thess. 2:1ff.; 1 Cor. 2:1ff. (11:2); Acts 20:31. Cf. also Heb. 13:7.

[37]Rev. 2:5; cf. Heb. 10:32, and Gal. 4:13ff.

[38]Likewise, *e.g.*, 1 Thess. 1:4ff.; 2:13; 1 Cor. 1:26ff.; Gal. 3:1ff.; Col. 1:5f.

[39]1 Cor. 15:1ff.; cf. 1:18ff.; Rom. 1:2ff.; etc.

[40]Likewise one could cite in this regard such names as Dibelius, K.L. Schmidt, Schniewind, and Hoskyns.

of the different writings or groups of writings. The reaction against this tendency manifested itself around 1900.[41] At that time scholars emphasized that the content of the New Testament was not in essence theology but religion, not doctrine but life. It was not christological dogma but the cult of Christ that was fundamental. After World War I, there was a certain reaction against over-emphasis upon the subjective and psycho-sociological aspect of religion. It can be said that today the principal accent is placed on the "kerygma" as that which unifies the multitude of "doctrinal conceptions," of types of piety, and of social settings reflected in the New Testament. I believe that something both correct and important has been brought to light. This, however, should not be taken to imply that the New Testament contains primarily *kērygma*, a preaching in the sense of proclamation, a message publicly announced by a herald. *Kērygma* is, in the first place, the missionary message. The verb *kēryssein* refers to the announcement of Christ where he is not as yet known. The central content of the epistles and of the preaching to the communities was certainly the same as that of the missionary preaching. But the faithful already knew the message; they had been made participants, they had been made part of the divine work of which the kerygma was a proclamation. That is why, precisely when it is a question of the very core of the gospel, the preaching to the communities was more recollection than proclamation. Thus what we understand generally by "to preach" - namely, to deliver a sermon in the church - no longer corresponds to the *kēryssein* of the New Testament, but rather closely to *hypomimnēskein*, to restore to memory.[42]

The fact that the missionary message leads to a call to conversion and baptism makes this difference quite clear. The words addressed to the communities, on the contrary, presuppose that they have already received baptism, and exhort the baptized to hold fast to that in which they have been made participants - regardless of whether baptism is understood as purification, as regeneration, or as death and resurection with Christ. We find in the epistles numerous reminders of baptism. They seem to have

---

[41]Cf. W. Wrede's critique of B. Weiss, H.J. Holtzmann and others in his manifesto *Über Aufgabe und Methode der sogenannten Neutestamentliche Theologie* (Göttingen: Vandenhoeck und Ruprecht, 1897).

[42]Cf. 2 Tim. 2:14; Titus 3:10; Jude 5; 2 Peter 1:12 (cf. 1:13, 3:1); 1 Clem. 62:2 (*hypomimnēskein*); 1 Cor. 4:17 (*anamimnēskein*). Words such as *didaskein* and *parakalein* can also be used for "to preach

held a definite place and to have received a somewhat traditional formulation as the basis for exhortation.[43]

Baptism was administered in the name of Jesus Christ. The gospel was the message concerning him. Basically, to recall the gospel and baptism is to evoke the memory of Jesus as Savior and Lord. 2 Timothy says it very clearly: "Remember Jesus Christ, risen from the dead, descended from David, as preached in my gospel" (2 Tim. 2:8). To "remember Jesus Christ" does not mean to preserve in memory an image of him but to let this memory form our thoughts and actions. Let us notice also the brief formula accompanying the name of Christ: "risen from the dead, descended from David." We possess many such christological formulas. They consist principally of participles or relative clauses and at times also declarative or causal clauses, designating some of the important events which made Christ significant for the faithful: his birth, passion, death, resurrection, etc.

These formulas are like brief resumes of the purport of the gospel. In other cases they could be the reflection of confessions of faith of the same type as the second article of the Apostles' Creed.[44] They could also serve to motivate an exhortation, as does this well-known passage from Philippians 2:6 "who, though he was in the form of God, did not count equality with God a thing to be grasped." A passage like this is not, properly speaking, a doctrinal christological formula. It is a call to the faithful: as Christians they live in Christ - that is why they ought to remember him and let him determine their attitude. Here we do not have a confession of faith; we could say that it is an "anamnesis of Christ," a commemoration of Christ. One finds similar formulas in the prayers of the early church and in its thanksgiving, hymns, and praises.[45] There Christ and the salvation of God are remembered in the same way that Israel remembered the mighty deeds of its God in former times. To pray and to give thanks in the name of Jesus does not mean simply that one made use of the formula "in the name of Jesus," but that in

---

[43]Cf. Rom. 6:1ff.; 1 Cor. 1:12ff.; 12:13; Eph. 1:10, 14, 2:1ff.; Col. 1:12-14; 2:9-15; Titus 3:5-7; 1 Peter 1:3ff., 23, etc. Cf. E.G. Selwyn, *The Epistle of St. Peter* (London: Macmillan, 1946), 389-393.

[44]For style, see E. Norden, *Agnostos Theos* (Leipzig: Teubner, 1931), 250ff.; 263ff. For more recent literature, cf. J.N.D. Kelly, *Early Christian Creeds* (London: Longmans, 1950) and V. Neufeld, *The Earliest Christian Confessions* (Grand Rapids: Eerdmans, 1963).

[45]Passages such as Phil. 2:6-11; Col. 1:9-15; 1 Tim. 3:16; 1 Peter 1:18-21; 2:21-25; 3:18-22 reflect hymnic style, but they have an epistolary function and serve to recall the memory of Christ in the communities where the letters are read. Their antecedents may be homiletical as well as liturgical.

prayer and thanksgiving one mentioned the name of Jesus and generally also what made him Savior and Lord of the church (cf. e.g., Act 4:24-30).

"Remembrance" and "commemoration" have then held a central place in early Christian worship, in the preaching to the churches, and in thanksgiving and prayer. We also find a trace in the New Testament of the celebration of Sunday as the Lord's Day in memory of his resurrection.[46] And very early Christians commemorated Jesus at the feast of Passover.[47] The Lord's Supper was central to these occasions as well as worship of the early church in general. In the course of its celebration the "commemoration" of Jesus was most firmly established. "Do this in remembrance of me," we read in the very words of institution as Paul and possibly Luke report them to us.[48]

Historians of liturgy belonging to diverse confessions agree in seeing in *anamnēsis*, commemoration, a fundamental theme or, one can justifiably say, *the* fundamental theme of the celebration of the Lord's Supper in the early church. The commemoration was not something that took place essentially within individual believers, in their subjective memory. The celebration itself, i.e. thanksgiving, sacrifice, and sacrament (*mystērion*) was a commemoration, an *anamnēsis* of the death and resurrection of Jesus where the history of salvation was re-presented by the sacramental commemoration.[49]

In liturgical terminology, the word *anamnēsis* subsequently designated a particular part of the Mass, that which follows immediately the words of institution and begins, in the Roman rite, with the words: *Unde et memores....* This section of the Mass is ancient, but originally the *anamnēsis* was not confined to this particular element.[50] This is clear from the oldest fairly

---

[46]Acts 20:7; 1 Cor. 6:2; Rev. 1:10. Cf. Ign. Magn. 9; Barn. 15:8ff.

[47]Cf. *e.g.* O. Casel, "Art und Sinn der ältesten christlichen Osterfeier," *Jahrbuch für Liturgiewissenschaft* 14 (1943), 1-78. For more recent literature, cf. W. Huber, *Passa und Ostern* (Berlin: Topelmann, 1969).

[48]1 Cor. 11:24-25; Luke 22:19b.

[49]Cf. O. Casel, *Das Gedächtnis des Herrn in der altchristlichen Liturgie* (Freiburg, 1922) and "Das Mysteriengedächtnis der Messliturgie im Lichte der Tradition," *Jahrbuch für Liturgiewissenschaft* 6 (1926), 113-204. G. Dix, *The Shape of the Liturgy* (Westminster: Dacre Press, 1943), 161, 215, 234ff. J.A. Jungmann, "Das Gedächtnis des Herrn in der Eucharistia," *TQ* 133 (1953), 387-399. P. Brunner, "Zur Lehre vom Gottesdienst der im Namen Jesu versammelten Gemeinde," *Leiturgia* (ed. K.F. Müller; Kassel: J. Stauda Verlag, 1954), esp. 358ff.

[50]Cf. Casel, *Das Gedächtnis*, 130: "(The Anamnesis)...is the solemn, liturgical expression of the idea that the celebration of the mass is the memory of the redemptive death."

detailed eucharistic liturgy which we find in "The Apostolic Tradition" of Hippolytus, dating from the beginning of the third century. The passage that corresponds to what was later called *anamnēsis* reads: "In remembering his death and resurrection, we offer Thee the bread and the cup, giving thanks to Thee...."[51] Thus it is quite evident that the entire thanksgiving that preceded, indeed the whole celebration, is an *anamnēsis*, a commemoration of the death of Christ and of his resurrection. This theme is predominant in the eucharistic liturgy of Hippolytus more than in any later liturgy. After the introductory dialog between the celebrant and the faithful - as we find it today in the *sursum corda* - there follows the thanksgiving proper: "We render thanks unto Thee, O God, through Thy Child (*pais*) Jesus Christ, whom in these last times Thou didst send to us as Savior, Redeemer, harbinger of Thy will, he who...." The whole prayer that follows is then one "commemoration" of Christ as the Word of God "through whom everything has been created, who was incarnate, and who when He was betrayed to suffering that He might abolish death and rend the bonds of the devil...Taking bread and giving thanks to Thee said: Take eat...."

By taking the mid-second century apologist Justin as an intermediary link, we can trace the ceremony of the supper described by Hippolytus back to Paul himself.[52] On this point Paul represents the Pauline communities; we could even say the pre-Pauline communities. By the words "Do this in remembrance of me," Justin understood the word *poiein* not purely and simply in the general sense of "to do," but as a cultic term, to celebrate, or - less likely - to sacrifice.[53] Admittedly it is doubtful whether this

[51]According to G. Dix, *The Treatise on the Apostolic Tradition of St. Hippolytus of Rome* (London: SPCK, 1937), 8ff. Cf. H. Lietzmann, *Mass and Lord's Supper* (tr. Dorothea H.G. Reeve; Leiden: Brill, 1953-69), 47 and 142f.

[52]In his work cited above, Lietzmann demonstrated that we can trace a line from Hippolytus via Justin back to Paul. Cf. also F.L. Cirlot, *The Early Eucharist* (London: SPCK, 1939) 74-77.

[53]According to Justin's interpretation, the bread and the cup are the objects of sacrificial "doing" (Dial. 70:4; cf. Apol. 66:3 and the allusions to Mal. 1:10-12 in Dial. 41 and 117). But the eucharistic commemoration is not only intended to recall the sacrifice of Christ before God; by words and action Christians themselves "remember" Christ and his death (Dial. 117:3; Apol. 67:1). The sacrificial aspect is overstressed by F. Cirlot (*The Early Eucharist*, 102, 106ff., 104ff., 222ff.) and, to some extent, by G. Dix (*The Apostolic Tradition*, 73ff., and *The Shape of the Liturgy*, 161). In 1 Cor. 11:24-25 a sacrificial interpretation is less likely even though v. 25 reads most smoothly if *potērion* is taken to be the antecedent of the second as well as of the first *touto*, since it is also the unexpressed object of *pinēte*. The translation would then have to be something like, "Make this, (bread, cup) my memorial." Unfortunately the work of K.H. Bartels (*Dies tut zu*

interpretation is Paul's, but in any case the celebration of the Lord's Supper was for him also a commemoration of Christ. In order to explain the words of institution, he adds, "For as often as you eat this bread and drink the cup, you proclaim the Lord's death until he comes." The verb *kataggellein* used here indicates that Paul had also oral proclamation in view.[54] No doubt he alludes to the thanksgiving over the bread and wine. In the thanksgiving, the death of Jesus is commemorated before God. And this same act, the death of Jesus, is also proclaimed to the faithful. We can also reconstruct to some extent the form of this commemoration of Christ in the Pauline communities. One illustration is the passage in Philippians 2 cited above; another is the hymn-like passage in Colossians 1 that speaks of giving thanks to God for the redemption that has been given us in his Son; "He is the image of the invisible God, the first-born of all creation." Such "commemorations" of Christ correspond in form and type to the eucharistic thanksgiving formulas of Hippolytus. As Lietzmann in particular has made clear, there is reason to suppose that it was by similar words that Christ was remembered at the Lord's Supper even in the time of Paul.[55]

---

meinem Gedächtnis. Zur Auslegung von I Kor 11:24f. [Mainz, 1959]) was not accessible to me.

[54]On *kataggellō* and related words, cf. J. Schniewind, *TDNT*, I, 70-73. In the Psalms, words for recalling (*hizkir, mimnēskō, mnēmoneuō*) and proclaiming (*higgid, anaggellō, kataggellō*) are used synonymously (*e.g.* Ps. 71[70]: 16-17). What is recalled and proclaimed in prayer and praise addressed to God is thereby also made known to the worshipping community and to the world. In 1 Cor. 11:25 the phrase "until he comes" simply indicates that the commemoration of Jesus is to take place in the interim between Jesus' death and his coming. Cf. "Eschatology and History," in my book *The Crucified Messiah* for analogous phrases in Jewish documents. J. Jeremias (*The Eucharistic Words of Jesus* [tr. N. Perrin; New York: Scribners, 1966] 237-255) has proposed that the phrase "in remembrance of me" be translated "...that God may remember me" and understood as a prayer for the parousia. This presupposes a false opposition between human and divine remembrance and is too narrow. The eucharistic commemoration should rather be taken to imply a prayer that God may remember Jesus and be gracious to the beneficiaries of the covenant in his blood.

[55]This holds true even though it remains doubtful whether any of the christological "hymns" in the New Testament are actually derived from a eucharistic prayer. The exact wording was open to variation, so that any reconstruction of "liturgical fragments" in the New Testament remains precarious. Style and phraseology, patterns and themes may have been much the same whether a thanksgiving or a hymn was used at baptism, at the Lord's Supper, or on some other occasion. We do know, however, that Christ was commemorated in the eucharistic thanksgiving in which God was praised both for the gifts of creation and for salvation through Christ. Cf. Did. 10; Justin Dial. 41:1 and 117:3; Hippolytus' *Apostolic Tradition*, and Const. Apost. VIII, 12:7ff. The parallelism between creation and salvation through Christ is already found in New Testament passages like Col. 1:15-20 and Heb. 1:2-4 (cf. Phil. 2:6-11).

At that time there would have been no contradiction between commemorative celebration and Christ's real presence in the bread and wine. It was the bread and wine consecrated by the commemorative thanksgiving that gave a share in his body and blood. Even if ecstatic phenomena, glossolalia, etc., played a part, nevertheless the theme of commemoration dominated the worship of the early church. The church of Christ possessed no sacrificial cult. Just as the complete revelation had been given once for all, so also the perfect sacrifice had been offered once for all. What had happened was not simply an event in the past; it was also a present reality in the church which remembered her Lord and proclaimed his death until he might come.[56]

Early Christianity was not only faith and worship, but also a way of life. Those who became Christians received not only the evangelical message, but also prescriptions concerning the manner in which they ought to behave. Perhaps from the beginning, in any case at a very early time, baptismal instruction included the fundamentals of Christian conduct. The introductory chapters of the Didache illustrate one form of this instruction. We read: "You must not forsake the commandments of the Lord, but you shall keep the teachings you have received, neither adding to them or taking from them."[57] In the epistles, the exhortations are in large measure the reflection of such "catechisms." The exhortations are often, as we have already said, a recall both to the precepts that the Christians received and to the obligations of their baptism in Christ. Some early Christian writers termed such catechetical instruction the "precepts of the Lord."[58] In such contexts sayings of Jesus are not infrequently quoted. To cite one of his sayings was to appeal to the supreme authority. It is precisely by this practical application that the words of

---

[56]The Agape-Eucharist prayers in the Didache do not contain any rehearsal of saving events but rather thanksgiving for knowledge and life, granted through Jesus, and prayers for his coming. One may guess that the celebration in the early Jerusalem church, or in Johannine circles, was more like that of the Didache than like the tradition of Paul, Justin, and Hippolytus. But even so, the thanksgiving would include commemoration of Jesus. Thus, the distinction between two types of celebration should not be overstressed. Cf. E. Schweizer, "Das Abendmahl, eine Vergegenwärtigung des Todes Jesu oder ein eschatologisches Freudenmahl?" *TZ* (1946), 81-101.

[57]Did. 4:13; cf. chs. 1-7 *passim*. Allusions to basic catechetical instruction are found in passages like 1 Thess. 4:1ff.; 2 Thess. 3:6; Rom. 6:17; Eph. 4:20ff.; Heb. 6:1; 1 John 3:11; 2 John 6; from a later date, Justin Apol. 61:2 and 65:1.

[58]Cf. *e.g.* Barn. 2:1, 10:11 (*dikaiōmata*); Pol. Phil. 4:1; Ign. Rom. (*entolē*); 1 Clem. 8:4; 17:3 (*entolai*). Similar expressions are found in 2 Peter 3:2; 2:21 and already in 1 Cor. 14:37; Gal. 6:2; 1 John 2:3.

Jesus were preserved and transmitted. We see it already in Paul.[59] I cite, in particular, the manner in which an otherwise unknown saying of Jesus is introduced in one of the discourses of Paul related in Acts: "Remembering the words of the Lord Jesus, how he said: 'It is more blessed to give than to receive.'" Clement and Polycarp used similar quotation formulas: "Remember the word of Jesus when he said...." This was evidently a customary form of citation.[60] Even here "to remember" does not mean to retain in memory an inert concept but to bring to mind the words of Jesus in order to live by them: "being no hearer that forgets but a doer that acts," as James expresses it.[61]

In addition to their use in exhortations, the words of Jesus are also cited in the eschatological teaching as predictions of what must happen.[62] But this is not the place to consider this aspect of the question. What is clear, in any case, is that the manner in which the sayings of Jesus are transmitted is similar in many respects to the manner of transmitting traditions in Judaism. The essential difference concerning the mode of transmission lies in that for Christians Jesus was not merely a link in the chain of succession. He was a unique Master; his word was the word of the living Lord.

Thus we encounter the memory of Jesus in the epistles of the New Testament and in the apostolic fathers primarily in two different modes: first, his commemoration as Savior as announced in the gospel; second, the memory of his words as a rule of conduct. One finds in the hellenistic world certain analogies: the commemorative meal for the deceased, the cultic representation of myths in the mystery religions, the doctrinal tradition in the philosophical schools and in popular philosophy. Here we cannot dwell on the similarities or differences. Despite undeniable analogies in Hellenism there can be no doubt that one must seek the principal historical background in Judaism, in its cultic "commemoration" and in its tradition. The new element is that everything focuses on the memory of Jesus the Master who was at the same time Savior and Teacher. In light of Jesus the exodus from Egypt and the law itself take second place as matters belonging to a by-gone age which have now found fulfillment in their superior--

---

[59]1 Cor. 7:10; 9:14; cf. 7:11, 25.

[60]Acts 20:35; 1 Clem. 13:1ff.; 46:7; Pol. Phil. 3:2. Cf. also Luke 24:6, 8; Acts 11:16; John 2:22; 15:20; 16:4; Matt. 26:75; Justin Apol. 14:4.

[61]James 1:22ff.; cf. 2 Clem. 17:3.

[62]1 Thess. 4:13ff.; cf. Mark 13 and parallels; Did. 16; Barn. 4 (N.B. v. 14); Pol. Phil. 7:1.

the bringer of the end time.[63]

From our gospels we can infer that the transmission of the words of Jesus was accomplished in a relatively independent fashion paralleling that of the kerygma. Earlier scholarship deduced the existence of a special written document, the logia source; many scholars today believe that the sayings were transmitted orally. Matthew and Luke were the first to make the logia tradition integral to the gospel. The gospels themselves, particularly Mark and John, give the preponderant place to the recital of the passion and resurrection, towards which everything converges. But the gospels also relate a series of detached episodes about the life of Jesus prior to the passion. Outside the gospels, we find few traces of such narrative in the first century documents. I must say a few words about the gospels in closing.

Writing for pagan readers, Justin Martyn calls the gospels *apomnemonēumata tōn apostolōn*, the memoires of the apostles, or more precisely, "the memoires that have been drawn up by the apostles and those who have come after them."[64] Apomnemoneumata were a literary form well known in antiquity; they were a collection of loosely connected episodes from the lives of illustrious men whom the author had known. The "Memorabilia" of Xenophon about Socrates are today, as in antiquity, the most illustrious example. Justin certainly had them in mind; he is the first to parallel Christ and Socrates (Apol. I 5, 3ff., Apol II. 10, 6-8). As has often been noted, this characterization of the gospels is slightly misleading.[65] However, it is necessary to recognize that for his own purpose, namely to give to the non-initiated a notion of what the gospels contain, Justin could hardly have chosen a more suitable expression. Papias, bishop of Hierapolis, had already expressed some ten years before Justin an analogous point of view concerning the gospels. With ardor Papias himself gathered the recollections of early times, and he informs us that Mark recorded in writing what he recalled of Peter's accounts of what the Lord had said and done.[66] Basically, Luke has the

---

[63]The discussion reported in bBerakoth 12b (end) on the question whether or not in the days of the Messiah one will remember (in the benedictions) the Exodus from Egypt is interesting as a term of comparison.

[64]Dial. 103:8; cf. Apol. 66:3; 67:3; Dial. 100:4, etc.

[65]Cf. K.L. Schmidt, "Die Stellung der Evangelien innerhalb der allgemeinen Literaturgeschichte," *Eucharisterion für H. Gunkel* (Göttingen: Vandenhoeck und Ruprecht, 1923), II, 50-134.

[66]Euseb. *H. E.* III, 39, 15.

same point of view, even if he lacks knowledge of writings with direct apostolic authority. He proposes to write a coherent, connected account conforming to what has been "delivered to us by those who have been from the beginning eyewitnesses and ministers of the word."

Strong objections have been raised against considering the gospels as "memoires," "recollections," and it has been made clear that they do not pretend to be retrospective historical accounts, but precisely "gospel," preaching, witness of faith. My late teacher Ragnar Asting was an extreme representative of this point of view. In his posthumous work on the preaching of the early church, he endeavored to show that the gospels did not intend to be accounts of past facts, but a prolongation of revelation where what was recounted becomes present reality by the very fact of preaching and reading. Consequently the historical question, "What really happened?" was irrelevant and foreign to the subject.[67]

The assertion contains some truth. The decisive message of the gospels is that which comes at the end, the message of the resurrection of Jesus. For the early church, the gospel was not a memory of the historical Jesus but a message concerning the Resurrected One. The apostles were not primarily traditioners; they were Jesus' messengers, his spokesmen. It has futher been demonstrated that the framework of the Markan account is determined less by geographic-chronological development than by the apostolic kerygma.[68] But if one draws too sharp a distinction - either the gospel message or the "recollections of the apostles" - one introduces an opposition that early Christianity did not know. On the contrary, for the evangelists - and we dare add, for the apostles themselves - it was precisely the encounter of the apostles with the resurrected Christ that revived their recollections of his earthly life. The account of the choice of a replacement for Judas illuminates the question. It was necessary for the one who was to be a witness of the resurrection to come from among the "men who have accompanied us during all the time that the Lord Jesus went in and out among us" (Acts 1:21). In the missionary preaching, as we see by the speeches related in Acts 2 and 10, Jesus' mighty works were cited as proof that God was with him, and possibly

---

[67]Cf. R. Asting, *Die Verkündigung des Wortes im Urchristentum* (Stuttgart: Kohlhammer, 1939), esp. 742ff.

[68]For various opinions, cf. K.L. Schmidt, *Der Rahmen der Geschichte Jesu* (Berlin: Trowitzsch, 1919); R.H. Lightfoot, *Locality and Doctrine in the Gospels* (London: Harper, 1938); C.H. Dodd, *The Apostolic Preaching and its Development* (London: Hodder and Stoughton, 1936).

special stories served as examples.[69] But above all it must have been in the assembly of the faithful that one recounted how Jesus traversed the countryside healing the sick and casting out demons, how he had been opposed and unrecognized, and how he had come to the aid of his disciples.[70] These events were not recounted because of a detached historical interest; nevertheless, the stories betray a concern to remember past events. In faith in the resurrected Lord, one calls to mind his mortal life, poor yet rich with hidden splendor. He was remembered in the certainty that he remained exactly what he had been then. Thus there is no contradiction in the view that the gospels contain "the memoires of the apostles" and are the "cultic, popular books" or the "books of the popular cult," following K.L. Schmidt's designation. The early Christian cultus was precisely a "commemoration" of Jesus; it is interesting that Justin, who uses the term memoires, is the first to inform us of the formal way in which the gospels served as books for reading in worship.[71]

What the first three evangelists only imply, John has consciously made explicit. There it is twice mentioned that the disciples did not understand at first what Jesus had said or done, but later, when he was resurrected from the dead, his disciples remembered and they believed (2:22, 12:15). Of the Paraclete, the Holy Spirit, it is said that he will recall to the disciples the teaching of Jesus (15:25). These words are like a key to the gospel of John. The gospel does not intend to give a neutral sketch of the life of Jesus; but neither does it intend to be philosophical reflection nor, as a recent German commentary would have it, existentialist revelation that never reveals anything but that Jesus is the revealer.[72] The gospel is intended to be a witness and thereby an inspired "commemoration" of the life and work of Jesus, in which everything radiates with the light of the resurrection. Without any doubt, the tradition is more thoroughly recast in this light in John than in any of the synoptics. But there is no essential differences.

The historical critic will conclude from this that what is

---

[69]M. Dibelius (*From Tradition to Gospel* [tr. B.L. Woolf; New York: Scribners, 1934]) maintained too exclusively that missionary preaching was the *Sitz im Leben* of the gospel tradition.

[70]According to Mark 8:14-21 the disciples failed to understand and remember properly during the earthly life of Jesus. We should probably add that after the resurrection they did remember and understand (cf. 9:9; 14:9; Luke 24:6-8).

[71]Justin Apol. 67:3.

[72]R. Bultmann's important commentary on John is at this point extreme. Cf. my review of Bultmann's *Theology of the New Testament*, in *The Crucified Messiah* (Minneapolis: Augsburg, 1974) 90-128.

to be sought in the gospels is first of all the disciples' memory of Jesus, not the life of Jesus. The question whether or not it is possible on these foundations to reconstruct an image of the "historical Jesus," is beyond the scope of this essay. But any answer would have to realize that we are incapable of producing a biographical account of his life. Today only outsiders and novelists dare to undertake such an enterprise. We can, however, construct for ourselves an idea of his message and teaching and of the impression that he produced both on his disciples and on his adversaries. We cannot retreat from a minute examination of the sayings and stories as they are variously preserved. But it will never be possible to draw a sharp line of demarcation between pious imagination and historical tradition. We have the latter only in the framework of the former. If the recollections of Jesus have been preserved for us, it is because he was preached as crucified Messiah and resurrected Lord. What *mnēmosyne* would have been able to tell about Jesus of Nazareth would have been very little indeed if Jesus had not been commemorated by those whose faith was in the Risen Lord and who broke the bread *eis anamnēsin Christou*.

CHAPTER 2

FORM-CRITICAL OBSERVATIONS ON EARLY CHRISTIAN PREACHING

The writings of the New Testament are studied today not in literary isolation but as far as possible in their context within the whole life of the early church. The order of the day in New Testament scholarship is not source-criticism but the recovery of the more or less fixed forms of traditional material taken over by the New Testament writers. Men like A. Seeberg, E. Norden, and H. Gunkel were, each in his own way, pioneers in this new orientation of research. Nearly everywhere today one hears of kerygma, confessions of faith, liturgical and catechetical traditions. This situation results from the confluence of scholarly developments in the history of religions field and in form criticism with renewed interest in theology, church life, and liturgy.

Many fruitful insights have been produced, but fashionable theological movements always have their dangers. In the use of terms like kerygma, confession of faith, and liturgical formula, a measure of caution is desirable, lest they lose their precise meaning. In the new Testament there are numerous christological affirmations, many of which are cast in high prose; but not all are kerygmatic, not all are liturgical, and not every statement about Christ is a confession of faith.[1]

To go further, even after we have differentiated between the missionary proclamation and early Christian preaching (preaching

---

[1]For example, in O. Cullmann's fine little book (*The Earliest Christian Confessions* [tr. J.K.S. Reid; London: Lutterworth Press, 1949]), the concept "confession" is much too broad.

within the Christian congregation), we have still to determine the forms and functions of this preaching. For the preaching of the Word of God had many forms in the congregations and was characterized by such words as *parakalein, didaskein, lalein.* Occasionally *kēryssein* and *euaggelizesthai* can also apply to congregational preaching - the gospel must always be heard anew - but these words remain, as a rule, terms for the fundamental message of the apostolic mission. The community preaching is distinguished from the missionary proclamation in that it does not bring the message of Christ to those who have not yet heard it, but recalls to believers the message they have already heard. The missionary preaching culminates in a call to baptism; in contrast the community preaching calls for a recollection of the baptism that has already occurred. Thus words like *epanamimnēskein* or *hypomimnēskein* can be used to refer to such preaching.[2] We have few, if any, direct sources for the preaching of the early Christian community (though possibly Hebrews or 1 John). However, the distinction between the Word preached and the Word written in letters and epistles can hardly have been very great. We may therefore suppose that many passages in the letters of the New Testament correctly convey preaching. The aim of preaching, expressed briefly, is to instruct, to console, to exhort, and to admonish the community in order to preserve it and to build it up as the church of God in Christ and to prepare it to meet the coming Lord. Surely, preaching was largely practical and parenetic. But naturally it was also necessary, even within the community preaching, to refer to the Christ event and to Jesus Christ himself.

In considering such references to Christ we will pursue only one line of approach. We will examine some fixed patterns within the New Testament letters which serve to introduce christological statements and which, it may be assumed, had their *Sitz im Leben* in preaching. Two such preaching types have already been noted by Rudolf Bultmann.[3] I will suggest a few more without trying to be exhaustive. For the sake of brevity I have tried to give names to the various patterns, but what matters are the observations, not the nomenclature.

---

[2]Cf. my article "Anamnesis," in this volume, and K. Stendahl, "Kerygma und Kerygmatisch," *TLZ* 77 (1952), 715-719.

[3]*Theology of the New Testament* (tr. K. Grobel; New York: Scribners, 1951), 105ff.

1. *The Revelation Pattern.* Theme: Present from eternity - now revealed.

The pattern exists in two variations:

(a) The typical Pauline formulations speak of the mystery that was earlier hidden but has now been revealed (1 Cor. 2:6ff.; Col. 1:26f.; Eph. 3:4-7, 8-11). The pattern is employed in the secondary doxology of Romans 16:25f. and is echoed in the eulogy in Ephesians 1 (the eternal decree of God in Christ in 1:4-5 and its eschatological realization in 1:6-14). But it can scarcely be doubted that it belongs originally to discourses within the believing community unfolding the mystery and wisdom of God. The eschatological newness and the heavenly riches of the revelation proclaimed in the gospel are to be brought home to the hearers. Here, everything focuses on the revelation and salvation in Christ. In Colossians 1:26f. it is even said that the content of the mystery is "Christ in us", Christ himself preached among the Gentiles and thereby present. The transition from participle (*to apokekrymmenon*) to finite verb (*nun de ephanerōthē*) might indicate underlying fixed formulation. 1 Corinthians 2:6ff. shows that this preaching type is not in itself specifically christological but serves to proclaim a secret wisdom. The crucifixion of Christ is cited as proof that the wisdom of God has remained hidden to the *archontes*. But it shows at the same time that the Pauline wisdom discourse actually has no other content than the "word of the cross." What has been revealed and should be perceived is "the gift bestowed on us by God."

(b) In the Pastoral epistles and the non-Pauline letters, the concepts of "mystery" and "hidden" are missing. The pattern is varied freely: what was promised, given, etc. before the foundation of the world, now at the end time has been revealed (2 Tim. 1:9-11; Titus 1:2f.; 1 Peter 1:18-21, cf. 10-12; 1 John 1:1-3; Ign. Magn. 6:1; Herm.Sim. 9:12). The statements either concern the salvation revealed in Christ and can then become directly christological passages (2 Tim. 1:9ff.), or they speak simply of Christ himself "who was with the Father before the aeons and appeared at the end" (Ign. Magn. 6:1; cf. 1 Peter 1:18ff.: *proegnōsmenou-phanerōthentos*; 1 John 1:1ff.). The prolog of the Gospel of John may also be cited in this connection. While the structure of the synoptic Gospels corresponds to the apostolic kerygma as it is reproduced in the speeches of Acts, the Gospel of John with its prolog is related more to the "revelation pattern" of preaching. There, of course, the key term is not *ephanerōthē*, but *sarx egeneto*. Even the passage on the creation of the world through the Logos does not come from the preaching type discussed here; one may compare the liturgical or hymnic texts found in Colossians 1 and Hebrews 1. But the revelation pattern does cast some light upon the place of the prolog as the beginning of the Gospel.

2. *The Soteriological Contrast Pattern*

This second preaching type of Bultmann's is also dominated by the opposition between "once" and "now" (*pote-nuni de*). But here the contrast is anthropologically and soteriologically oriented: "Once you were - but now you are" (Eph. 2:11-22; 5:8; Gal. 4:8f.; Rom. 6:17-22; 7:5f.; 11:30; 1 Peter 2:10; cf. Gal. 3:23ff.). It can also be expressed: "Once you were - but now God (Christ) has ... you" (Col. 1:21f.; Eph. 2:1-10; Titus 3:307; cf. Gal. 4:3ff.; Col. 2:13f.; 1 Peter 1:14ff.; 2 Clem. 1:6ff.).

As Bultmann has observed, the pattern can be linked to a catalog of vices (Titus 3:3ff.; cf. 1 Cor. 6:9ff.; Col. 3:5ff.; 1 Peter 4:3f.). In this connection some passages stress the mercy of God (Rom. 11:30; Eph. 2:4; Titus 3:5; 1 Peter 2:10; cf. 1 Peter 1:3). The change from the "once" prior to faith to the "now" of faith is marked by baptism, which is often expressly mentioned in this preaching type. The same is true in other texts which do not so strongly stress the contrast to prior existence (e.g. Rom. 6:1ff.; Heb. 10:19ff.). Whether or not the language is expressly about baptism, the transformation from unfaith to believing existence is made possible and brought about by God's act in Christ. Even within this preaching type direct statements about the Christ event are to be found (Ga. 4:3ff.; Eph. 2:13ff.; Col. 2:13ff.).

Further, it should not be overlooked that the contrast between former existence estranged from God and the new life in faith is a dominant theme in particular epistles (above all Col. 1:12-21; 2:8-15; 2:20ff.; 3:5ff.; Eph. 1:15-2:22; 1 Peter 1:13-2:10). Also in Romans the contrast between "once," the paganism and under the law (1:18-3:20), and "now," after the revelation of the righteousness of God (3:21-8:39), is basic to the structure of the epistle.[4]

This preaching type is intended to help believers understand what the existence newly offered to them in Christ really

---

[4]One may compare with this the structure of Bultmann's exposition of Pauline theology in his *Theology of the New Testament*.

means and entails, in contrast to their former life as pagans or Jews. The emphatic contrast between once and now contains a call to a thanksgiving rooted in knowledge (e.g., Eph. 2; Col. 1:12ff.), to steadfastness without falling back into Jewish legalism or pagan vice (e.g., Gal. 4; Col. 2-3), and thus also to a new way of living that corresponds to the renewal already given in Christ (e.g., 1 Peter; Titus 3:3ff.; Col. 3:5ff.).

3. *The Conformity Pattern*. Theme: Just as Christ - so you also.

Examples:

kathōs kai ho Christos	Rom. 15:7f.; Eph. 5:2, 25, 29; Col. 3:13; cf. Eph. 4:32
kai gar ho Christos	Rom. 15:2f.; cf. Mark 10:44f.
hoti kai Christos	1 Peter 2:21ff.; 3:18ff.

Some Johannine statements are in harmony with these formulations, both in content and terminology (John 13:34; 15:21ff.; 1 John 4:9ff.; etc.).

The pattern has its function within exhortation and serves to introduce allusions to Christ in this context. Christ is not seen simply as a model to be imitated; his conduct is prototypical precisely to the degree that it is of saving significance. What is important is Christ's surrender for us, his incarnation and his death, which imply salvation. Therefore it would be better to speak of *conformitas* and not *imitatio* because of later connotations of the term.

This pattern can serve to introduce quite detailed statements about Christ (cf. Eph. 5:25-27; 1 Peter 2:21-24; 3:18-22). It is indeed possible that actual quotations, perhaps fragments of hymns, were introduced in this way.[5] However, the introductory phraseology undoubtedly stems from the preaching style. Philippians 2:5-11 is also to be mentioned in this connection. For no matter how the expression *ho kai en Christō Iēsou* is to be precisely interpreted, it has the function of providing a transition from the exhortation to the christological statements, much as the usual formula *kathōs kai ho Christos*. Not stylistically, but in substance, 2 Corinthians 8:9 is in harmony with this preaching pattern (cf. also Heb. 3:1ff.; 12:2f.).

---

[5]Cf. R. Bultmann, "Bekenntnis - und Liedfragmente im ersten Petrusbrief," *Coniectanea Neotestamentica XI in honorem A. Fridrichsen* (Lund: Gleerup, 1947), 1-14.

4. *The Teleological Pattern*

In a whole series of christological statements final clauses are connected with a *hina (hopōs)*. This pattern belongs not only to preaching; it is found also in hymnic texts (e.g., Phil. 2:9f.). Such final (or consecutive) clauses are also found in the preaching types we have already discussed. But the pattern also occurs frequently in other places and in variant forms:

(a) "Christ...for us-so that we...": 1 Thess. 5:9f.; 2 Cor. 5:14f., 21; Gal. 3:13f.; 4:4f.; 1 Peter 2:21, 24; Ign. Trall. 2:1. Cf. Rom. 8:3f.; 2 Cor. 8:9; John 17:19.

(b) "Christ...for us-so that he...": Gal. 1:4; Eph. 5:25f.; Titus 2:13f.; 1 Peter 3:18; John 11:41f.; Ign. Smyrn.1.

(c) Without "for us" and similar variations: Rom. 14:9; Eph. 2:15f.; 4:10; Heb. 2:14f.; Barn. 5:1, 6f., 11; 7:2. Cf. John 10:17; 3:15-17.

(d) A special form: "...manifested-so that...": 1 John 3:5, 8; 4:9. Cf. Titus 2:11f.; Barn. 14:5.

Stauffer has collected a portion of this material under the heading "The Paradoxical Incarnation Formulae in Paul and his Successors."[6] He accurately observed the paradox: the protasis speaks of "the burden of the unencumbered," and the apodosis of "the unburdening of the encumbered." This applies in general to the passages gathered under (a) and (b) above and also to the passages from Barnabas. But the type should not be called an "incarnation-formula," because many of the examples are teleological passion formulas (1 Thess. 5:9f.; 1 Peter; etc.). It is also questionable whether or not the type is specifically Pauline; the paradoxical formulas under (a) and (b) are the most likely to have a peculiarly Pauline twist.

That the stylistic characteristics of this pattern belong to preaching seems clear primarily because the main emphasis lies on the final clause, sometimes prepared for by an *eis touto (gar)* (Rom. 14:9; 1 John 3:8; Barn. 5:1; cf. 1 Peter 2:21). The writer (or preacher!) gives additional emphasis to his concern by stressing that it corresponds to the goals of Christ's saving act (cf., e.g., Rom. 14:8f.; Gal. 3:13f.; 4:4f.; 2 Cor. 5:12ff.; 1 Thess. 5:9f.; 1 Peter 2:19ff.). The purpose clauses almost invariably have a soteriological content and/or motivate exhortations

---

[6] *New Testament Theology* (tr. J. Marsh; London: SCM Press, 1955), 343, cf. 246.

which comfort and admonish. Believers ought to know that they have access to salvation, righteousness and life because Christ came and died precisely for this purpose (Gal. 1:4; 2 Cor. 5:21; 1 Peter 3:18; Heb. 2:14f.; Barn. 5:1; etc.). Often the deliverance of the church is set forth as the goal of the saving activity of Christ (Eph. 2:15f.; 5:25f.; Titus 2:14; Barn. 5:7; Ign. Smyrn. 1:21 cf. Gal. 3:13f.). Occasionally, the clauses are directed toward the eschatological future (1 Thess. 5:9f.; Rom. 14:9). The idea is pervasive that the believers should learn to understand their own existence from the purpose of Christ's self-surrender. This also includes the possibility of a new life in obedience and the obligation to it: "And he died for all, that those who live might live no longer for themselves but for him who for their sake died and was raised" (2 Cor. 5:15; cf. Rom. 8:3f.; Eph. 5:27; Titus 2:14; 1 Peter 2:20-24). Therefore it can scarcely be doubted that this christological pattern as well had a function within hortatory preaching - probably there above all.

5. The simplest form for alluding to Christ is the addition of some phrase like *en kyriō, dia tou onomatos tou kyriou hēmōn Iēsou Christou* to the verb which introduces the paraenesis most often, *parakalein*.[7] In the Pastoral Epistles such allusions to Christ are expanded in the direction of creedal statements: *diamartyromai enōpion tou theou kai Christou Iēsou, tou...* (2 Tim. 4:1; cf. 1 Tim. 6:13; 5:21).

In oral preaching as in the extant letters there is a whole series of other possibilities for referring to Christ. Among these would be the homiletic use of kerygmatic, confessional, and liturgical formulations (cf., e.g., Rom. 3:24f.; 4:24f.; 8:33f.; 1 Thess. 4:14; 1 John 2:1f.). Perhaps other fixed patterns will also be discovered that may be especially characteristic for the community's preaching style. I have not mentioned here such things as the allusions to the parousia of Christ, the proclamation of Christ in early Christian prophecy (Revelation), and interpretation of scripture (Hebrews, Barnabas). However, through my observations I hope to have offered some supplement to what Bultmann has written in his *Theology of the New Testament*.

---

[7] C. Bjerkelund, *Parakalô* (Oslo: Oslo University Press, 1967), esp. 162-168. Cf. Rom. 15:30; 1 Cor. 1:10; 2 Cor. 10:1; 1 Thess. 4:1; 2 Thess. 3:12.

CHAPTER 3

THE PASSION NARRATIVE IN MATTHEW

The passion narrative in Matthew is a suitable point of departure for a discussion of synoptic questions and problems in gospel criticism, chiefly because of the unusual simplicity of the data for source criticism at this point. The Matthean passion is very close to the Markan. Every episode in the Markan account is also found in Matthew, with the exception of two informative notes (Mark 14:51f.; 15:21b) and some descriptive details (Mark 14:3-4, 7, 12-25, 40, 56-9, 67; 15:7, 44-5; 16:1-5). Still, it is even more noteworthy that the outline and order within the Matthean and Markan passion narratives are without exception identical. To a great extent a verbatim or almost verbatim correspondence can be found. To compare Matthew and Mark to Luke and John makes the similarity between the first two especially striking. They contain two variations of one and the same account.

The great majority of the critics have assumed that Matthew is dependent on Mark. Attempts to prove dependence the opposite way have been uniformly unconvincing.[1] Alternately, one could propose the use of a common source, an Ur-Markus. But within the passion story such a hypothesis would mean only a superfluous complication of the picture; such an Ur-Markus would be only a pallid double for our Mark. It is extremely unlikely that Matthew used written sources other than Mark for the passion narrative. We can be confident at *this* point, as at perhaps no other that we

---

[1]Cf. *Der Evangelist Matthäus* (Stuttgart: Calwer, 1929) and above all *Markus, der Evangelist für die Griechen* (Stuttgart: Calwer, 1935). A. Schlatter defended the priority of Matthew without success.

possess the author's sole written source.

Precisely because the source-critical situation is so simple at this point, it is all the more important to recognize that this result of critical analysis cannot resolve every problem in the Matthean passion narrative. The existence of scholars who defend the priority of Matthew confirms this.[2] Moreover, whoever rejects Matthean priority must concede that some weighty evidence supports it. Almost all of the observations may be reduced to a common denominator: within the passion narrative, as elsewhere, Matthew has a more "Jewish" character and stands closer to the original Palestinian milieu of the gospel message than does Mark. This fact cannot counterbalance the weight of the evidence that speaks for the priority of Mark, but it does require an explanation. Source-critical assumptions alone cannot provide a satisfactory explanation.[3] In addition to the literary dependence on Mark and the editorial work of the first evangelist, we must pay serious attention to the significance of Matthew's church environment: his geographical and historical situation, existing traditions, liturgy, preaching, and school concerns.

We may almost take for granted that the "church of Matthew" had some knowledge of Jesus's passion prior to its acquaintance with the written Gospel of Mark. Still, the fragments of the Gospel of Peter illustrate how the tradition continued to grow and change even after all four gospels were known. We must thus reckon with an intermingling of written and oral tradition and understand Matthew's literary revision of Mark within the framework of early Christian history.[4] In what follows I shall attempt to elaborate and establish these theses.

---

[2]B.C. Butler (*The Originality of St. Matthew* [Cambridge: Cambridge University Press, 1951])argues almost exclusively from the sayings of Jesus. But cf. more recently W. Farmer, *The Synoptic Problem* (New York: Macmillan, 1964) and D.L. Dungan, "Mark - The Abridgement of Matthew and Luke," *Jesus and Man's Hope* (ed. D.S. Buttrich; Pittsburgh: Pittsburgh Theological Seminary, 1970), 51-98.

[3]In this respect J. Finegan (*Die Überlieferung der Leidens - und Auferstehungsgeschichte Jesu* [Giessen: Töpelmann, 1934]) is also unsatisfactory. The early form critics began to see the interrelationships among the synoptics within the history of traditions framework. Cf. G. Bertram, *Die Leidensgeschichte Jesu und der Christuskult* (Göttingen: Vandenhoeck und Ruprecht, 1922), as well as M. Dibelius, *From Tradition to Gospel* (tr. B. Woolf; New York: Scribners, 1935) and R. Bultmann, *The History of the Synoptic Tradition* (tr. J. Marsh; New York: Harper and Row, 1963).

[4]Cf. the correct and fruitful statement of the problem by G.D. Kilpatrick, *The Origins of the Gospel according to St. Matthew* (Oxford: Clarendon Press, 1946) as well as by K. Stendahl, *The School of St. Matthew* (1954. 2 ed. Philadelphia: Fortress, 1968). The high probability of an interplay between written and oral sources has been established by the Old Testament discussion initiated by H.S. Nyberg and carried forward chiefly by Scandinavian scholars.

The special traditions of Matthew are only secondarily inserted into the Markan order. This is obviously the case in the account of Judas' death (27:3-10). Not only does it break the connection between 27:2 and 27:11, but it also stands at the wrong place chronologically; in 27:3-10 the chief priests and elders are in the temple, while immediately before (27:2) they are with Pilate. If this verifies the priority of the Markan version, there can still be no doubt that Matthew used traditional material with a long prehistory.[5] The core must go back to the tradition localized in Jerusalem, as evidenced by the etiology in 27:8. Even if none of the details is historical, the account of the horrible end of Judas reflects the impression the betrayal made upon the early Palestinian church.

The account of the miracles at the death of Jesus is also a later insertion. This is shown by the premature mention of the appearance in Jerusalem of the resurrected saints after the resurrection of Jesus (27:51b-54). A secondary tradition is presented in the apologetic legend of the guards at the tomb (27:62-6; 28:2-4, 11-15). It obviously arose in connection with discussions that were carried on with the Jews. Because the legend is incompatible with the intended anointing of the body of Jesus (Mark 15:1), it is at least conceivable that the legend presupposes a version of the story of the empty tomb in which the anointing did not occur (cf. John 20).[6]

Thus the special traditions prove, on the one hand, that Matthew is secondary to Mark and, on the other, that Matthew also knew oral traditions in addition to the written Markan account. Moreover, the special traditions influenced the redaction of the material taken over from Mark. This is clearest in the story of Judas in which 26:15 (Zech. 11:12) anticipates the report of the betrayer's death (cf. 26:23-5). The motif of the guard at the tomb (no theft of the corpse!) is anticipated in Matthew's peculiar emphasis on the soldiers' keeping watch at the cross (27:36 replacing the chronological reference in Mark 15:25).

In the largest portion, about four-fifths of the Matthean passion, Matthew recasts Mark. Many of the differences are hardly

---

[5]Cf. Kilpatrick, 44-46; Stendahl, 120-126 and 196-198.

[6]The story probably reached its present form in a community well acquainted with Mark. For in the words of Jesus in Matt. 27:63, *meta treis hēmeras* agrees with Mark 8:31; 9:31 and 10:34. Matthew himself uses *tē tritē hēmera* which is more exact chronologically, but he did not find it necessary to make the correction in his rendering of a statement of Jesus' enemies.

based on deliberate corrections but simply on the adaptation of the language and narrative style within the passion story to Matthew's characteristic mode.[7] Especially remarkable is the frequent reappearance of narrative sentences from Mark in the form on statements in direct address in Matthew; I consider this a decisive proof of Matthean dependence.

The eucharistic pericope presents the most formal example; Matthew 26:27 has *piete ex autou pantes* in contrast to the *epion ex autou pantes* of Mark 14:23. In a similar fashion the chronological reference of Mark 14:1 reappears in Jesus' words in Matthew 26:2; *meta duo hēmeras to pascha ginetai*. Even elsewhere Matthew has shaped or expanded statements in direct address from Markan material.[8] In part this may be no more than the hand of the evangelist. But the preference for direct discourse may well reflect the style of subsequent retelling of the story in the written text. Within the eucharistic pericope for example, the adaptation to direct address had already occurred in liturgical recitation.

Even where Matthew does not employ direct address one finds alongside verbal correspondences free reminiscences from Mark. For example, the phrase *palin apelthōn prosēuxato ton auton logon eipōn* is found in the second petition in Gethsemane in Mark, but in the third in Matthew (26:44). The phrase *ezētoun pseudomartyrian* in Matthew 26:59 is an anticipation of the characterization of the witnesses in Mark 14:56f.[9] Perhaps Matthew even takes for granted that his readers are familiar with the Markan account when he speaks simply of going to a certain man (*pros ton deina*) in the account of the preparation for the passover meal (26:18). In any case, 26:67-68 presuppose the blindfolding of Jesus reported by Mark; only in that way does the question *tis estin ho paisas se* make sense. This confirms that the Markan gospel is known not only to the author of Matthew but also to the community within which and for which he writes.

---

[7]*E.g. tote* or *de* for *kai, eipen* or *ephē* for *legei,* a preference for *idou, ho legomenos, symboulion lambanein,* conjunctive participles, frequent mention of the name Jesus. Cf. Finegan, 37f.

[8]Cf. Matt. 26:36, 38-40, 42 and 26:15, 65f.; 27:21. A complete list is given as Appendix I in *NTS* 2 (1955).

[9]Further examples: 27:15 (*tō ochlō*, cf. Mark 15:8); 27:32 (*exerchomenoi* cf. Mark 15:20 *exagousin*)and 21 *erchomenon*; 27:50 (*aphēken*) cf. Mark 15.37 *apheis*); 27:55 (*pollai*, cf. Mark 15:41); 27:60 (*megan* cf. Mark 16:4). In such cases it is not necessary to assume an intentional redaction; the similarities of phraseology may simply be unconscious reminiscences.

It often remains uncertain to what extent the reshaping of the Markan narrative rests on the redactional work of the evangelist and to what extent it occurred in the community even before the story was once again fixed in writing.[10] The question is not vital, for the first evangelist is an independent author to a much less degree than is Luke; rather, he is the preserver of tradition, a scribe, and he stands within a living tradition.

Agreements of Matthew and Luke against Mark are not numerous and almost exclusively concern the choice of words.[11] That Luke should have known the Gospel of Matthew is extremely improbable. All agreement ceases with the end of Mark. No agreement with the special material in the Matthean passion is found in Luke. Both evangelists make Pilate a witness to the innocence of Jesus, but they do it in entirely different ways. However, small agreements occur in spite of mutual independence. Luke frequently omits Markan statements that are also missing in Matthew; this fact enhances the importance of the agreements. A second common source, such as a passion narrative in Q, is not a real possibility.[12]

In some cases, the evidence supports Streeter's hypothesis that the agreements arose through a secondary harmonization within the textual tradition;[13] in others it remains completely conjectural.[14] But in order to be able to explain all data in this way the whole textual history must be reconstructed using a presupposition from literary analysis: agreements of Matthew-Luke against Mark are secondary; agreements of Matthew-Mark against Luke and Luke-Mark against Matthew are primary. This is not advisable. The harmonizing of the copyists was scarcely conscious or methodical. Rather, they adapted the text being copied to the wording familiar to them. Matthew and Luke would have done the same thing in their reproduction of the Markan text. However, the other wording to which they had access was not fixed in writing but was an oral tradition continuing alongside Mark or arising from Mark. The accumulation of minor agreements in a few pericopes is noteworthy:

---

[10]A. Debrunner (*Coniectanea Neotestamentica XI in honorem Antonii Fridrichsen* [Lund: Gleerup, 1947], 45-49) concludes from the use of *aparti* in Matt. 26:29, 64 that an intermediate stage lies between Mark and Matthew.

[11]The "minor agreements" are chiefly found in these pericopes, Matt. 26:39-42, 50-52, 58, 63-64, 68, 75 (?); 27:54-55, 57-60. Cf. Appendix II in *NTS* 2 (1955).

[12]E. Hirsch (*Die Frühgeschichte des Evangeliums*, Tübingen: Mohr, 1941, vol. II, 236-249) has argued for this.

[13]Cf. above all B.H. Streeter, *The Four Gospels* (London: Macmillan, 1927), 293-331.

[14]Cf. Streeter, 325ff.; Bultmann, 272f.

the trial before the council with mocking, the denial of Peter and, above all, the burial. The common "omissions" - for example, the second cock-crow or the scheme of the days of the passion week - could possibly be explained as peculiarities of the written Markan version that were not able to hold their own over against the wider stream of tradition.[15]

Within the passion story, agreements between Matthew and John against the others are more significant and interesting than those between Matthew and Luke: the mention of the name of Caiaphas, the account of a plot to kill Jesus, Judas' greed, the identification of the betrayer, emphasis on Jesus' sovereign power at the arrest, the inscription placed on the cross, the name 'Jesus' in the inscription, Joseph of Arimathea as a disciple of Jesus, the newness of the tomb, and the appearance of the resurrected Jesus to the women at the tomb. The wording of parallel pericopes, and some cases of the stereotyped phraseology furnish additional points of contact.[16]

No single hypothesis is sufficient to explain all John's contacts with the Matthean version of Markan material and with his special traditions. Some may be accidental; others may be ascribed to a "tendency" common to both evangelists. But such explanations are not sufficient. Besides the burial episode and the christophany at the tomb, the logion in the account of the arrest is of primary importance: *apostrepson tēn machairan sou ton topon autēs* (Matt. 26:52); *bale tēn machairan eis tēn thēkēn* (John 18:11). Such similarities do not demand John's literary dependence on Matthew. That there were points of contact between the pre-Johannine and pre-Matthean traditions is more probable. It is difficult to say this with certainty because the possibility also exists that elements of Matthew's text have been orally transmitted to John. If this is true, and there are some indications that it is at least part of the truth, it would prove that details from Matthew have passed into an oral tradition to be fixed again in writing by John. In any case, the agreements between Matthew and John are evidence of the interplay of written and oral tradition.

---

[15]Cf. Mark 14:40b, 51f., 72 (cf. v. 30); 15:21, 44f.; 16:3. This explanation of the omissions within the passion story becomes more probable when viewed in light of Matthew's and Luke's common omissions in earlier chapters.

[16]Matt. 26:3-5, 7, 9, 15, 23, 25; 27, 29, 37, 51, 59, 60, 62. Cf. Appendix III in *NTS* 2 (1955). P. Borgen, "John and the Synoptics in the Passion Narrative," *NTS* 5 (1958-59), 246-259.

We should also mention Matthew's Semitisms at this point. Matthew generally improves Mark's Greek. However, there are a few cases where the language of Matthew has the more Semitic character. We find names such as *Mariam* and *nazōraios*, foreign words such as *rabbi* and *korbanas*, biblical idioms such as *ekteinas tēn cheira* (26:15) and the paratactic construction *katabatō nun· apo tou staurou kai pisteusomen* (27:42), where Mark's subordinate clause is better Greek. Several other typically Matthean idioms and phrases are considered Semitisms by experts in the field.[17] Influence from the Hebrew Old Testament is present not only in the formula quotations in 27:9-10 but also in the designation of Joseph of Arimathea as a wealthy man (27:57; cf. Isa. 53:9). Matthew presupposes an audience familiar with the peculiarity of the Galilean dialect (26:73). Such observations do not prove the priority of Matthew over Mark or the existence of an Aramaic proto-Matthew. Rather, the assimilation and influence of Greek gospel literature within a Semitic-speaking area appears to be a recurring phenomenon in the early church. Such assimilation does not exclude the possibility that a chain of indigenous tradition continued parallel to it. Examples of this include the Aramaic Gospel of the Nazarenes and possibly the old Syriac versions and the Semitisms of Codex D.[18]

Consequently, we may assume that the Matthean gospel took shape in a bilingual or trilingual community. Certainly the liturgical language of that community was Greek. But, that community combined its use of the Greek Mark with a "school" activity which still worked with texts and traditions in Hebrew and Aramaic.[19]

Matthew relates the passion more closely to the Old Testament than does Mark. This is not surprising. Even before a written passion story was available, texts from the Old Testament (e.g. Ps. 22) were read as descriptions of the passion of Jesus,

---

[17]On the Semitisms in Matthew, cf. primarily M.-J. Lagrange, *Evangile selon Saint Matthieu* (3rd ed.; Paris: Gabalda, 1927); further Butler, 147-156. Cf. also M. Black, *An Aramaic Approach to the Gospels and Acts* (Oxford: Clarendon, 1946), 99f. on Matt. 28:1; E. Lohmeyer, *Das Evangelium des Matthäus* (Meyer; Göttingen: Vandenhoeck und Ruprecht, 1956) on 26:10, 13, 23, 28, 69 and other passages.

[18]Cf. Black, esp. 178-205, 212-221, where the persistence of oral tradition is noted. Concerning other contributions to the complex of problems, cf. A.E.J. Klijn, *A Survey of the Researches into the Western Test of the Gospels and Acts* (Utrecht, 1949), 27ff., 146-150.

[19]The conclusion of Kilpatrick (103: "Our community was Greek-speaking") has been modified somewhat by Stendahl's investigations in *The School of St. Matthew*.

and this practice continued even later, as best exemplified by the Epistle of Barnabas. The allusions to the Old Testament peculiar to Matthew, or made more explicit by him, show how the references were occasioned by previously existing traditions. The Old Testament texts, for their part, helped to shape the accounts.[20]

As an aid to the reconstruction of the course of events, the chief value of the Matthean passion lies in the light it throws upon the Markan passion narrative. There are, however, a few passages where historical considerations favor the priority of Matthew. That Matthew knows the name of the high priest Caiaphas has little if any significance. But the form on the name "Jesus Barabbas" (27:16-17 codex Θ, etc.) is so striking that it must be not only an original Matthean text but also an authentic historical tradition.[21] In the episode of the mocking of Jesus by the soldiers, historical probability argues for the scarlet robe of Matthew (27:28) in contrast to the purple of Mark.[22] The reference to Elijah (27:47ff.) seems to presuppose the Hebrew "Eli, Eli" in the cry from the cross; this text is better supported in Matthew than in Mark. In the trial scene Matthew seems to offer the older tradition when he omits from the words of Jesus the addition *cheiropoiēton-allon acheiropoiēton* (26:61); the same is true when he leaves out the assertion that statements of the witnesses who quoted these words did not agree (Mark 14:59).[23]

In such cases, the greater historical probability is no certain proof that old, authentic tradition has been preserved. The impression of historical accuracy could be the result of improvement by the redactor. Indeed, in the passion narrative of the "historian" Luke this may well be the case. But Matthew is hardly interested in the historically probable. One must therefore

---

[20]Cf. 26:15; 27:3-10 (on this Stendahl, 196f.); 27:43 and further 26:67 (Isa. 50:67); 27:12 (Isa. 53:7?); 27:34 (Ps. 69:22); 27:57 (Isa. 53:9 MT). Psalm 31:14 seems to have had an influence on the form of Matt. 26:3-4; the psalm (cf. esp. vs. 12-19) could be read with Psalms 22 and 69 as a description of the passion. Finally, Luke 23:46 alludes to Ps. 31:6. Cf. K.H. Schelkle, *Die Passion Jesu in der Verkündigung des Neuen Testaments* (Heidelberg: F.H. Kerle, 1949), 86ff. The minor variants in the citations 26:31, 54; 27:35, 46 support the relative independence of Matthew from Mark.

[21]T.W. Manson has called my attention to the possibility that the full name "Jesus Barabbas" may have stood in the primitive text of Mark 15:7 as well.

[22]Cf. R. Delbrück, "Antiquarisches zu den Verspottungen Jesu," *ZNW* 41 (1942), 132f.

[23]Cf. J. Wellhausen (*Das Evangelium Matthaei* [Berlin: Reimer, 1904], 141f.), who surmises that Matthew has preserved the original even in 26:67.

allow for acquaintance with traditions independent of Mark.

My concern here is not to decide individual cases. It is rather to show the complexity of the problem, and to indicate how many factors must be taken into account even in an area of the synoptic problem where the source-critical question can be answered clearly and simply. We will not succeed if we follow a purely literary approach. To be sure, the Matthean passion is a revision of the Markan account, but the reshaping is not simply the result of the literary activity of a redactor. It has its *Sitz im Leben* within a specific church which esteemed Mark's gospel and which possibly read it in worship. But in this milieu, oral tradition was still living and the study of the Old Testament was pursued.[24] Here and there the possibility exists that the secondary Matthean version contains an authentic tradition, but what is more important is that it shows how a specific church community understood and interpreted the passion of Jesus.

With this I come to the second part of my exposition: the theology of the passion narrative in Matthew. There is the danger at this point of over-interpretation; not all deviations from Mark are determined by a theological tendency. However, in the composition as a whole and in many details, a specific understanding of the passion story characteristic for Matthew emerges. What is at stake in this interpretation is the significance of the passion of Jesus for the church in its relationship to the synagogue.

As in the other gospels, so in Matthew: the passion story is dominated by the conviction that Jesus suffered as the Messiah. Jesus' passion is his road to enthronement. Matthew depicts the appearance of the Resurrected One on the mountain as a revelation of the already enthroned Christ to whom all power has been given, who gives to his disciples the great commission. Corresponding to Mark's description, Jesus' suffering is portrayed as the road of the humiliated Christ: rejected by the leaders of Israel, betrayed by Judas, forsaken by his disciples, condemned by the council, denied by Peter, mocked by many - up to the cry of forsakenness on the cross, "My God, My God--." As in Mark, the passion of Jesus is portrayed in conjunction with Old Testament psalms of suffering; Jesus walks the road prescribed for him so that scripture may be fulfilled (26:54, 56). Matthew emphasizes more strongly than does Mark how Jesus' own word is also fulfilled

---

[24]Here we may conjecture that Matthew was already revered as an apostle and guarantor of tradition before the first gospel was accredited to him. This would explain the identification of the tax collector with Matthew (9:9 and 10:3).

(26:2; cf. 27:63; 28:6). A motive for the insertion of the Judas story (27:3-10) was a concern to show that the word of woe concerning the betrayer has been fulfilled (26:24). Matthew emphasizes the voluntary character of Jesus' suffering. An example of this is the modification of the Gethsemane pericope (cf. esp. 26:42). A saying of Jesus is the signal that first sets the whole event in motion (26:1-2; cf. 26:18, 25 and also 26:50). These are all familiar observations; Dibelius, for example, has shown how in Matthew Jesus in the midst of the passion remains the Son of God endowed with power.[25]

The hearer of Matthew's story hardly doubts for a moment that twelve legions of angels would have been at the disposal of Jesus the Christ if he had prayed for them. But that was a moral impossibility (26:53; cf. 26:61, *dynamai*). The crucifixion is not a profound mystery in the same way as in Mark; the account is constantly illuminated by the faith of the church. The resurrection follows as self-evident. In Mark the anticipation of Jesus' resurrection in 27:53 would be impossible, or at least stylistically inappropriate. In contrast, the hearers of the Matthean account know all the time that he who was crucified is resurrected. The messiahship of the Crucified One is thus understood from the perspective of the Christian faith.[26] Luke (23:2) and John (19:12) refer each in his own way to the political aspect of the messianic question. In Matthew such historical reflections are remote. He makes the Jews condemn and mock Jesus as the Christ of the Christian confession, *ho Christos ho huios tou theou* (26:63-6). Jesus' self-confession, identical with the Christian confession, is a blasphemy in Jewish ears as is the assertion that the Crucified One is God's son (27:40, 43). In the trial before Pilate it is not so much a question of the King of the Jews (27:11; cf. Mark) but rather of *Iesous ho legomenos Christos* (27:17, 22).[27] The identity of the crucified Jesus as the Christ of Christian confession is presented in constant opposition to his rejection by the Jews.[28]

---

[25]*From Tradition to Gospel*, 196-199.

[26]G. Bornkamm ("Matthaus als Interpret der Herrenworte," *TLZ* 79 [1954], 341-346) comes to a similar conclusion from other material. Cf. his article "End Expectation and Church in Matthew," *Tradition and Interpretation in Matthew* (tr. P. Scott; Philadelphia: Westminster, 1963), 15-51.

[27]Cf. also the reminiscences of the Christian kerygma in 27:63, 64; 28:7.

[28]As a rule Matthew designates Jesus' opponents as *hoi archiereis kai hoi presbyteroi (tou laou)* (26:3, 43; 27:1, 3, 12, 20; 28:11f., ef. 21:43), no doubt in order to emphasize that they acted as official leaders of the Jews. The legal aspect of

Of primary importance is the Barabbas episode. The care with which it is reworked demonstrates its significance for the Matthean passion. From the beginning the pericope is dominated by a question that poses the alternative: who do you want me to release for you, Jesus Barabbas or Jesus who is called Christ? With its acclamation, the mob concurs with the judgment of its leaders; this is indeed already the thought of Mark, but in Matthew it is set forth even more clearly.[29] From a special tradition Matthew added the reference to Pilate's wife (27:19) in which the Gentile woman declares Jesus to be innocent. More important, however, is the elaboration of the pericope by Pilate's self-exoneration and the assuming of guilt by the Jews (27:24-25). Here the existence of any special tradition is open to doubt. An interpretation of the event is set in direct discourse: the Jews declare themselves responsible for the death of Christ. Pilate's declaration of innocence and the Jew's acceptance of responsibility are stylized in accordance with an ancient phraseology whose origin lies perhaps in the institution of blood vengeance. It played a role primarily within the sphere of sacred law; God is the avenger of innocent blood. Similar formulas are used in rabbinic legal procedure, where they serve primarily to exonerate the tribunal and to incriminate possible false witnesses.[30] In Matthew not only the term *haima athōon* in 27:4 (23:35) but also the maxim of 26:52, alluding to Genesis 9:6, belongs to the same complex of ideas.

Within the Matthean passion narrative an etiological interest appears at several points (27:8, 28:15). This interest also stands in the background in the Barabbas pericope. Judas

---

the passion is also emphasized by the oath at the trial (26:67) as well as by Matthew's designation *ho hēgemōn* for Pilate (27:2, 11, etc.). The *grammateis* appear only in 26:57 and 27:41, whereas in Mark they appear also in 14:1, 53 and 15:1. Could it be that the scribes were the contemporary opponents of the evangelist, while the chief priests and elders were considered the principal adversaries of Jesus?

[29] P. Seidelin "Den synoptiske Jesu," *Bidrag til Kristologien*, (eds. L. Berner *et. al.*; Bringstrup, 1951) gives a few hints concerning the results of his unpublished studies on the passion story and writes among other things, "The real point of the Barabbas episode is to eliminate Pilate from the question of guilt, because he was not a Jew, did not belong to the people, and was therefore irrelevant to this confrontation" (63).

[30] Cf. 2 Sam. 1:16; 3:28f.; 14:9; 1 Kings 2:31-33, 44-45; Lev. 20:9; Deut. 21:5ff.; Sus. 46 Theod; As. Mos. 9:7; Mishnah Sanhedrin 4:5; Test. Levi. 16:3; Acts 5:28; 18:6; 20:26. Cf. K. Koch, ed., *Um das Prinzip der Vergeltung in Religion und Recht des Alten Testaments* (Darmstadt: Wiss. Buchgesellschaft, 1971), esp. the essays by Koch and H. Reventlow.

perishes because he is guilty of the innocent blood of Jesus; but for Matthew even the Jews of his time stand under the blood guilt that they have incurred. He probably understood the fall of Jerusalem as a corroboration of that guilt (cf. 22:7). That the assignation of guilt to the Jews is not a negligible aspect of the passion story for Matthew is confirmed by the preceding chapters of the gospel. The parables in 21:28-22:14 and the speech in 23 are especially important in this connection. At its conclusion (23:35f.) we hear of the "righteous blood" that shall come upon this generation. What one might call the theme of the passion narrative is stated in Matthew's conclusion to the parable of the vineyard: "The kingdom of God shall be taken away from you and given to a nation producing the fruits of it" (21:23).[31]

On the positive side, the blood of Jesus--of which the Jews have made themselves guilty--is seen as the blood of the (new) covenant, which is shed for many for the forgiveness of sins. The eucharistic pericope has a central place within the passion story. An indication of this is the reshaping of the account of the preparations for the Passover meal (26:17-19). According to Matthew, what is to be prepared for is not the eating of the Jewish Passover lamb but the first paschal feast of the new covenant; Jesus' kairos is near and he will celebrate Passover with his disciples in order to institute the Eucharist. The eucharistic pericope itself (26:26-29) is brought into relation to the contemporary celebration of the church even more clearly than in the parallel traditions.

The entire passion (and resurrection) story has an etiological significance; it explains the origin and the continuing basis of the church's existence as the people of the new covenant, as the evangelizing, baptizing, and teaching community (28:19). Matthew emphasizes the failure of the disciples, though not quite as sharply as Mark.[32] The foundation of the church's existence is not the faithfulness of the disciples but the faithfulness of Jesus and the forgiveness of sins through his blood. However, a paraenetic motif also appears in Matthew's portrayal of the disciples and their failure; he warns against false certainty and calls for faithfulness to the confession of Christ.[33]

---

[31]Cf. Seidelin, 64f.: on Mark, M. Kiddle, "The Death of Jesus and the Admission of the Gentiles in St. Mark," *JTS* 35 (1934), 45-50.

[32]As examples of modification, cf. the omission of Mark 14:40b and the insertion of *idein to telos* in Matt. 26:58 and *pikrōs* in 26:75.

[33]Cf. 26:22-25, 29 (*meth hymōr*), 31-35 (*en emoi-tes poimnēs-en soi*), 38, 40 (*met emou*), 58, 69-75; 27:57 (*emathēteuthē*); 28:8, 17.

For Matthew, disciples from all nations constitute the new community, as emphasized clearly at the conclusion of the gospel. Within the passion story the events at the death of Jesus prepare for this (27:51-54). The earthquake and the resurrection of the deceased saints, related to Jewish interpretations of Ezekiel 37, testify to the eschatological significance of the death of Jesus.[34] This special Matthean tradition is inserted between Mark 15:38 and 39 so that the event is illuminated in three ways: (1) The rending of the temple veil signifies the end of the earthly temple service and judgment upon Judaism. (Also, the providing of access to God? cf. Heb. 10:19f.). (2) The resurrection of the saints points to the fulfillment of the promises made to the pious of the old covenant. (3) The confession of the centurion and his men that the crucified Jesus is Son of God foreshadows the conversion of Gentiles to Christ.

Matthew did not write his Gospel exclusively for Jewish Christians, but for the universal church.[35] The evangelist and many members of his community were obviously of Jewish descent. But the separation of Jesus' disciples from the Jews is complete. Matthew 28:15 speaks of "the Jews" in an almost Johannine way. However, it is no accident that Matthew speaks of the Jews in this way only after the crucifixion, because the breach is first consummated by it. The people of the new covenant is the church from all nations. Thus, the church as represented by Matthew understands itself in terms of the passion and resurrection of Jesus; and conversely, the passion story of Jesus is related to the peculiar existence of the church separated from the Jewish nation.[36] To this church also belongs the Old Testament as it is fulfilled in the history of Jesus. Consequently, one could say that in Matthew the passion of Jesus stands at the mid-point

---

[34]Cf. H. Riesenfeld ("The Resurrection in Ezekiel xxxvii and in the Dura-Europos Paintings," *Uppsala Universitets Årsskrift* [1948], 11) where the correspondence between Matt. 27:51-53 and the representation of Ezek. 37 in the synagogue at Dura is demonstrated.

[35]K.W. Clark ("The Gentile Bias in Matthew," *JBL* 66 [1947], 165-172) even accepts a Gentile Christian background for the author.

[36]W. Hillmann (*Aufbau und Deutung der synoptischen Leidensberichte* [Freiburg i. Br., 1941]) comes to a similar conclusion though he approaches the problem quite differently: The first evangelist "takes up the question of his readers, which has to do above all with the internal and external vindication of the Christian church, and he justifies this new community by appeal to the events and the teachings of Jesus, based on faith in his true Messiahship" (264).

of a triangle whose angles are Old Testament, church, and synagogue.[37]

We conclude with a brief word about the place of the passion narrative in the gospel as a whole. On the one hand, Kähler's expression "passion narratives with an extended introduction"[38] proves to be true for Matthew much less than for Mark; the preceding chapters, above all the speech compositions, carry much too great a weight for that. On the other hand, it would also be one-sided to view chapters 26-28 with B.W. Bacon as an epilog to the five-fold work and to understand Matthew as a catechetical handbook.[39]

The passion narrative is linked to the teaching of Jesus by means of 26:1: "And it happened when Jesus had finished all these sayings." In the same way, Jesus' teaching is bound to the resurrection by 28:20, the word of the Resurrected One: "Teaching them to observe all that I have commanded you." It is certainly not accidental that both passages remind one of formulations at the end of Deuteronomy.[40] The evangelist understood his work as a sort of counterpart to the Pentateuch.

The passion of Jesus can only begin when Jesus has ended his teaching ministry. Those disciples added after Easter must learn to keep what Jesus commanded during his teaching in Israel. The whole post-Easter church stands under the word that was addressed only to Israel before the passion. But like the kingdom, this word is taken from the Jews and given to a nation which must learn to keep the commandments. On this basis must be explained the co-existence of apparent particularism and universalism in Matthew. The problem can be illustrated by means of Chapter 10. The logia gathered there are obviously put together as instructions for the contemporary church; however, the command to go only to the lost sheep of the house of Israel stands at the beginning of the chapter. For

---

[37]On this cf. A. Oepke (*Das neue Gottesvolk* [Gütersloh: Bertelsmann, 1950]) who speaks, for example, of a "peculiar ... dialectical, triangular relationship" (42f.). Cf. now W. Trilling, *Das Wahre Israel* (Leipzig: St. Benno Verlag, 1959) also R. Hummel, *Die Auseinandersetzung zwischen Kirche und Judentum im Matthäusevangelium* (München: Kaiser, 1966).

[38]*The So-called Historical Jesus and the Historic, Biblical Christ* (tr. C. Braaten; Philadelphia: Fortress, 1964), 80, note 11.

[39]One major point of departure for this theory is the five-fold occurrence of the concluding formula: 7:28; 11:1; 13:53; 19:1; 26:1. Cf. B.W. Bacon, *Studies in Matthew* (New York: Holt, 1930), 80-82; repeated by Stendahl, 25. Regarding Matthew as a "handbook," cf. Stendahl, 20-29.

[40]On Matt. 26:1, cf. Deut. 31:1 (LXX), 24; 32:44f. On Matt. 28:20, cf. Deut. 29:8; 30:8, 10, 16; 31:12; 32:46.

Matthew this specific command is applicable only to the pre-Easter situation. But Jesus' disciples in all nations must learn to keep all that he commanded on the occasion of the sending out of his apostles to Israel. Both belong together for Matthew: Jesus is *Christos* and *Didaskalos*, crucified Son of God and New Moses. This is in accord with the double character of the book as "gospel" and "handbook."

CHAPTER 4

THE PURPOSE OF MARK'S GOSPEL

In spite of the objections which have been advanced, there is still good reason to regard Mark as the earliest of our four Gospels. Not one of the many attempts to reconstruct written sources for Mark has been generally accepted. Form critical studies suggest, however, that not only the smallest units of tradition but also more inclusive complexes of tradition were available to the evangelist in a fairly fixed form. The general framework is provided by a pattern used in kerygmatic summaries of the message concerning Jesus and those events which were connected with his name, from the baptism by John up to the resurrection. Thus it is clear that the evangelist did not have a completely free hand in dealing with tradition. Yet Mark's Gospel has such a distinctive literary and theological character that the evangelist's work cannot be confined to the collecting and editing of already existing tradition. We must ask what readers he has in mind and what he has intended with his Gospel.

Generally speaking one can say that the Gospel must be written with the "intention to preserve that tradition which was applied on various occasions to the upbuilding of the church."[1] As a reaction against the *Tendenzkritik* of the Tübingen school there was some justification for saying that this Gospel has no other "tendency" than that which every Gospel must have.[2] But such general characterizations of Mark's purpose are insufficient,

---

[1]H. Mosbech, *Nytestamentlig Isagogik* (Copenhagen: Gyldendalske Boghandel, 1946-49), 199, cf. 182f.

[2]A. Jülicher, *Einleitung in das Neue Testament* (7th ed. by E. Fascher; Tübingen: Mohr, 1931), 300.

and more recently scholars have rightly sought to move beyond them. In general the question of the individual Gospel's composition and "theology" has attracted increasing attention, and several monographs and articles have been devoted to Mark in particular.[3] Despite these contributions the problem of purpose remains. There is still good reason to outline a suggested solution, although the problem demands penetrating and detailed study.

Any attempt to make a detailed separation between tradition and redaction must necessarily be hypothetical, since in Mark's case we have no earlier writing for comparison. Conjectured symbolism and typology provide an even shakier foundation upon which to construct Mark's purpose. The point of departure for determining the purpose of the Gospel ought to be observations whose accuracy cannot be doubted. There is reason to focus attention on three features which are so characteristic of Mark's Gospel that any plausible theory of the document's purpose must be able to explain them.

1. *Selection of Jesus' sayings.* Mark has not tried to be complete, as have Matthew and Luke. But neither has he totally excluded sayings material, something which could perhaps be explained by postulating that the sayings tradition had a form and function different from that of narrative material. Since Mark has chosen some sayings and excluded others, the selection must be determined by the evanglist's intention.

2. *The "Messianic Secret"* and related conceptions. Since W. Wrede these features have attracted a good deal of attention.[4]

---

[3]Cf. *e.g.* R.H. Lightfoot, *The Gospel Message of St. Mark* (Oxford: Clarendon, 1950). A.M. Farrer, *A Study in St. Mark* (Westminster: Dacre Press, 1951). Ph. Carrington, *The Primitive Christian Calendar: a Study in the Making of the Marcan Gospel* (Cambridge: Cambridge University Press, 1952); reviewed by W.D. Davies, "Reflections on Archbishop Carrington's 'A Primitive Christian Calendar,'" *The Background of the New Testament and its Eschatology* (eds. W.D. Davies and D. Daube; Cambridge: Cambridge University Press, 1964). H. Riesenfeld, "On the Composition of the Gospel of Mark," *The Gospel Tradition* (tr. E. Margaret Rowley; Philadelphia: Fortress Press, 1970). W. Marxsen, *Mark the Evangelist* (tr. D. Juel, et al.,; Nashville: Abingdon, 1969). G. Schille, "Bemerkungen zur Formgeschichte des Evangeliums. Rahmen und Aufbau des Markus-Evangeliums," *NTS* 4 (1957), 1-24.

[4]W. Wrede, *Das Messiasgeheimnis in den Evangelien* (Göttingen: Vandenhoeck und Ruprecht, 1907) ET. *The Messianic Secret* (Greenwood, S.C.: Attic, 1972). As representative of the later discusssion, cf. esp. H.J. Ebeling, *Das Messiasgeheimnis und die Botschaft des Markus-Evangelisten* (BZNW 19; Berlin: Töpelmann, 1939). Further E. Percy, *Die Botschaft Jesu* (Lund: Gleerup, 1953), 271-299; E. Sjöberg, *Der verborgene Menschensohn in den Evangelien* (Lund: Gleerup, 1955) esp. 100-132; and G. Minette de Tillesse, *Le secret messianique dans l'évangile de Marc* (Paris: Editions du Cerf, 1968).

It has become clear that the ideas did not originate with the evangelist. He has taken over and developed motifs which were present in the tradition. It is possible that the idea of the hidden Son of man goes back in some form to Jesus himself. The background is in Jewish concepts of eschatological mysteries, including notions of a hidden existence of the Messiah (or the Son of man) before his public manifestation. But the emphasis and shape which these concepts have received must result from some particular concern of the evangelist.[5]

3. *The Ending of the Gospel*. The secondary endings of Mark show that at an early stage something was felt to be missing. In modern research as well it has often been assumed that an original conclusion has been lost. But it appears that Matthew and Luke did not know any other ending to Mark than the one which is attested in our earliest manuscripts. An intentional scribal omission is unlikely in view of the great deviations between the other Gospels, and the conjecture of an external cause for the loss of the text is a mere expedient. Today there is a rising tendency to assume that 16:8 is the original ending.[6] The puzzling conclusion which tells about the women who fled from the empty tomb and who remained silent because they were afraid cannot be explained as an accident; it harmonizes too well with the Gospel's presentation of the messianic secret and its overall character as a "book of secret epiphanies" (Dibelius).[7]

It is appropriate to begin with this last point. If the evangelist has concluded his work with the words of 16:8, the account must point beyond itself. That is evident also from the angels' message: "But go, tell his disciples and Peter that he is going before you to Galilee." Following Lohmeyer's *Galiläa und Jerusalem* (1936), several scholars have assumed that these words need not refer to the risen Christ's revelations to the disciples, but to the Parousia. Such a localizing of the Parousia is not really in harmony with what is otherwise said about the coming of the Son of man. But even if this interpretation should

---

[5]Cf. Sjöberg, 219: "The expressions of the messianic secret peculiar to Mark have turned out to be Mark's creations in almost every case. But the fact of the hidden Messiah is nevertheless firmly anchored in tradition."

[6]Cf. *e.g.* O. Linton, "Der vermisste Markusschluss," *Theol. Blätter* 8 (1929), 229-234. H. Mosbech, "Markusevangeliets avslutning," *SEA* 5 (1940), 56-73. R.H. Lightfoot, 80-97, 106-116.

[7]Cf. W. Nauck, "Die Bedeutung des leeren Grabes," *ZNW* 47 (1956), 251, note 45.

prove correct, the Gospel presupposes that the silence of the women was not the last of the Easter events. After Jesus' resurrection, during the time before the end, the Gospel is to be proclaimed to all nations (13:10; 14:9). What remained hidden during Jesus' earthly life will be preached in public (9:9). What Mark knows but does not say is that although the angel's message was not communicated, the risen Christ himself appeared to his disciples. It seems best to understand the words "tell the disciples and Peter" as hinting at appearances both to Peter and to the twelve. In this connection it is of secondary importance whether or not Mark knew of an appearance to the women on their flight from the tomb or whether he has localized the appearances to the disciples in Galilee or in Jerusalem.

Not only the account of the women at the tomb, but also the evangelist's whole picture of the disciples points forward toward a decisive turning point which occurred when the risen Lord revealed himself. It is conceivable that this unveiling of the mystery was treated as a genuine *arcanum* which should not be committed to writing and thereby be exposed to profane readers. But such a hypothesis is not supported by what we otherwise know about the treatment of the resurrection message in primitive Christianity. Even in Mark, Jesus' resurrection from the grave is proclaimed clearly enough. That the Gospel mentions neither the fact nor the manner of the appearances does not mean that Mark intended to veil the secret. It must rather mean that his readers were already informed.

Thus there is reason to maintain that Mark presupposes the readers' knowledge of the events subsequent to the women's flight from the empty tomb. In other words, the book is intended for Christian readers who already believe the message about Jesus and his resurrection. The written Gospel points beyond itself to the living word in the church, that message which the disciples were commissioned to proclaim when the risen Christ appeared to them. The goal is not to awaken faith but to recall the character of the resurrection as a mystery and wonder which could elicit fear and awe. The conclusion suggests that the evangelist did not intend to write an "aid for mission work,"[8] but writes for believers and wants to clarify for them what faith and the Gospel really involve.

The so-called messianic secret (better: the Christ-mystery) is not a literary device intended to maintain suspense

---

[8]Thus Jülicher-Fascher, 308.

by keeping something hidden from the reader until he learns the solution of the enigma. The Christ-mystery is a secret only for those persons who appear in the book. The readers know the point of the story from the very beginning: it is the Gospel of Jesus Christ. They know that Jesus was the stronger one who would come after John and baptize with the Holy Spirit, the one in whose name they themselves have been baptized. It has never been concealed from them that during his entire earthly life Jesus was the beloved Son in whom God was well pleased. They know the answer to the disciples' astonished question: "Who can this be?" They know that when Jesus died, forsaken by men and by God, it happened in order that the scriptures should be fulfilled: the Son of man gave his life as a ransom for many. Mark is not presenting the solution to something which has been an unanswered riddle; he is emphasizing the mysterious character of something with which his readers are familiar.

Wrede claimed that the messianic secret was an attempt to harmonize the earlier view that Jesus became the Messiah only at the resurrection with the later view that Jesus' earthly life had a messianic character. This understanding of the messianic secret as a transitional device hardly explains the origin of the motif and certainly does not explain its function in Mark.[9] More widespread than Wrede's explanation of the messianic secret is the view that it is apologetic in character.[10] According to this interpretation, the injunctions to silence and the theme of divine hardening of hearts explain Jesus' rejection by his own people though he was the Messiah and a great worker of miracles. But if the concern had been apologetic, one would have expected Matthew and Luke to have made greater use of the idea. In fact, the other two synoptics do have an apologetic tendency, each in its own way, which it is difficult to find in Mark. Further, Israel's unbelief does not play the role in the second Gospel that the theory presupposes. Matthew shows how Jesus' life and passion are the foundation of the church's existence in its opposition to the synagogue, and at the same time he emphasizes that the new people stand under the command of Jesus and will appear before his judgment seat. Luke-Acts tells how God's promises to Israel were fulfilled in Jesus, and how the salvation promised Israel

---

[9]Cf. the critical objections of Ebeling, Percy and Sjöberg.

[10]The explanation offered by T.A. Burkill in a series of articles and in his book *Mysterious Revelation* (Ithaca: Cornell University Press, 1963) is a variant of this theory. It has been criticized by Ebeling, Percy and Sjöberg.

was extended to the Gentiles. In Mark, the portrayal of the Jews is more differentiated than in the other Gospels. The relation to the Jewish people is neither a present conflict as in Matthew nor a problem of salvation history as in Luke.

Mark presupposes the church and the Gentile mission, but his interest is concentrated on Jesus himself. The contrast between "you" and "those outside" in Mark 4:11 cannot be identified with the contrast between the church and the synagogue. It has to do more generally with the division between believers and non-believers. Together with the injunctions to silence and the messianic secret in general, the distinction between public teaching in parables and esoteric interpretations serves to elucidate the gospel's character as a revealed mystery. Jesus and his word become genuine revelation and salvation only for the chosen circle to whom the secret is given.

The connection between the messianic secret and the crucifixion must be different from that which proponents of the apologetic theory have supposed. Mark's stress on the mystery of Jesus' life must be closely associated with the peculiar character of the Markan passion story. Mark does not give prominence to Jesus' sovereign power in the midst of suffering as do Matthew and John, nor does he portray Jesus as the exemplary martyr as Luke does. In Mark, the picture of Jesus as the hidden, contradicted and misunderstood Messiah reaches its high point in the passion story. There Jesus is depicted as the rejected one who was betrayed, deserted and denied by his own, slandered, condemned, spit upon and ridiculed, mocked as he hung on the cross, even by those who were crucified with him. Not the physical suffering but the expulsion from human fellowship is stressed again and again. Even his cry in deepest need and loneliness, "My God, my God...!" elicits only a crude joke. The concealing of Jesus' messiahship is not an apologetic theory intended to explain how Jesus was rejected. The case is just the reverse. In Mark, the historical fact that Jesus was spurned by the majority of Jews serves to illustrate the mysterious character of the revelation and salvation given in him. It has to do with "what no eye has seen, nor ear heard, nor the heart of man conceived, what God has prepared for those who love him."

Partly in line with the interpretation advanced here, H.J. Ebeling has made the evangelist's kerygmatic intention the basis for his explanation of the messianic secret in Mark.[11] He believes the secret to be a literary device which serves to stress

---

[11]Cf. note 4 above.

the greatness of the revelation in which the readers participate as they hear the Christian message. Against this interpretation it has rightly been maintained that Ebeling has overemphasized the purely literary at the expense of content and religious meaning. It has been further objected that it is not legitimate to place the evangelist's kerygmatic intention in any exclusive contrast to historicity.[12] Ebeling writes in a somewhat inflated style, without sufficient precision, which is shown not least by his use of the fashionable word "kerygmatic." The worthwhile element lies in the emphasis that there must be a close connection between the messianic secret and the evangelist's "message" or purpose. But he misses the mark because his understanding of revelation and proclamation as an always contemporary call to decision is one-sided. Mark writes for those who are already in the church and have received the secret of God's kingdom as a gift. His goal is not to persuade readers to believe in the message but to remind them of what is contained in it in order that they might understand what has been given to them. The purpose is not kerygmatic in the word's narrower sense, but rather theological or - to coin a word - anamnetic.[13]

That the evangelist has Christian readers in mind is evident especially from his description of the relation of the disciples to the Christ-mystery. As often pointed out, it is a two-sided relationship. The secret of the kingdom of God is given to the disciples; they recognize that Jesus is the Messiah and are instructed concerning the necessity of suffering. An inner circle receives special revelations. Nevertheless, we constantly hear that the disciples lack faith and do not understand. There are certain hints that their insight gradually increases; but even so, they fail in the hour of crisis. Contrasted to those outside, the disciples are the recipients of revelation. Despite this fact, they form the dark background against which the figure of Christ appears. Mark does not go as far as the author of the letter of Barnabas, who says that the disciples were sinful beyond measure (5:9). But Mark's picture of the disciples can also serve to illustrate Jesus' words: "I came not to call the righteous, but sinners." Not their own fitness, but Jesus' call and God's gift make them Jesus' disciples and recipients of the mystery of God's kingdom. Not because of their fidelity, but despite their failures they became after the resurrection the bearers of Jesus' message and the kernel of the church.

---

[12]Percy, 288ff.; Sjöberg, 118ff.
[13]Cf. my essay "Anamnesis," in this volume.

Mark's picture of the disciples cannot without qualification be regarded as typical of his view of Christians. He markedly contrasts time prior to the resurrection with time after the resurrection. It was during the time of Jesus' earthly life that the miracles, the messiahship, and the necessity of suffering were to be kept hidden; during this time the disciples lacked understanding and faith. Throughout Mark's Gospel, the messianic secret expresses an understanding of the "history of revelation" (Percy), according to which the decisive and complete revelation of the mystery, the realization of God's saving plan, first occurred with Jesus' death and resurrection. The Easter events place a dividing line between the period when Jesus lived as the hidden and misunderstood Messiah, and the time when he is openly proclaimed as the Crucified and Risen One. But this does not mean that the possibility for failure among Jesus' followers has ceased, that the dark picture of the disciples' behavior during Jesus' life on earth was only to be a foil for an all the more radiant picture of the church which lives in faith in the risen Lord. The conclusion of the Gospel shows on the contrary that even when the message that Jesus is risen is proclaimed by angels, those who hear can react in a manner which is no more adequate than that of the disciples when Jesus was among them.

If it were the case that the disciples' misunderstanding only provided contrast to the understanding which is now granted the church, the same should apply to the disciples inability to work miracles.[14] But even if we retain the full force of the sayings concerning the boundless possibilities open to believers, it is unlikely that Mark thought these possibilities were realized in the church. His emphasis on the disciples' shortcomings cannot be fully explained as stemming from Mark's view of the "history of revelation." The additional feature is paraenetic. This paraenetic concern was already present in tradition, most clearly in the Gethsemane narrative: "Watch and pray that you may not enter into temptation." Mark makes it something of a continuing theme. The members of the church who have partaken of the full revelation and salvation must see to it that they do not fall short, misunderstand and fail as the disciples did in the time before the resurrection. Ferdinand Kattenbusch once wrote: "The

---

[14]J. Coutts ("The Authority of Jesus and of the Twelve in St. Mark's Gospel," *JTS* n.s. 8 [1957], 111-118) has observed that the disciples' inability to perform miracles should be added to the features noted by Wrede.

Twelve are 'authorities' for the learning church, *types* for the celebrating 'church'."[15] With reference to Mark one might add: they are examples intended to serve as a warning to a complacent church lacking in faith.

What is said here about the Christ-mystery in Mark can be illuminated by analogous conceptions in the epistles. Ephesians and Colossians, and texts like 1 Corinthians 2:6-16 and 1 Peter 1:1-12 imply that the presentation of the gospel's content as a mystery had its setting in preaching to the community rather than in missionary proclamation. But there is a significant difference. The epistles speak of the mystery which was hidden from angels, powers and principalities. But according to Mark, the demons knew who Jesus was. Especially in the Pauline letters, the Christ-mystery is placed within a cosmic framework which is missing in Mark. But the difference has to do mostly with the forms of perception. If one inquires as to what function the conceptions have, the similarity becomes more pronounced. The ignorance of the angelic powers underlines the hiddenness of God's plan, now revealed in Christ for man's salvation. Mark achieves the same end by stressing that the demons were forbidden to make Christ known though they recognized Jesus to be God's Son, while men did not understand the secret of his person and suffering.

In the epistles too the purpose is practical and paraenetic: Christians are urged to realize the greatness of the revealed mystery and to conform their lives to the pattern provided by the salvation granted them. In 1 Corinthians 2 Paul speaks of God's mysterious wisdom which was hidden from the rulers of this age but is revealed to Christians through the Spirit. Paul's stress on this wisdom contained in the word of the cross, which he was unable to unfold fully in Corinth, is meant to put to shame those Christians who are quarreling and fighting, who brag about their leaders and want to be great themselves. It is not inconceivable that a similar concern lies behind Mark's emphasis on the messianic secret and related concepts.

This leads us to the third feature which in the introduction I maintained would have to be explained by any theory of the purpose of Mark's Gospel: the selection from the tradition of Jesus' sayings. The first large collection of sayings material is in Chapter 4. The parable discourse is Mark's principal example of Jesus' public preaching and an illustration of the message

---

[15]*Festgabe für Karl Müller*, (1922), 347, note 1. Cf. O. Linton, "Das Problem der Urkirche," UUA (1932), 96-100.

which was thematically summarized in 1:15. At the same time this discourse serves to interpret those events which the adjacent chapters discuss: Jesus' work in Israel is the hidden beginning of that which will be completed in God's coming kingdom. The eschatological outlook is clearest in the parables of the seed growing secretly and of the mustard seed (Mark 4:29, cf. Joel 3:13 [M.T. 4:13]; Mark 4:32, cf. Ezek. 17:23 etc.). In the parable of the sower, the concluding progression, thirty, sixty, even a hundredfold, also points beyond earthly conditions to the harvest present in God's kingdom when afflictions and persecution, the cares of the world and delusions of riches have all passed away. The insertion of the words about the secret of God's kingdom between the parable and its interpretation (4:11-12) corroborates that for Mark the parable of the sower also deals with the kingdom of God.

In Mark 4 there is an obvious connection between the messianic secret and the selection of sayings material. The very fact that the parable is interpreted only for the disciples is taken to indicate that the mystery of the kingdom of God is given to them - and thereby to the church.[16] For those standing outside everything is in parables, and the mystery remains hidden. The interpretation gives the parable of the sower a paraenetic turn which is not apparent in the story itself.[17] But for Mark the paraenesis is something which belongs to the esoteric revelation, Jesus' word to his church. The power of God's kingdom is operative in the word, but the person who has heard it must take care how he receives and keeps it. The inserted sayings in 4:21-25 underscore further that Jesus' proclamation includes both promise and warning for the church's members.

The distinction between public and private teaching also plays a significant role in Mark even apart from Chapter 4 (7:1-23; 10:1-12, 17-31). A series of controversy dialogs shows how Jesus was opposed, thereby pointing forward to the passion story. As "apophthegms" (in Bultmann's terminology), such stories may have belonged, perhaps right from the beginning, with the narrative

[16]On the composition of Mark 4, cf. *e.g.* E. Percy, "Liknelseteorien i Mark 4:11f. och kompositionen av Mark 4:1-34," *SEA* 12 (1947), 242-262; W. Marxsen, "Redaktionsgeschichtliche Erklärung der sogenannten Parabeltheorie des Markus," *ZTK* 52 (1955), 255-271; T.A. Burkill, "The Cryptology of Parables in St. Mark's Gospel," *NovT* 1 (1956), 246-262; B. Noack, *Markusevangeliets Lignelseskapitel* (Copenhagen: G.E.C. Gads Forlag, 1965).

[17]Cf. my essay "The Parables of Growth" in this volume.

material rather than with the sayings tradition in a narrower sense. In any case, this material falls into line with the picture of Jesus as the hidden and rejected Christ.

The longest uninterrupted discouse of Jesus is the eschatological speech in Chapter 13. According to Mark, it was directed to the inner circle of four disciples. Jesus' predictions and warnings for the time after his departure thus appear as mysterious revelation. But the second person plural includes more than the four individuals; the sayings are meant for all Christians (cf. v. 37). At the same time the discourse refers in the third person to "the elect," using a current term for those who will be saved, the eschatological community. We have no right to make an unqualified identification of "you" and "the elect;" there is no guarantee that those who hear the word and are present in the congregation will also endure to the end and be saved. The stress lies on the exhortations to persevere and to be watchful during the afflictions and persecutions which are coming. As far as the evangelist is concerned, such trials do not belong to a distant future but to the present which he himself and his church are experiencing. It is possible that he thought of himself as standing at the end of the beginning of the tribulations (13:8-13). However, in this connection it is neither possible nor necessary to go further into the interpretation of Mark 13. What is important with respect to the purpose of the Gospel is that the instructions concerning the eschatological mysteries function as admonitions addressed to those who are living during the time of distress, which is also a time of growth.

Mark 13 is often referred to as the "little apocalypse" or the like, a term which unwittingly isolates the section from the rest of the Gospel. With respect to the evangelist's composition, it would be more appropriate to refer to "Jesus' farewell discourse according to Mark."[18] In Mark 13 we encounter various motifs common to early Christian and even Jewish farewell discourses and "testaments."[19] In view of the difference in style and outlook, the many correspondences between Mark 13 and John 14-17 are

---

[18]That Mark 13 is a farewell discourse was, to my knowledge, first stated by F. Busch, *Zum Verständnis der synoptischen Eschatologie: Markus 13 neu untersucht* (Gütersloh: Bertelsmann, 1938), 44.

[19]This becomes quite evident when Mark 13 is compared with the texts and themes analyzed by J. Munck in his article "Discours d'adieu dans le Nouveau Testament et dans la litérature biblique," *Aux sources de la Tradition Chrétienne* (Neuchâtel: Delachaux and Niestlé, 1950), 155-170. It is strange that Munck did not include Mark 13 in his own study.

remarkable.[20] The placement of the eschatological discourse immediately before the passion story is certainly not accidental. Attention has also been directed to certain pertinent points of contact between Chapter 13 and Chapter 14-15, e.g. the role which the saying about being "handed over"(*paradidosthai*) plays both in the eschatological discourse and in the passion story.[21] The idea can hardly be that Jesus' sufferings began to fulfill the predictions concerning afflictions in the end time. Nevertheless, one can say that the farewell discourse contributes to the understanding of the passion story: Jesus sufferings and resurrection inaugurate the time of distress before the end of the world. Believers live in that time, and they are called to endure to the end and to be watchful.

It is evident from a series of "scholastic dialogs" in Mark 8-10 that there actually is an inner connection between the eschatological tribulations and Jesus' own sufferings. Here one finds the sayings about the Son of man being rejected and put to death coupled with the call to deny oneself and follow Jesus.[22] The same mentality which shows itself in the disciples' inability to understand the necessity of Jesus' sufferings also comes out in their narrowmindedness (9:38-39 and 10:13-16; cf. 10:48) and in their desire for their own greatness (9:33-34 and 10:35, 41). If they had really understood the mystery of suffering, such an attitude would have been impossible. Mark's composition suggests that in the church, where the death of Jesus is no longer an obscure secret but is revealed as the basis of salvation, self-seeking ambition and spiritual arrogance should be excluded.

This sketch does not pretend to give a complete or detailed explanation of the form and purpose of Mark's Gospel. I have outlined for the reader's consideration a possible explanation of three features: the Gospel's apparently singular ending, the concepts associated with the messianic secret and, to a certain extent, the selection from the sayings tradition. The evangelist is not writing with a missionary aim but wants those who already believe to understand the proper significance of the Gospel. He reminds them that the Christ in whom they believe is the one who lived as the hidden Son of man and died as the rejected Messiah. The emphasis on those points in the narrative which

---

[20]Cf. *e.g.* G.R. Beasley-Murray, *Jesus and the Future* (London: Macmillan, 1954), 234-238.

[21]Cf. R.H. Lightfoot, 47-59.

[22]Cf. N. Perrin, *What is Redaction Criticism?* (Philadelphia: Fortress, 1969), 40-56.

evoke fear and astonishment is a cry to awaken, addressed to a church in danger of taking the Gospel for granted. This call to faith, to endurance in affliction, and to watchfulness is combined with a warning against self-assurance and ambitious strivings.

It is rather commonly assumed that the Gospel of Mark was written in Rome sometime during the sixties, shortly after Peter had been martyred. If one gives free reign to his historical imagination, one might combine what is said here about the evangelist's purpose with Oscar Cullmann's picture of conditions in the Roman congregation in the sixties. For Cullmann surmises that controversy, envy and jealousy within the Roman church were partially responsible for the martyrdoms of Peter and Paul.[23] If this is correct, it would undeniably provide a vivid background for Mark's Gospel with its picture of the disciples' shortcomings and of their lack of faith and understanding. Cullmann's highly attractive reconstruction remains conjectural. Mark emphasizes the Gospel's character as mystery partly as a warning against self-sufficiency and ambitious striving. But such tendencies have been apparent at various times both within and without the Roman church. Therefore it is not advisable to place any special weight upon the possibilities of fixing the chronological and geographical background. My effort to determine the purpose of the Gospel must be evaluated apart from the historical reconstruction suggested above.

One final consideration should be added. Hugo Odeberg once wrote that "we suffer from a construction of history which actually treats the synoptic Gospels as if they were the oldest sources and for that reason places the Pauline material between the synoptics and the Gospel of John."[24] If the proposal sketched here is correct, it will contribute to the critique of the "construction of history" of which Odeberg speaks. The Gospel of Mark, with its notion about the messianic secret, can no more be interpreted as if it represented an early stage of the conformation of an originally non-dogmatic Jesus tradition to later ecclesiastical norms. Mark presupposes a Christianity which was already "ecclesiastical" and "dogmatic;" and he provides a certain corrective by recalling that the Jesus confessed by the church as God's Son is the one who was misunderstood and deserted by his very

---

[23]O. Cullmann, *Peter, Disciple, Apostle, Martyr* (tr. F.V. Filson; London: S.C.M. Press, 1953), 89-112. Cf. also page 75 where reference is made to earlier articles by Cullmann, Mollard and Fridrichsen.

[24]H. Odeberg, *Tillbaka til Bibeln* (Lund: Gleerup, 1944), 108.

own, the one who died lonely and forsaken on the cross. It was precisely in this way that he revealed and realized God's hidden plan of salvation.

CHAPTER 5

THE STORY OF ABRAHAM IN LUKE-ACTS

The author of the two books to Theophilus is often called the historian among New Testament authors.[1] And certainly Luke, as we may call him without prejudging his identity, was more of a historian than the other evangelists. But there were many types of historians in ancient as in modern times. To classify Luke among the historiographers, therefore, does not say very much either about his literary intentions or about his concept of history. What can be known about these matters has to be inferred from observations we can make concerning the outline of his two volumes, his style, his use of sources and traditions, etc., in comparison with other relevant literature. Important results have been achieved by modern researchers, pioneered by such men as H.J. Cadbury and Martin Dibelius. Among their successors Paul Schubert has had the advantage of uniting in his person some of the best traditions of German and of American scholarship.[2] But despite their important contribution, many questions remain controversial.

Luke begins his narrative with the announcement of John the Baptist's birth and ends with Paul's imprisonment in Rome. But it seems reasonable to assume that study of his references

---

[1]Cf. e.g. C.K. Barrett, *Luke the Historian in Recent Study* (Philadelphia: Fortress, 1970).

[2]The present study was inspired to a great extent by discussions with Paul Schubert, as well as by his essay "The Structure and Significance of Luke 24," *Neutestamentliche Studien für Rudolf Bultmann* (BZNW 21; 2nd. ed.; Berlin: Töpelmann, 1957), 165-186. The immediate topic of my article, however, was not touched in our conversations.

to Old Testament narratives may throw important light on his understanding of history. Luke's account of the things which had been accomplished is told as a story of John the Baptist, Jesus, Peter, Paul, and other apostles and evangelists. In a similar way, he considers the history of Israel to be bound up with individual persons, of whom Abraham, Moses, and David are the most outstanding. The figure of Moses is closely connected with the law, and that of David with the messianic hope. For reasons of simplicity, I prefer to concentrate on the story of Abraham as Luke relates it and refers to it.

In "Philo's Place in Judaism,"[3] Samuel Sandmel wrote: "To see what the writer makes of Abraham is often to see most clearly what the writer is trying to say." This statement may be applied to New Testament as well as to Jewish authors. To Paul, Abraham is the father and prototype of Christian believers. In Galatians 3 he seeks to demonstrate that God, in granting his Spirit to Gentiles who believed the apostolic message, has acted according to his promise to Abraham. In Romans 4 the story of Abraham is adduced in order to prove the thesis that a man is justified by faith apart from works of the law. And yet, Paul insists in Romans 9-11 that the word of God has not failed; in spite of their disobedience, the Israelites remain "beloved for the sake of the fathers."[4] Putting the accent in quite a different way, James finds that Abraham's faith was at work in his actions, and draws the conclusion that a man is justified by his deeds and not by faith in itself (2:20-24). To John, Abraham was a witness to Christ before his coming.[5] To the author of Hebrews he is an example to be imitated, as one of those who inherited the promises through faith and patience (6:11ff.). His migration and endurance illustrate the essence of faith, as defined by the

---

[3]"Philo's Place in Judaism," *HUCA* 25 (1954), 209-237 and 26 (1955), 151-332. The quotation is taken from vol. 25, 237. For earlier literature, cf. J. Jeremias, *TDNT*, I, 8-9.

[4]Paul's interpretation of the Abraham story is now under discussion. Cf. e.g. U. Wilkens, "Die Rechtfertigung Abrahams in Römer 4," *Studien zur Theologie der alttestamentlichen Überlieferung* (Neukirchen: Neukircher Verlag, 1961); G. Klein, "Römer 4 und die Idee der Heilsgeschichte," *EvT* 23 (1963), 424-447, and "Individualgeschichte und Weltgeschichte bei Paulus," *EvT* 24 (1964), 126-165.

[5]Cf. my articles "The Johannine Church and History," in this volume; "Manndraperen og hans far," *NTT* 64 (1963), 129-163, esp. 145-148; "Der Erstgeborene Satans und der Vater des Teufels," *Apophoreta. Festschrift für E. Haenchen* (BZNW 30; Berlin: Töplemann, 1964), 70-84, esp. 77-78. W.A. Meeks has drawn my attention to the possibility that "Abraham's works" in John 8:39 may include his hospitality (Gen. 18). Cf. 1 Clem. 10:7 *dia pistin kai philoxenian*.

writer (11:8-19, cf. 11:1). But the certainty of our hope and the superiority of Christ's priesthood over against that of Aaron are also argued on the basis of the biblical account of Abraham (6:13-7:10).[6]

Thus, in various ways the story of Abraham is used as a vehicle for interpreting the gospel message and its significance. Paul and John, the author of Hebrews, and James, all tend to make Abraham a protagonist of the Christian faith as each of them understands it. In an opposite, yet analogous, way, the rabbis visualize Abraham as a chief rabbi, and Philo depicts him as a Jewish philosopher. In comparison, Luke's portrait of Abraham more closely approximates one drawn by a historian. In his writings there is much less obviously Christian reinterpretation of the biblical account than in other parts of the New Testament. "Our father Abraham" in Luke-Acts remains the father of the Jews and is not said to be the father of Christian believers.[7] He is not presented as a prototype and model to be imitated. Apart from references to Abraham in the sayings of Jesus and John the Baptist, Luke is usually content to summarize and paraphrase biblical texts. Certainly, he too uses Abraham as a part of this theological argument, but he does so by means of establishing a connection and continuity between the history of Abraham and the events of which he himself is writing.

All allusions to Abraham in Luke-Acts are found in hymns, sayings, or speeches. The material can easily be subsumed under a small number of headings:

a. The God of Abraham, Isaac, and Jacob, the God of the fathers: Luke 20:37; Acts 3:13; 7:32; cf. Acts 5:30; 22;14; 24:14.

b. God's covenant, oath, and promise to Abraham;

---

[6]Cf. H. Koester, "Die Auslegung der Abraham-Verheissung in Hebräer 6," *Studien zur Theologie der alttestamentlichen Uberlieferung*, 95-109.

[7]Cf. Luke 1:73; 16:24; Acts 7:2. Only in addressing Jews are Abraham, Isaac, Jacob and their descendents called "our fathers" (Luke 1:55, 72; Acts 3:13; 5:30; 7:32; 13:17; 22:14; 26:6). "Our fathers" can also refer to the twelve patriarchs (Acts 7:11, 12, 15), to the Exodus generation (Acts 7:19, 38, 39, 44), or to Israelites of later epochs (Acts 7:45; 5:10). The term "your fathers"more often has negative connotations (cf. Luke 11:47-48; Acts 7:51-52; 28:25), as has "their fathers" (Luke 6:23, 26). However, according to the best manuscript evidence "your fathers" is used also in Acts 7:25. There does not seem to be sufficient evidence for the sharp differentiation between two groups of fathers as suggested by A.F.J. Klijn, "Stephen's Speech -- Acts VII. 2-53," *NTS* 4 (1957/58), 25-31, on the basis of the variant reading "your fathers" in 7:39.

Luke 1:55; 1:72-73; Acts 3:25; 7:2-8; 7:17; cf. 3:17, 32; 26:6.

c. Children of Abraham: Luke 3:8; 13:16; 19:9; Acts 13:26; 13:33 v. 1; cf. 3:25.

d. Abraham in the hereafter: Luke 13:28; 16:22-31; 20:37-38.

e. Miscellaneous: The genealogy of Jesus, Luke 3:34; the tomb which Abraham bought, Acts 7:16.

The picture transcends that of the Septuagint mainly insofar as Abraham is taken to be an eschatological as well as a historical figure. This feature is taken over from earlier Gospel tradition. Luke 20:37-38 is derived from Mark 12:26-27; Luke 13:28 is paralleled by Matthew 8:11. The story of the rich man and Lazarus must come from a special source, oral or written. It possibly alludes to some popular tale.[8] The image of Abraham's bosom is, in any case, familiar also to the rabbis.[9] Similar ideas are also found in Old Testament Pseudepigrapha. The Testament of the Twelve Patriarchs contains several allusions to the patriarchs as living after their death.[10] According to 4 Maccabees 12:17 the seven martyred brethren said: "For if we die in this way, Abraham, and Isaac, and Jacob shall receive us, and all the fathers shall praise us."

Some details indicate that Luke's rendering of the sayings of Jesus has been influenced by a phraseology used in Greek-speaking Judaism as represented by 4 Maccabees. To the answer given to the question of the Sadducees, Luke adds "for they all live to him" (*pantes gar autō zōsin*) 20:38. This comes very close to two passages in 4 Maccabees 7:19: "Unto God they die not, as did not our patriarchs Abraham, and Isaac, and Jacob, but they live unto God" (*zōsin tō theō*), and 16:25: "Men dying for God, live unto God" (*zōsin tō theō*) as live Abraham, and Isaac, and Jacob, and all the patriarchs." In Luke 13:28: "When you see Abraham, and Isaac, and Jacob, and all the prophets in the kingdom of God," the phrase "and all the prophets" seems to be a Lukan addition, corresponding to "all the patriarchs" (or "fathers") in 4 Maccabees 15:25 and 13:17. To Luke, fathers and

---

[8]Cf. K. Grobel, "Whose Name was Neves," *NTS* 10 (2963/64), 373-382, with literature cited.

[9]Cf. Bill. II, 225-226; R. Meyer, *TDNT* III, 825-826. Apostolic Constitutions VIII, 41:2 seems most likely to be influenced by Luke 16:22.

[10]T. Levi 18:14; T. Judah 25:1; T. Benj. 10:6.

prophets belong together.[11] Since he regards all the prophets as martyrs,[12] the affinity to the martyr-ideology of 4 Maccabees is rather close, although there can hardly be any question of direct literary dependence. Luke does not share the philosophical pretentions of the writer of 4 Maccabees, who proves the thesis that reason is master of the passions by means of the noble conduct of Eleazar, the seven brethren, and their mother, who all behaved like true children of Abraham.[13] The similarities must be due to a common background, reflected in a common terminology.[14]

To Luke, Abraham is most often the primary recipient of God's promise to the fathers. The words *epaggelein, epaggelia* etc., are only occasionally found in the Septuagint; there is, in fact, no exact Hebrew equivalent. But the notion of God's promise to Abraham is common to the Lukan writings, the Pauline epistles, and the Epistle to the Hebrews. The terminology probably goes back to Greek-speaking Judaism.[15] The figure of Abraham in Hebrews comes rather close to that of Luke in other respects as well. The main accents are put upon God's oath and promise, and upon Abraham's migration and sojourn as a foreigner in the promised land.[16] He is placed within a succession of prophets and martyrs reaching from Abel to Christ and to the present day.[17] As each of the two writers makes the Christian adaptation in his own characteristic way, most of the common features are likely to go back to slightly Hellenized Jewish versions of the story of Abraham.

Luke's affinity with Hellenistic Judaism is confirmed by his own comprehensive survey of Abraham's history, found in the speech of Stephen, Acts 7:2-8. This, however, does not mean that the biblical account has been fundamentally changed. There are

---

[11]Cf. 1:70-72; 10:24; 11:47a, 50; Acts 3:21, 25.

[12]Luke 6:23; 11:47-51; 13:33-34; Acts 7:52.

[13]4 Macc. 6:17, 22; 9:21; 13:12; 14:20; 15:28; 17:6; 18:1, 20, 23.

[14]*ho patrōos theos*, Acts 24:14; cf. 4 Macc. 12:18; Jos. Ant. 9:256, 12:278. *hoi patriarchai* Acts 7:8; cf. 4 Macc. 7:19; 16:25; T 12 Patr., inscr. *thygatēr Abraham* Luke 13:16; cf. 4 Macc. 15:28.

[15]Cf. Schniewind/Friedrich, *TDNT* II, 579-581. The term *hai epaggeliai tōn paterōn* found in T 12 Patr., T Joseph 20:1; Apost. Const. VII 35:10; 37:11; VIII 12:23, 24 may reflect the prayer language of the Greek-speaking synagogue.

[16]Heb. 11:11-12; cf. Acts 7:5, 8.

[17]Heb. 6:12-18; 11:2-12:11; cf. Acts 7:2-60; Luke 11:47-51. For other points of contact, cf. P.M. Jones, "The Epistle to the Hebrews and the Lucan Writings," *Studies in the Gospels: In Memory of R.H. Lightfoot* (ed. D.E. Nineham; Oxford: Blackwell, 1958), 113-143.

few, if any, traces of those accretions to the story which are known from writers such as Artapanus or Eupolemus,[18] Philo, and Josephus, as well as from Palestinian midrash.[19] In his short summary Stephen -- that is, the Stephen of Luke -- has left out a number of tales: Abraham in Egypt, Abraham and Lot, the battle with the kings, Hagar and Ishmael, the three men and the destruction of Sodom, and, most remarkable of all, the sacrifice of Isaac. The account is concentrated upon Abraham's migration, God's promise, the covenant of circumcision, and the birth of Isaac. This means that the texts which serve as a basis are Genesis 11:27-12:9; 13:15; 15 (in part), 17, and 21:1-4. Thus the summary stresses those themes which are fundamental to the whole outline of Israel's ancient history, starting with God's revelation to Abraham and leading up to the conquest of the promised land; these themes are most common in biblical recapitulations and references to the fathers.[20]

Stephen's account of Abraham has definitely and, I think, consciously been given a biblical flavor. At several point we find Septuagint phrases which in the Pentateuch are not related to the story of Abraham. *ho theos tēs doxēs* is taken from Psalm 28 (29):3; *oude bēma podos*, from Deuteronomy 2:5; *en gē allotria* from Exodus 2:22 or 18:3; and the end of the citation from Genesis 15:13-14 is an adaptation of Exodus 3:12. Even *Mesopotamia, gē Chaldaion, metōkisen,* and *edoken klēronomian* are Septuagint phraseology, but are not used in the Genesis story of Abrham. To current, though not biblical, Jewish terminology, belong phrases like *ho patēr hēmōn Abraham, diathēkē peritomēs* and *hoi (dōdeka) patriarchai*.

At some points the biblical account is altered in a somewhat more substantial manner. In Acts 7:2-3 God is said to have appeared to Abraham before he settled in Haran; the vision of Genesis 12:7 and the commandment of Genesis 12:1 are both transposed to the situation of Genesis 11:31. Thus God's revelation is made

---

[18]Eusebius, Praep. Evang. 9:17-18. The fragment attributed to "Eupolemus" must be of Samaritan origin. A book on Abraham and the Egyptians was attributed to Hecataeus; cf. N. Walter, *Der Thoraausleger Aristobulos* (TU 86; Berlin: Akademie Verlag, 1964), 187-188 and 195ff.

[19]On these traditions cf. Sandmel, *op. cit.*, and G. Vermes, *Scripture and Tradition in Judaism* (SPB 4; Leiden: Brill, 1961), 67-126.

[20]Cf. esp. Josh. 24:2-4; Ps. 104:8-11; Neh. 9:7-8; G. von Rad, "The Problem of the Hexateuch," *The Problem of the Hexateuch and Other Essays* (tr. E.W.T. Dicken; New York: McGraw-Hill, 1966).

the starting point of Abraham's migrations.[21] A minor point is the identification of Mesopotamia with the land of the Chaldeans; according to ancient and more usual terminology Haran is located in Mesopotamia.[22] Furthermore, Abraham is said to have left Haran after the death of his father. This is a consequence which a reader would draw from the Genesis account if he did not pay serious attention to the number of years given in Genesis 11:26, 11:32, and 12:4.[23] An unparalleled confusion is found in Acts 7:16, where Abraham's purchase of the cave at Hebron is mixed up with Jacob's purchase of a piece of land at Shechem.[24] All these are points of detail. Of theological significance is the underscoring of the facts that Abraham had neither any ground of his own nor any children when God promised to give the land to him and his posterity.[25] But unlike the author of Hebrews, Luke does not spell out the religious lesson to be learned.

The most remarkable element in Acts 7:2-8, in contrast with similar summaries, is the prominent place given to a full quotation of Genesis 15:13-14, with some important variations. More attention is usually paid to Genesis 15:6, 7-12, and 17-20, but in Stephen's speech no special importance is assigned either to Abraham's faith or to his nighttime vision. We may safely assume that the divine word about the history of Abraham's posterity has been placed intentionally in the foreground. At this point, if anywhere, the specific emphasis in Stephen's reproduction of the biblical story must be discernible. Although most commentators have not paid sufficient attention to it,[26] the specific function of the citation within the whole outline of the speech is not difficult to see. The oracle in Acts 7:6-7 predicts the succeeding events in the history of Israel, and the

---

[21]God's initiative is also stressed in Gen. 15:7; Neh. 9:7; Heb. 11:8; Philo, de Abr. 162-67; Jos. Ant. I, 154. But Haenchen may be right that there is not sufficient reason for speaking of a school tradition. Cf. *The Acts of the Apostles* (tr. B. Noble *et. al.;* Philadelphia: Westminster, 1971), 278, note 1.

[22]Cf. Judith 5:7; Jos. Ant. I, 152.

[23]Cf. Philo, de migr. Abr. 177. According to the Samaritan chronology, Terah died at the age of 145 (not 205); thus it supports the view that he was dead when Abraham left Haran. On this and similar points, cf. the commentaries and H.J. Cadbury, *The Book of Acts in History* (New York: Harper, 1955), 102-104.

[24]Gen. 23:16-17 and 50:13; Gen. 33:18-19 and Josh. 24:32. It is possible that a Samaritan local tradition, that all the (twelve?) patriarchs were buried at Shechem, has been reinterpreted and made a proof of Abraham's lack of property in the land of the Jews.

[25]Acts 7:5; Cf. Heb. 11:9-13.

[26]Cf., however, B.W. Bacon, "Stephen's Speech: Its Argument and Its Doctrinal Relationship," *Yale Bicentennial Publications: Biblical and Semitic Studies* (New York: Scribner's, 1902), 211-276, esp. 237ff.

following parts of Stephen's speech tell about the realization of God's word to Abraham. The story of Joseph (Acts 7:9-16) reports how it came to pass that Abraham's posterity became aliens in a land belonging to others who enslaved and maltreated them (7:18-19). The story of Moses (7:20-36) tells how they were led out, while God judged the nation which had enslaved them. Thus, the history of Israel is understood as a history of prophecy and fulfillment. Stephen also sets forth the way in which God kept his promise to give the land to Abraham and his posterity, although he had no offspring (7:5). Abraham became the father of Isaac and, through him, of Jacob, and the twelve patriarchs (7:8). In Egypt the people grew and multiplied (7:18). At the time of Joshua they took possession of the land, dispossessing the nations (*en tē kataschesei tōn ethnōn* 7:45, cf. *eis kataschesin*).[27]

The importance of the scheme of prophecy and fulfillment is confirmed by a number of references to Abraham in the speech of Stephen. The burial of the fathers at Shechem (in the tomb that Abraham had bought) serves to illustrate that they were aliens (7:16, cf. 7:6). Most remarkable is the phrase, coined for this purpose, which introduces the Exodus story: "But as the time of the promise drew near, which God had granted to Abraham" (7:17). This is a direct reference to the prediction in 7:6, taken up again in 7:20: "At this time (*en hō kairō*) Moses was born." Further, it is carefully pointed out that at the burning bush God revealed himself with the words: "I am the God of your fathers, the God of Abraham and of Isaac and of Jacob" (7:32). Here again, God's words -- promise and commission -- precede the realization which occurs (7:30-34, 35-36). But the Exodus event did not bring God's word to its final fulfillment: "This is the Moses who said to the children of Israel: God will raise up for you a prophet from your brethren as he raised me up" (7:37).

At this point it becomes clear why Stephen does not need to give any directly christological or eschatological interpretation of God's promises to Abraham. Here God's word to Abraham is seen as the beginning of a history in which partial realizations are interconnected with new promises, until the coming of the Righteous One, of whom all the prophets spoke (cf. 7:52). In Stephen's speech Moses and, to some extent, Joseph are seen as types of Christ, but the typology is subordinated to the recurring pattern of prophecy and fulfillment.

---

[27]The phrase is taken from Gen. 17:8; cf. Gen. 48:4; Ezek. 33:24, etc.

When close attention is paid to the function of the citation in Acts 7:6-7 within the whole speech, it also becomes obvious that the alteration at the end must be due to some specific reason. The Septuagint text of Genesis 14:14b reads: "But afterwards they shall come out hither with much baggage." For this, Acts 7:7b substitutes: "And afterwards they shall come out and worship me in this place." The phrase is taken from Exodus 3:12: "And you (the Israelites) shall worship God upon this mountain," and adapted to Genesis 15:14b and 16, "and they shall come back here." Thus, according to Stephen's quotation of Scripture, the goal of the Exodus is neither the worship of God at Mount Sinai, nor the possession of Canaan itself but, much more, worship of God in the land promised to Abraham and his posterity. This means that just as Acts 7:6-7b is a prediction of Israel's coming to Egypt and the Exodus (Acts 7:9-38), so the final clause in 7:7b points forward to the events in the time from Joshua to Solomon and even later. The correspondence is clear; it is not so much the conquest of Canaan as the worship performed there which is the center of interest (Acts 7:44ff.).

This observation may be of considerable importance for the solution of one of the most vexing problems confronting interpreters of Stephen's speech. Often the remark in Acts 7:47 "But it was Solomon who built a house for him," followed by the remark "yet the Most High does not dwell in houses made with hands," and a citation from Isaiah 66 has been taken -- even by outstanding commentators -- to imply a radical opposition to the temple.[28] If this interpretation were correct, there would be a sharp contrast between Stephen's point of view and that of Luke himself. But Luke is not likely to have been aware of any such contradiction, and therefore it seems reasonable to look for other possibilities of exegesis.

Although I cannot go into detail here, I will suggest an approach to the problem. The argument of Acts 7:44ff. may be summarized in the following way: The tent of witness, made according to the heavenly model, accompanied the fathers in the wilderness and was brought into the land under Joshua. This state of affairs remained unchanged until the days of David. He found favor in the sight of God and asked leave "to find a

---

[28]Thus Bacon, "Stephen's Speech," 270, etc.; M. Simon, *St. Stephen and the Hellenists* (London: Longmanns & Green, 1956), 50-58. But cf. the critique of J.C. O'Neill, *The Theology of Acts* (London: SPCK, 1961), 72-83.

habitation for the God (or house)[29] of Jacob." That is, he asked for the fulfillment of God's word to Abraham," and they shall worship me in this place." With B.W. Bacon one may even say that David brought the divine promise to "the verge of fulfillment."[30] "But Solomon built a house for him." It might seem as if this brought the prediction to its definite realization, the temple of Solomon being the place for Israel's worship. But no! "The Most High does not dwell in houses made with hands."

If this paraphrase adequately summarises the main points, the argument in Acts 7:44-50 runs fairly parallel to that of Hebrews 4:31-11 or, more especially, of 4:8-9: "For if Joshua had given them rest, God would not speak later of another day. So then, there remains a sabbath rest for the people of God." By analogy we may paraphrase Acts 7:47-50 as follows: Solomon built a house for him. But had Solomon's temple been the fulfillment of David's prayer for a "dwelling-place," and its cult the worship of which God spoke to Abraham, the prophet would not have said: "Heaven is my throne and earth my footstool. What house will you build for me, says the Lord, or what is the place of my rest? Did not my hands make all these things?" One might even venture a conjecture and assume that to Luke the true answer to David's prayer in Psalm 131 (132):5 was given in verse 11 of the same psalm: "The Lord swore to David a sure oath (*alētheian*) and shall not make it invalid: (One) from the fruit of your body I will set on your throne (LXX)." We may also compare 2 Samuel 7: David intended to build a house for God, but through Nathan he was told that God should make him a house and raise up his offspring after him. These texts are of considerable importance for Lukan christology and may even be in the background of Acts 7:47-48.[31] We are

---

[29]*tō oikō Jakōb* is the reading of the best Egyptian uncials and of the bilingual D. It may be due to a conscious interpretation and adaptation of the Septuagint text of Ps. 131 (132):5: Asking leave to find a habitation for the God of Jacob, David asked at the same time for a "dwelling place," a permanent place of worship, for the house of Jacob. For this use of *skēnōma* cf. Ps. 131 (132): 7; 14 (15):1; 42 (43):3; 83 (84):1. Cf. also 2 Sam. 7:10.

[30]"Stephen's Speech," 270.

[31]Cf. M. Simon, *St. Stephen*, 52: "It is, however, obvious that 2 Sam. 7, Nathan's prophecy, is also in Stephen's mind." But I doubt that Simon is correct in taking Nathan's prophecy to imply a radical opposition to the temple and in assuming that Stephen understood it that way. Cf. R.A. Carlson, *David the Chosen King* (tr. E.J. Sharpe & S. Rudman; Stockholm: Almqvist & Wiksell, 1964), 106-128. On the promise to David in the Lukan writings, cf. Luke 1:32-33; Acts 2:30; 13:23ff.; etc. E. Lövestam, *Son and Saviour* (tr. M.J. Petry; Lund: Gleerup, 1961).

told that Moses and the prophets announced the coming of the "Righteous One" (7:37, 52). May we not conclude that God's word to Abraham, "they shall worship me in this place," was fulfilled not by the erection of Solomon's temple but by the rebuilding of the "dwelling of David" (Acts 15:16 = Amos 9:11)? Thus, Stephen himself would be the representative of the true worship of God in Jerusalem, the worship performed by the disciples who gathered in the name of Jesus, both in the temple and in houses.[32]

If my proposal is not totally wrong, there is no contradiction between the speech of Stephen and the general outlook of Luke. Much more, there is another passage in Luke-Acts which strongly supports the interpretation proposed here, viz. the Benedictus, Luke 1:68-75. Here the Lord God of Israel is praised because he has redeemed his people, just as he had said through his holy prophets: "To perform the mercy promised to our fathers, and to remember his holy covenant, the oath which he swore to our father Abraham, to grant us that we, being delivered from the hand of our enemies, might serve him without fear, in holiness and righteousness before him all the days of our life." Here the messianic redemption is described in terms reminiscent of the deliverance from Egypt and is seen as the fulfillment of God's oath to Abraham.[33] The final goal is said to be worship in holiness and righteousness. According to Luke's understanding, the same true worship, made possible by the coming of Christ, must be envisaged also in the promise granted to Abraham, that "they shall worship me in this place."

When the thematic function of the quotation in Acts 7:6-7 has been recognized, it is no longer possible to hold the opinion "that the major part of the speech (7:2-34) shows no purpose whatsoever."[34] The speech contains a philosophy, or rather, a "theology of history," dominated by the motif of prophecy and fulfillment. Even the opposition to the temple is subordinate to the demonstration of a continuity in history, reaching from Abraham

---

[32]Cf. Acts 2:42, 46-47; 4:24-31; 5:12, 42, etc.

[33]Luke 1:72f, cf. Ps. 106:10. B.W. Bacon already pointed out the close relations between Stephen's speech and the Benedictus ("Stephen's Speech," 237-38, 244, 270).

[34]M. Dibelius, *Studies in the Acts of the Apostles* (tr. Mary Ling; London: SCM, 1956), 168; cf. p. 169: "The most striking feature of this speech is the irrelevancy of its main section." He is followed by Haenchen, *Acts*, 287; H. Conzelmann (*Die Apostlegeschichte* [Tübingen: Mohr, 1963], 45-51) has seen that the idea of the promise, its fulfillment, and its rejection, is a main theme of the speech. But he does not draw the consequences and still speaks of an underlying layer "whose sense lies in the tracing of history as such (!)" (50).

through Moses to Jesus and on to Stephen, his suffering witness. The assumption that Luke has made use of some existing summary of Israel's history might still hold true, but there are reasons for doubt. I know of no other recapitulation of biblical history in which the idea of successive fulfillment of prophecies is so prominent, whereas this is a favorite theme of Luke's.

In Stephen's speech the Jewishness of Abraham is not concealed but emphatically pronounced. Abraham is "our father," the father of Jews (7:1). Finally it is stressed that God gave "the covenant of circumcision" to Abraham, and that Isaac, Jacob, and the twelve patriarchs were circumcised on the eighth day (7:8). But this Jewish flavor is in full harmony with good Lukan theology. Its function is to make it clear that the promise given to Abraham and now fulfilled in Jesus first and foremost belonged to Abraham's posterity, circumcised Jews living in the land of Israel. "The promise is to you and to your children" (Acts 2:39; cf. 3:25, etc.).

Stephen confronts the Jews of Jerusalem with their own sacred history, showing that God has kept his promises. But the history has also another aspect, that of constant disobedience and opposition to God and his messengers. The Bible itself provided materials for this point of view,[35] but Stephen sharpens it, contending that by their betrayal and murder of Jesus the Jews of Jerusalem have created a solidarity between themselves and the contemporaries of Moses and the persecutors of the prophets. Over against this continuous resistance to the prophetic Holy Spirit[36] stands the succession of righteous sufferers, Joseph, Moses, the prophets, Jesus, and Stephen himself.[37] The conclusion to be drawn is, evidently, that along this line the divine promises are brought to fulfillment, while those who reject Jesus and his witnesses disinherit themselves from God's promise to the offspring of Abraham. The modern reader may doubt whether Stephen's speech conforms to the historical situation; but certainly it fits

---

[35]Cf. 1 Sam. 12:6-15; Psalms 78 and 106; Jer. 2; Ezek. 20; Neh. 9. Even in Exodus through 2 Kings the whole history of Israel is seen by and large as a series of transgressions. Among later recapitulations, CD 2:14-6:11 is of special interest. Cf. 1QS 1:21-23. A more remote parallel is the speech in which Josephus confronted the besieged Jews with the history of their people (Bell V, 375-419).

[36]7:51; cf. Ps. 106:33, Neh. 9:30, CD 5:11.

[37]In Luke's portrait of Stephen (Acts 6:5, 8, 10; 7:55ff.) we find some of the same, typical features of the wise, inspired, and persecuted man of God, as in his portraits of Joseph, Moses, and Jesus (Luke 2:40, 52; 24:19; Acts 2:22-23, 3:14, 10:38).

Luke's literary and theological purpose. The account of Stephen's speech and martyrdom is given as the last preaching of the early apostles and evangelists in Jerusalem. Stephen's own history is the continuation of that history which began with God's revelation to Abraham; it leads to the preaching in Samaria and beyond.

Another recapitulation of Israel's history is found in Paul's speech in Pisidian Antioch (Acts 13:16-41). Here the patriarchal story does not comprise a section in itself. But as the election of all Israelites goes back to that of Abraham, it is included in the initial phrase, "The God of this people Israel chose our fathers" (13:17).[38] The summary covers the period from the Exodus to David, from whose seed God brought a savior to Israel, as he had promised (13:17-23). Then Paul proceeds to the history of Jesus, concentrating upon the theme of the Davidic-messianic promise and its fulfillment by the passion and resurrection of Jesus.[39] But even here the election of Abraham and his descendants provides the wider context, as is made clear by the appositional expression in vs. 26: "Brethren, sons of the family of Abraham,[40] and those among you that fear God, to us has been sent the message of this salvation." What God promised to the fathers is proclaimed as fulfilled to the sons (13:32-33).[41] In the context, *tēn pros tous pateres epaggelian* cannot exclusively refer to God's promise to the patriarchs, but must include both the promise given to David and later prophecies. However, Luke seems to think all messianic prophecies reiterate and unfold the one promise to the fathers, first given to Abraham.[42]

The speech in Acts 13, like that of Stephen in Acts 7, has been placed at a crucial point of Luke's narrative. The audience consists of Jews and proselytes gathered in a diaspora synagogue. At the end they are warned: "Beware, therefore, lest there come upon you what is said in the prophets: Behold, you scoffers, and wonder, and perish" (13:40-41, citation from Hab. 1:5). But we learn that they did not take heed. The fulfilled

---

[38]Election of the fathers: Neh. 9:7; Ps. 105:6; 2 Macc. 1:25; Ps. Sol. 9:9; 4 Ezra 3:13; cf. Schrenk, *TDNT* IV, 169f.

[39]Cf. Lövestam, *Son and Saviour*.

[40]*huioi genous Abraham*. The term *genos Abraham* is not found in translations from the Hebrew Bible, but cf. 1 Macc. 12:21; T Napth. 1:10; Jos. Ant. V, 113; Apost. Const. VII, 33:7.

[41]Manuscript evidence supports the reading, but this hardly makes sense, in spite of Acts 2:39.

[42]Cf. Luke 1:55, 70-74; Acts 3:13, 18, 21, 25; 26:6.

promise had first to be proclaimed to the "sons of the family of Abraham." When they rejected it, Paul and Barnabas turned to the Gentiles (13:44-49, with citation of Isa. 49:6).

The speeches of Stephen and Paul are preceded by those of Peter. The Abraham-theme holds a prominent place in one of them, the speech in the temple, Acts 3:12-26. Here the kerygma is condensed into the statement that "the God of Abraham and of Isaac and of Jacob, the God of our fathers, glorified his servant Jesus, whom you delivered up and denied in the presence of Pilate" (3:13). Thus, God fulfilled what he had foretold by the mouth of all the prophets from old (3:18, 21-24). At the end, Peter addresses his hearers with the words: "You are the sons of the prophets and of the covenant which God gave to your fathers, saying to Abraham, 'And in your posterity shall all the families of the earth be blessed'" (3:25). In this citation of Genesis 22:18 (12:3) Luke has replaced the *ta ethnē* of the Septuagint with *hai patriai*, thus indicating that the Jews are included among those who shall be blessed in the "posterity" of Abraham, i.e., the Christ, Jesus.[43] "God, having raised up his servant, sent him to you first" (3:26a). The blessing is taken to mean the forgiveness of sins granted to those who turn away from their wickedness (v. 26b; cf. v. 19). However, the Genesis citation, even in its modified form, makes Peter's speech end with a universal outlook. It also contains a warning, viz., the words of Deuteronomy 18:19, quoted in v. 23: "And it shall be that every soul that does not listen to that prophet shall be destroyed from the people."

Peter's speech resulted in the first arrest of the apostles (Acts 4:1ff.). In fact, it foreshadows and prepares for the theme which is taken up and developed in Acts 7 and 13: The promise of God was given to Abraham, reiterated and spelled out by Moses and the prophets, and fulfilled through the passion and resurrection of Jesus. Apostles and evangelists bore testimony to this, first to the Jews. But their message was rejected by the majority, while Gentiles believed and became participants in what had been promised to Abraham and his posterity. The references to Abraham serve to bring this out, not only in the interrelated speeches of Peter, Stephen, and Paul, but also in the two-volume work of Luke as a whole.

---

[43]Cf. Gal. 3:16; Conzelmann, *Apostelgeschichte*, 35. The reader of Acts would hardly get the impression that merely the "claims of the land" are meant (against Haenchen).

The very beginning of Luke's narrative, the announcement of Zechariah, recalls the story of Abraham. In an archaizing, biblical style the birth narratives of Luke report announcements of what is going to happen and of events which include new promises.[44] The whole story is full of allusions to biblical prophecies as well as to the expectations of pious Jews. Abraham is directly referred to in the hymns of Mary and Zechariah (Luke 1:54-55 and 72-73). The relevant passage from the Benedictus has already been quoted as akin to the Abraham section of Stephen's speech. In the Magnificat the text runs: "He has helped his servant Israel, in remembrance of his mercy, as he spoke to our fathers, to Abraham and to his posterity for ever." As it is not possible to give a detailed exegesis, it may in this context be sufficient to point out that the phrases in the Magnificat and the Benedictus have been modeled upon the pattern of references to Abraham in hymnic and historical texts of the Old Testament.[45]

According to the prophecy of Isaiah 40:3-5, John the Baptist prepared the way of the Lord, announcing the coming of One who was mightier than he (Luke 3:1-17). The saying that God is able to raise up children to Abraham from the stones (3:8) is reported as a warning to the Jews. It foreshadows the coming events, even though Luke never draws the conclusion that Gentile believers are made spiritual children of Abraham.[46] In the major sections of the Gospel there are not many references to Abraham, but some of them are peculiar to Luke and characteristic of his outlook. The argument for a sabbath healing is strengthened by the point

---

[44]Cf. the analysis by Schubert, "The Structure," 178-179. P. Benoit, "L'enfance de Jean-Baptiste selon Luc 1," *NTS* 3 (1956/57), 169-194.

[45]Exod. 32:13; Mic. 7:20; Ps. 105:8-11, 42; 1 Chron. 16:5-18; Neh. 9:7-8; Exod. 2:24; 6:3-4, 8; 33:1; Lev. 26:42; Deut. 1:8; 9:5, 27, etc.; 2 Kings 13:23; Jer. 11:5. In intertestamental literature this type of reference is less frequent than might be expected; cf. Sir. 44:21; 1 Macc. 4:10; 2 Macc. 1:2; Ps. Sol. 9:9; As. Mos. 3:9; T Levi 15:4. The general tendency is rather to stress the exemplary conduct, the temptations, and the apocalyptic visions of Abraham; cf. e.g. Sir. 44:19-20; Judith 5:6ff.; 8:26; 4 Ezra 3:13-14; Bib. Ant. of Ps. Philo 23:4-7; 32:1-4. If the Magnificat and the Benedictus should go back to Jewish hymns, as several scholars have assumed, this would illustrate what is in any case probable: Luke has been able to find and use materials which were akin to his own outlook while, on the other hand, his own points of view are largely traditional.

[46]It is hardly fortuitous that, in contrast to Matt. 8:11-12, Luke does not directly say that many shall come from east and west to sit at table with Abraham, Isaac and Jacob in the kingdom of God. Luke 13:27-27 contains two distinct sayings regarding a) the exclusion of Jesus' Jewish contemporaries from communion with the patriarchs and prophets, and b) the coming of men from east and west and from north and south. Luke never speaks of a "change of peoples" in the same way as Matthew (21:43).

JESUS IN THE MEMORY OF THE EARLY CHURCH

ESSAYS BY

NILS ALSTRUP DAHL

AUGSBURG PUBLISHING HOUSE
Minneapolis, Minnesota

that the woman who had for eighteen years been "bound by Satan" was a daughter of Abraham (13:16). To Zacchaeus Jesus is reported to have said: "Today salvation has come to this house, since he also is a son of Abraham" (19:9). Both stories illustrate how God's promise to Abraham was fulfilled for his children through the ministry of Jesus.

Even the idea of the lives of the patriarchs in the hereafter has been integrated into Luke's theology of prophecy and fulfillment: they live unto God forever. The God of the fathers is the God who raises the dead and who has now raised Jesus. Thus the apostolic message of Christ's resurrection is the proclamation of what was promised to the fathers and what Israel has been hoping for.[47] This theme is carried through to the end of Acts, even though the name of Abraham is not mentioned after the speeches of chapters 3, 7, and 13 which we have analysed. To Jewish accusations, Paul gives the answer: "Now I stand here on trial for hope in the promise made by God to our fathers" (26:6). Even his mission to the Gentiles is considered to be part of the continuous history which originated with God's revelation to Abraham. This is also made clear by the words of Ananias: "The God of our fathers appointed you to know his will, to see the Just One and to hear a voice from his mouth; for you will be a witness for him to all men of what you have seen and heard" (22:14-15). To Gentile audiences the apostle preaches first of all the truth of biblical monotheism (Acts 14:15-17; 17:22-31).[48]

God's promise to the fathers, from Abraham onward, is a theme which runs through the whole of Luke's two-volume work. The first volume tells the story of Jesus, by whom the salvation promised to Israel was effected. The second volume contains the story of the apostolic preaching by which this salvation was brought to the Gentiles. In a rough sketch, Luke's ideas of mission to Jews and Gentiles may be summarized in three points:

---

[47]Cf. Luke 20:37-38; Acts 3:13, 25-26; 4:2; 5:30; 13:32-33; 24:14-15; 26:6-7, 22-23; 28:2. Is it a mere coincidence that Luke's emphasis on the God of the fathers as the one who raises the dead corresponds to the first two of the Eighteen Benedictions?

[48]There seems to be increasing agreement that these speeches, with their philosophical flavor, draw upon traditions of Hellenistic Judaism; cf. e.g. B. Gärtner, *The Areopagus Speech and Natural Revelation* (ASNU 21; Lund: Gleerup, 1955); J.-C. Lebram, "Der Aufbau der Areopagrede," *ZNW* 55 (1963/64), 221-243.

1. Salvation of Gentiles was from the beginning envisaged by God and included as part of his promises to Israel. Luke does not claim that the church has replaced Israel as the people of God, nor does he call Gentile believers Abraham's children.[49] Gentiles are saved as Gentiles. Luke takes care to adduce prophecies that really spoke of them.[50] This "proof-from-prophecy" has a double function: to prove the legitimacy of Gentile mission and Gentile churches, and to prove that Jesus is the Anointed One of whom the prophets spoke.

2. Luke wants to make it clear beyond doubt that in the course of events due respect has been paid to the priority of Israel. This is made clear by the birth stories, by the presentation of the ministry of Jesus and of the life and preaching of the earliest church, and by the stereotyped picture of Paul as everywhere beginning in the synagogue.[51] Luke even says that the number of believing Jews in Palestine was quite considerable (Acts 2:41; 4:4; 21:20). It would not be to the point to think that he simply assumes the mission to the Gentiles to result from the failure of the mission to the Jews.[52]

3. The priority of Israel is regarded as a matter of history; it is no longer a present reality for Luke and for churches like those of Corinth and Rome. The primary task, to proclaim the fulfillment of the promises to the Jews, *has* been carried out by the apostles; Paul's conversation with the Jews at Rome marks the end of it. (One might here compare the notion, widespread in early Protestantism, that even the task of proclaiming the gospel to all nations had been carried out by the apostles!) That so many Jews did not believe in Christ might seem to

---

[49] Acts 15:14 and 18:10 do not transcend the limits of the prophecy in Zech. 2:11; cf. my article "A People for His Name (Acts 15:14)," *NTS* 4 (1957), 319-327.

[50] Luke 3:6 (Isa. 40:5); Acts 2:17 (Joel 3:1 "all flesh"); 3:25 (Gen. 22:18); 13:47 (Isa. 49:6); 15:17 (Amos 9:12). Cf. biblical allusions and reminiscences in Luke 2:32; 4:24:27; Acts 1:8; 2:39; 10:34; 15:14; 26:17-18; 28:28. J. Dupont, "Le salut des Gentiles et la signification théologique de livre des Actes," *NTS* 6 (1959/60), 132-155. F. Hahn, *Mission in the New Testament* (tr. F. Clarke; Naperville: Allenson, 1965), 128-136.

[51] Cf. esp. Acts 13:46-48; 18:4-6; 28:17-31. For the pre-Pauline idea that the salvation of Gentiles would follow as a result of Israel's conversion to faith in Jesus, the Messiah, cf. J. Munck, *Paul and the Salvation of Mankind* (tr. F. Clarke; Richmond: John Knox, 1959).

[52] Thus Haenchen, *Acts*, 730: "The last chapter also is thus completely integrated into the total work, in that it bases the justification of the Gentile mission on the refusal of the Jews." But cf. latest German edition, 280-282.

jeopardize the "proof-from-prophecy," but Luke is able to show that even the obstinancy of the covenant people had been foretold by the prophets and by Jesus. It conformed to a constant pattern of biblical history.[53] Thus the main point would seem to be that the continuity with this history had in no way been broken, either by the emerging of Gentile churches, or by the exclusion of disobedient Jews.

For me, the study of Abraham in Luke-Acts has been a confirmation of Paul Schubert's thesis that "proof-from-prophecy" is a main theological and literary device of the work. It should be observed that this motif is in the foreground especially in those parts of the work at which there might seem to be some break in the historical continuity: the beginning of the gospel story, the passion and resurrection of Jesus, the transition from the ministry of Jesus to the activity of his apostles, the conversion of Cornelius, and the vocation, career, and imprisonment of Paul.[54] These are all points at which the hand of the author is easily discernible. Luke did not invent the Christian "proof-from-prophecy," but in a special way he made it a principle for the composition of a continuous historical work.

The model for his conception of sacred history as a series of predictions and events Luke found, no doubt, in the historical books of Holy Scripture. In the Pentateuch (viz., Tetrateuch or Hexateuch), God's promise to the fathers and the fulfillment of it is a main theme, I think *the* main theme. In the deuteronomic work of history (Deuteronomy-2 Kings) the word of God, announced by prophets and accomplished in due time is considered an active power at work in history.[55] Luke is

---

[53]Luke 1:34; 4:24-27; 6:22-23, 26; 8:10; 11:47-51; 13:23-30, 34; 14:24; 19:27, 41-46; 20:9-18; 21:20-24; 23:28-31; Acts 3:23; 4:25-28; 7:35-53; 13:40-41; 28:25-27.

[54]Cf. esp. Luke 1-2; 3:1-17; 4:16-30; 24; Acts 1:1-11; 10:1-11:18; 15:6-21. The passion of Jesus: Luke 2:35; 9:22, 31, 44, 51; 13:32-33; 17:25; 18:31-33; 19:14-17; 22:19-34. The vocation and career of Paul: Acts 9:1-18; 13:2; 16:6-8; 18:9-10; 20:23; 21:4, 11; 22:6-21; 23:11; 26:12-23; 27:9-11, 21-26, 41-44. H.H. Oliver ("The Lucan Birth Stories and the Purpose of Luke-Acts," *NTS* 10 [1963/64], 202-226) thinks that there is some question about the motif of "proof from prophecy": "Against it is the consideration that it has played no part in recent *redaktionsgeschichtliche* studies of Luke-Acts" (225). All the worse for redaction criticism if that is the case! The importance was already noticed by H.J. Cadbury, *The Making of Luke-Acts* (London: SPCK, 1927), 303-305. Cf. also E. Lohse, "Lukas als Theologe der Heilsgeschichte," *EvT* 14 (1954), 256-257.

[55]Cf. G. von Rad, *Studies in Deuteronomy* (tr. D.M.G. Stalker; London: SCM, 1953), 74-91, and *Old Testament Theology* (tr. D.M.G. Stalker; New York: Harpers, 1962), I, 339ff.

imitating biblical historiography. To say that is not to deny his Hellenistic affiliations (an unnecessary warning were it not the case that the struggle between "Hebraists" and "Hellenists" among New Testament scholars has caused some confusion). Luke consciously imitates the language of the Septuagint, but nonetheless writes the literary Koine of his day. In a similar way he writes "biblical history," but he does so as a Gentile Christian of Hellenistic culture and in Roman times. His interest in Abraham and his archaizing tendency in general bear the stamp of an age that looked back to classical times and considered antiquity an indication of value. Luke stresses the continuity between Abraham and the church of his own time, as some generations earlier Virgil had linked Roman history with that of Aeneas. The interest in "proof-from-prophecy," oracles, portents, and predictions, was not exclusively biblical.[56] The "father of history," Herodotus, had already paid considerable attention to oracles and the way in which they turned out to hold true.

But whatever the Greek, Hellenistic, and Roman components of Luke's historiography may have been, his own conscious intention was to write history in biblical style or, rather, to write the continuation of biblical history. This gives him a unique place even among the New Testament writers. Certainly, they all interpret the "Christ-event" within a frame of reference provided by biblical history, prophecy, and eschatology, as interpreted by contemporary Judaism.[57] The basic theme, that God's promise to Abraham was fulfilled in Christ and brought to the Gentiles by the apostolic preaching, Luke has in common with Paul and other writers after him. But Luke alone sets this forth in the form of a historical account which also includes recapitulations of the Old Testament history which is continued in the things now fulfilled. The apostolic preaching is to him not the revelation of an apocalyptic mystery, but a testimony to the most decisive events within a continuous series of predictions, occurrences, and new promises; the fulfillment of earlier prophecies is a guarantee that all that has been

---

[56]Luke himself is aware of this (Acts 16:16-18). His interests include the "popular" type prophets, of which Agabus was an example (Acts 11:28, 21:10-11).

[57]Cf. C.H. Dodd, *According to the Scriptures* (London: Nisbet, 1952); B. Lindars, *New Testament Apologetic* (Philadelphia: Westminster, 1961); and my essay "Eschatology and History in Light of the Qumran Texts," in *The Crucified Messiah* (Minneapolis: Augsburg, 1974), pp. 129-145.

foretold is to be established at the proper time.[58]

In the preface to his work Luke states that his purpose is that Theophilus should know the certainty (*tēn asphaleian*) of the things of which he had been informed. This can hardly be taken to mean merely that Luke wants to give an account which is outstanding according to the standards of historical accuracy. Interpreting the preface in the light of the whole work, we must much more assume that Luke wants to show the reliability of his account by demonstrating that everything has happened according to prophecies.[59] That is part of his task as historian, as Luke conceives it. Only with this in mind, I think, may we also say that for Luke the history of the church is its apology.[60] History, for Luke, has brought the prophecies to fulfillment, and the prophecies prove that the historical events happened according to the will of God.

Writing as a "biblical historian" Luke does not need to Christianize the portrait of Abraham in any direct and obvious way. The patriarch may remain the ancestor of Israel, the starting point of that sacred history of which the Gentile church is now the legitimate continuation. Luke, if I am correct, keeps closer to the Old Testament narratives and references to Abraham than does any other Christian or Jewish writer of his time. He gives very little room to legendary accretions and refrains from daring theological interpretations. In considering God's promise to Abraham as the first link in a series of prophecy and fulfillment, he is in full harmony with the outlook of Old Testament writers. Some details in the portrait of Abraham reflect the environment of a Hellenized, yet conservative type of Judaism. It is quite possible that Luke has taken over most of his references to the patriarch from sources at his disposal, Jewish or Christian. Yet with

---

[58]The difference between Luke's "Heilsgeschichte" and the eschatological interpretation of the "Christ-event" which, in spite of great variation, is common to Paul, Mark, Matthew and John, has been worked out by H. Conzelmann, *The Theology of St. Luke* (tr. G. Buswell; New York: Harper and Row, 1960). With his emphasis on the distinction between successive periods, however, he has unduly formalized Luke's conception.

[59]This is indicated by the phrase "the things which have been accomplished among us;" cf. Lohse, "Lukas als Theologe," 261ff. The term *asphaleia* in itself merely refers to the accuracy of the information (cf. Acts 21:34; 22:30; 25:26), but Theophilus had certainly already been informed that things had happened according to the Scriptures, and Luke feels that he is able to prove the accuracy of this.

[60]Cf. Haenchen, *Acts*, 732.

all his biblicism and traditionalism, Luke has made the whole material subservient to his own purpose; he rephrased and adapted it, and provided proper settings within the structure of his work. His way of dealing with the story of Abraham seems likely to be typical of his literary activity in general. He keeps rather close to his sources and wants to respect what he assumes to have been the historical facts. Yet, by means of redaction, rearrangement, and some minor changes, he is able to write history in such a way that he simultaneously sets forth his theology, whether he was conscious of this or not. In that respect Luke the historian had many and even outstanding followers among modern historiographers who have dealt with the same events -- no matter how greatly methods and ideas of history may have changed.

CHAPTER 6

THE PURPOSE OF LUKE-ACTS

Some twenty years ago W.C. van Unnik complained that scholars had neglected the question of the purpose of Acts.[1] Nobody would make such complaint today. A variety of theories have been discussed, modified, refined, or combined in various ways. Most of the recent contributions deal not with the purpose of Acts alone but rather with the purpose of the two-volume work conveniently called Luke-Acts. In these circumstances I find it impossible to attempt any survey of the history and present state of research.[2] I prefer to begin with some general remarks which are based upon fairly elementary observations and which should not be controversial. In the second part of this essay I shall turn to more problematical issues, especially questions raised by my former colleague Jacob Jervell.[3]

The author of Luke-Acts is likely to have been the first Christian author to publish a polished literary work. His stated purpose was to give an accurate and orderly account of events that had occurred. But the stated purpose need not be the only or even the major one. The shape of historical as of other literary works is conditioned by a variety of factors, including literary genres, patterns, and conventions, social and cultural

[1] "The 'Book of Acts' - The Confirmation of the Gospel," *Sparsa Collecta*, I (Leiden: Brill, 1973), 342 (repr. from *NovT* 4, 1956).

[2] For literature on Acts until ca. 1969, but with more attention to historicity than to literary composition and purpose, cf. W. Gasque, *A History of Criticism of the Acts of the Apostles* (Tübingen: Mohr, 1975).

[3] Jacob Jervell, *Luke and the People of God* (Minneapolis: Augsburg, 1972).

environment, and the material at the author's disposal as well as by his own personality and conscious purpose.[4] Yet, it is reasonable to assume that the purpose of Luke-Acts is reflected in the narrative rather than in some polemical, paraenetic, or other tendency to be abstracted from it.

The narrative is mainly composed of a number of more or less independent, self-contained dramatic episodes.[5] But these episodes are not simply joined together like pearls on a string. They are connected with one another, and to some extent with sayings of Jesus, by means of cross-references, predictions, portents, and summaries. Especially at important junctures, summaries, other general comments, and speeches contribute to the forward movement of the narrative as a whole. The author's redaction of known and conjectured sources and traditions has been analyzed in minute detail. Comparative studies of literary composition and techniques may prove equally valuable. Some work has been done in this area, but it is hardly more than a beginning. Minor Greek and Roman historians deserve more attention than they have received,[6] as do biblical and post-biblical Jewish historical and semi-historical narratives. Luke is frequently said to have been influenced by Hellenistic historiography. It may be more correct to say that he was himself a minor Hellenistic historian, albeit one who dealt with a very special subject matter and who imitated biblical rather than Attic style. Part of his purpose, I think, was to write a continuation of biblical history.

Luke-Acts is composed as one literary work in two volumes, but the separation between the two is not arbitrary. The first volume tells how the salvation promised to Israel was realized through the birth, life, passion, and resurrection of Jesus of Nazareth. The second volume tells how appointed witnesses proclaimed this salvation in Jerusalem, Samaria, and even wider circles, so that the word of God grew and even Gentiles became participants in that salvation. Throughout the narrative, the

---

[4]Cf. the outline of H.J. Cadbury's classical study, *The Making of Luke-Acts* (London: SPCK, 1961. [1st ed., 1926]).

[5]Cf. E. Plümacher, *Lukas als hellenistischer Schriftsteller* (Göttingen: Vandenhoeck & Ruprecht, 1972) 80-136.

[6]Cf. the important remarks by G. Bäärnhielm in his long review of B. Gärtner, *The Areopagus Speech and Natural Revelation* in *SEA* 20 (1955) 80-95. Plümacher's work (cf. preceding note) is hardly more than a beginning. For some analogies with biographies of philosophers, cf. C.H. Talbert, *Literary Patterns, Theological Themes, and the Genre of Luke-Acts* (Missoula: Scholars Press, 1974).

readers are made to understand that the course of events was directed by divine providence or, as Luke would have preferred to say, by the counsel (*boulē*) of God. A continuous series of promises and fulfillments connect the ancient history of Israel and the story of Jesus and his witnesses.

Luke tells the story of Jesus as the story of God's anointed whose coming was foretold by all the prophets from Moses onward, including Jesus' royal ancestor, David (cf. Acts 2:20; 3:22-24; 7:52). In the infancy story, the messiahship of Jesus is announced in fairly traditional terms (Luke 1:32-33, 68-75; 2:11). The words of old Simeon point forward to the continuation of the story in which it becomes increasingly clear that the Son of man had to suffer and be rejected (Luke 2:29-35; cf. 9:22f., 44f.; 17:25; 18:31-34; etc.). But it is not until after the resurrection, when the risen Lord opened their minds to understand the Scriptures, that the disciples realized that what had happened to Jesus conformed to what was written about the Christ (Luke 24:26-27, 44-47). At this point Luke has retained and even sharpened the idea of the "messianic secret" which is otherwise much more prominent in Mark (cf. Luke 9:45; 18:34; 24:25).

The conviction that Jesus was the Christ, whose coming was promised in the Scriptures, is common to all the evangelists. But unlike other New Testament authors, Luke does not simply draw a direct line from Old Testament testimonies to Jesus Christ. He does not only use terms like "the anointed," "the anointed of God," or "an anointed king" (e.g. Luke 9:20; 23:2); he can also develop the proof-from-prophecy in two steps: 1. The Christ had to suffer (but was not to see corruption). 2. It is Jesus who is the Christ (cf. e.g. Acts 17:2-3 and the interpretation of Psalm 16 in Acts 2:25-32; 13:35-37). Whereas the ancient kerygma, quoted by Paul in 1 Corinthians 15, stated that "Christ died for our sins in accordance with the Scriptures," Luke is interested in what we may somewhat anachronistically call "the Old Testament concept of the Messiah," in order to prove that it applies to Jesus and not to David or to anybody else. Moreover, Luke is also interested in the etymological meaning of the word *christos*, "anointed" (e.g. Acts 4:26-27, quotes from and comments upon Psalm 2). This relates to Luke's tendency to represent Jesus, more emphatically than the other evangelists, as a person filled with the Holy Spirit, with which he was "anointed" at his baptism (Luke 3:22; 4:1, 14; 10:21).[7]

Luke has used the episode of the rejection of Jesus in his home town as the occasion for an "inaugural address," (4:16ff.). Jesus reads the text of Isaiah 61:1: "The Spirit of the Lord is upon me, because he has anointed me..." and begins his sermon: "Today this scripture is fulfilled in your hearing." Thus, Luke makes his readers understand the following report about Jesus' preaching and healing ministry as the story of the Christ, who was anointed to bring good news to those in need (cf. e.g. Luke 6:20ff.) and sent to liberate those who were captives (possessed by evil spirits and bound by Satan), to give sight to the blind and to heal the sick. The whole Lukan picture of Jesus as the helper of the afflicted, the companion and savior of sinners, tax collectors, Samaritans and outcast Israelites corresponds with this initial proclamation of a "year of release." The importance of the anointing of Jesus as the Christ is confirmed by Peter's summary of the public ministry in Acts 10:36-39: "You know...how God anointed Jesus at Nazareth with the Holy Spirit and with power; and how he went about doing good and healing all that were oppressed by the devil, for God was with him."

According to Luke, the concept of the Christ includes both a royal and a prophetic component. As David was not only king but also prophet (Acts 2:30), and Moses not only a prophet but also ruler, judge, and deliverer (Acts 7:27, 35), so the Christ is -- by definition -- both the royal descendant of David, destined to rule for ever, and a man anointed by the Spirit, the prophet like Moses (Acts 3:28; 7:37). Thus, Luke is able to integrate Jesus' prophetic ministry of preaching and healing with his crucifixion and resurrection in such a way that the whole story corresponds to the biblical concept of the Christ as Luke understands it.[8] Both the royal and the more prophetic components of the concept support the thesis that the Christ by necessity had to suffer. Luke makes ample use of traditions that placed Jesus in a line of succession of prophets whose lot it was to be persecuted. In the speech of Stephen, Moses is represented as the prototype of the prophet who was rejected by

---

[7]The preceding section relies in part on W. Kurz, *The Function of Christological Proof from Prophecy for Luke and Justin* (forthcoming diss., Yale 1976).

[8]On Jesus and other prophets in Luke-Acts, cf. P.S. Minear, *To Heal and to Reveal* (New York: Seabury, 1976) and L.T. Johnson, *The Literary Function of Possessions in Luke-Acts* (unpubl. diss., Yale 1976).

his people (Acts 7:35, 39ff.). At the same time, "Davidic" psalms are used to prove that the Christ had to be rejected and to die before he could be enthroned at the right hand of God as Lord and Christ.

By means of his two-step proof-from-prophecy, Luke makes the passion and resurrection of Jesus the main evidence for his identity as God's anointed. One of the key proof-texts is the passage from Psalm 118:22 about the rejected stone that became the head of the corner (Luke 21:17; Acts 4:11). As is evident from the speeches in Acts 2-5, 10, and 13, the Lukan kerygma centers around the rejection of Jesus by the leaders of the people and his vindication by God. But the theme of reversal, the "turning of the tables," is already anticipated in the Magnificat and represents God's normal way of dealing with his people (esp. Luke 1:51-53, cf. also the stories of Joseph and Moses in Acts 7:9-13, 25-36). The first volume tells mainly about help and salvation for the poor, and suffering children of Abraham, to the exclusion of the rich and mighty. It also anticipates the story of the second volume by predicting that the kingdom is to be given to the apostles who had shared the trials of Jesus - in contrast to the leaders of Israel who had rejected him (Luke 22:28-29; cf. 12:32). In Acts the theme of reversal is repeatedly spelled out in the form of narratives about adversities that are turned into miraculous deliverances and result in further promotion of the gospel.[9]

The apparently contrasting but interrelated themes of fulfillment of the promises and of turning the tables pervade the entire two-volume work. The first episode is set in the Jerusalem temple, the last in Rome. The conclusion of the whole narrative is that the salvation promised to and realized in Israel has been sent to the Gentiles (Acts 28:28). This transition, however, only occurs gradually. The gospel story contains some portents of what was going to happen, but Luke limits the earthly ministry of Jesus to Israel. In this case the exception confirms the rule; it was at the recommendation of Jewish elders that Jesus healed the slave of a Gentile centurion (Luke 7:1-10). Even after the resurrection, Luke stresses, salvation in the name of Jesus was first preached to Israel and a considerable number of Jews did in fact believe. Thus, God's promises to Israel were fulfilled.

---

[9]Another forthcoming Yale dissertation, by David Adams, will deal with this theme.

The preaching to the Gentiles did not start until the Jews in Jerusalem had been given a chance to repent. A similar story is repeated in place after place. Paul first preaches in the synagogue and some Jews believe. Others react in a hostile way, and after that Paul turns to the Gentiles (cf. esp. Acts 13:46-48; 18:6; 28:23-28). The converted Gentiles do not become Israelites - or members of a "new Israel." They are saved as Gentiles, in fulfillment of promises that pertained to them (cf. Acts 3:25; 13:47; 15:17; Luke 2:32; 13:39).[10]

The addition of a second volume as a continuation of the gospel story was a literary innovation. But by writing "The Acts of the Apostles" Luke simply spelled out in narrative form what was already contained in summaries of faith: Christ was "preached among the nations, believed on in the world" (1 Tim. 3:16). The gospel, of which Paul became a minister, was "preached to every creature under heaven" (Col. 1:23). The same feature occurred in later formulations, including the secondary endings of Mark: "And they went forth and preached everywhere, while the Lord worked with them and confirmed the message by the signs that attended it" (Mark 16:20); "And after this, Jesus himself sent out by means of them, from east to west, the sacred and imperishable proclamation of eternal salvation" ("shorter ending," as translated in RSV, footnote to Mark 16:20).[11] The conversion of Gentiles could been seen as evidence that Jesus was indeed the Christ about whom it was written that the Gentiles should hope in him.[12]

Within the New Testament canon the second volume is called "The Acts of the Apostles," a title which refers to the apostles' mighty and miraculous acts. In the work itself, however, these acts are mainly important as evidence of the power of Jesus' name. With a Lukan formulation we might also say that the purpose was to show how the word of God "increased," or "grew and

---

[10]Cf. Jervell, 41-74 etc., and my articles "A People for His Name," *NTS* 4,(1957-58), 319-327 and "Abraham in Luke-Acts" (above).

[11]See also the referance to the testimony of appointed witnesses (Luke 24:47-48; Acts 13:31-32, etc.). Already Paul could include his own sending to the Gentiles in summaries of the gospel (Rom. 1:2-5; 1 Cor. 15:3-10). The pattern occurs in a stereotyped form in Eph. 3:2-10, Col. 1:23; 1 Tim. 1:11ff. and 2:5-7; 2 Tim. 1:9-11; Titus 1:2-3. See my article "Evangelium og Apostel," *NTT* (1943) 193-217.

[12]E.g. Rom. 15:12 (Isa. 11:10, cf. Gen. 49:10) and Gal. 3:13-14a (Gen. 22:18). See my *The Crucified Messiah*, 153f.

multiplied" (Acts 6:7; 12:24; 19:20). As a narrative about the growth of the word Acts is a confirmation of the gospel.[13] Especially the speeches, with their kerygmatic summaries and scriptural quotations, give Luke the opportunity to emphasize and to comment on the significance of the story told in the first volume. The stated purpose, that Theophilus should learn to know the unwavering truth (*tēn asphaleian*) of the things in which he had been instructed, cannot merely refer to the accuracy of historical information. The facts are much more certain because they occurred in accordance with God's promise and counsel.

Luke must have had much greater freedom in composing the second volume than the first. Reports about the early church in Jerusalem, about Peter and other apostles, and about Paul's conversion and successful missionary work, and so on, must have circulated already by the time of Paul himself, but such reports had hardly been fixed to the same degree as the Jesus-tradition.[14] It is, however, remarkable that Luke quite frequently not only tells about the experiences of the apostles and of Barnabas and Paul but also makes reference to the reports which they gave afterwards. In several cases we hear that those who heard the reports responded with prayer or by praising God and rejoicing.[15] We can safely assume that Luke hoped that his own comprehensive written report would have a similar effect. The chief purpose of Luke-Acts may simply be that Theophilus and other Gentile Christians should be strengthened in their faith, praise God for the salvation sent to them, and take courage, so that the number of believers might continue to increase.

I hope that my brief summary is fair and correct. It could easily be supplemented by more detailed observations, but it is time to turn to the more problematic issues. The general, positive purpose of Luke-Acts which I have tried to outline does not explain all the data. Most of the remaining problems relate to the seond half of Acts. If the purpose was simply to tell about the spread of the gospel from Jerusalem to Rome and from Jews to Gentiles, why does the narrative concentrate so exclusively

---

[13]Cf. van Unnik, note 1 above.

[14]Cf. esp. 1 Thess. 1:8-10; 2:14; Rom. 1:8; Gal. 1: 23-24, and see Jervell, "The Problem of Traditions in Acts," in *Luke and the People of God*, 19-39. An article of mine dating from 1940 on "Ordets vekst" (The Growth of the Word) was printed in *NTT* 67 (1966) 32-46.

[15]For reports about and reactions to events which have already been told, cf. Acts 4:23-31; 8:14; 9:27, 42; 11:7-18; 12:17; 14:27; 14:3-4, 7-9, 12; 21:19-20; 22:3-21; 26:2-29.

on Paul, to the exclusion of the later travels and preaching of Peter, Philip, or Barnabas? We do not even learn how the gospel came to Rome but hear only about Paul's arrival and conversation with Jews in the city. Furthermore, why do we hear so little about the success of Paul's mission to the Gentiles and so much about his preaching in the synagogues? In his speeches before a Gentile audience Paul preaches a strict monotheism (Acts 14:11-18; 17:16-32). The cause of his troubles is either false accusations leveled by unbelieving Jews or a conflict of interest with idolatry or with syncretistic magicians and mantics (Acts 19:23-40, cf. 13:6-11; 15:16ff.; 19:13-19).

Acts represents Paul as the chief instrument for the salvation of the Gentiles. But the precedent for baptizing uncircumsized Gentiles is set by Peter and the Apostolic Decree is enacted at the recommendation of James. The Lukan Paul remains a law-abiding Pharisee until the end. The reports about Paul's demonstrations of obedience to the law may possibly be explained by his principle to become as one under the law to those under the law (1 Cor. 9:20). But the qualification "though not being myself under the law" is conspicuously absent in Acts, as is Paul's whole doctrine of freedom from the law. At this point it will not do to say that the Lukan picture is only in conflict with existential interpretations of Pauline theology and not with Paul's own letters.[16] The rebuttal of charges of offenses against the law, the temple, and the Jewish nation comes into the foreground in Paul's speeches in Acts 21-26. But, as Jervell has successfully demonstrated, similar tendencies are latent throughout the entire work.[17] Luke did not include traditions about Jesus' critical attitude towards the law in his gospel, to give an example. Among early Christian writings, Luke-Acts is unique in its insistence that it was the God of the fathers who raised Jesus and in whose service Paul mediated salvation to the Gentiles.[18]

It is the great merit of Jervell's studies that he has so vigorously drawn our attention to these and similar features

---

[16]The difference between the Paul of the letters and the Paul of Acts has sometimes been overstressed (e.g. by Vielhauer, Haenchen, and Conzelmann), but their critics often fail to see the real differences (e.g. Gasque, 241-243, 283-291).

[17]On Paul and the law in Luke-Acts, see Jervell, *Luke* 133-207, and also his article "Den omskårne Messias" *SEA* 37-38 (1973-74), 145-155.

[18]Luke 1:68; 20:37-38; Acts 3:13; 5:30; 7:32; 13:17; 22:14; 24:14.

which had been unduly neglected in recent discussions of Luke-Acts, especially in Germany. Slogans like "delay of the parousia," "de-eschatologizing," distinction between various periods of *Heilsgeschichte*, "Early Catholicism," or *theologia gloriae* contain elements of truth, but they do not adequately explain the composition and purpose of the Lukan work.

Jervell's observations are, however, not entirely new. Some of them have played a considerable role in earlier discussions. In the nineteenth century, F.C. Baur and his school considered Luke a Paulinist who made concessions to Jewish Christianity and thereby contributed to the catholic synthesis. At a later date, some scholars explained the emphasis on the Jewishness of Paul and the representation of Christianity as the genuine Judaism as part of a political apologetic for Christianity as a *religio licita* which ought to be tolerated by the Roman authorities.[19] Others have argued that the data is best explained on the assumption that Luke-Acts was occasioned by the trial of Paul and published at the end of his two years of imprisonment in Rome.[20] None of these solutions is satisfactory; neither is the more recent theory of a veiled polemic against antinomian or gnostic trends among Gentile Christians.[21]

The problem as I see it is this: the whole narrative moves toward salvation for the Gentiles as its goal; it is therefore all the more remarkable that so much space and attention is devoted to covering the rear against Jewish objections and accusations. Part of the explanation is implicit in what I said in the main part of this essay. The rebuttal of Jewish charges is in line with the general proof-from-prophecy theme and with the argument from antiquity (an argument which was common in Christian apologetics at a time when age was valued more than modernity). The peculiarity of the Lukan apologetic -- compared to that of Matthew, Hebrews, Barnabas, or Justin -- is related

---

[19]Cf. esp. J. Weiss, *Über die Absicht und den literarischen Character der Apostelgeschichte* (Marburg and Göttingen: Vandenhoeck & Ruprecht, 1897). B.S. Easton, *The Purpose of Acts* (London: SPCK, 1936; also in his *Early Christianity*, London: Seabury, 1954).

[20]Thus not only conservative scholars but also A. von Harnack, *Neue Untersuchungen zur Apostelgeschichte* (Leipzig, J.C. Hinrichs, 1911).

[21]There may be elements of truth in the thesis of C.H. Talbert, *Luke and the Gnostics* (Nashville: Abingdon, 1966). Luke was certainly aware of a gnostic danger, cf. Acts 20:29-30. His purpose, however, is not to refute the gnostics but much more to prove that Paul himself had no responsibility for their antinomian teachings.

to the narrative form of presentation. In refraining from overt Christian reinterpretation of the figure of Abraham, the law of Moses, etc., Luke proves that he did, indeed, have a better historical sense than other early Christian writers.[22] The double pattern of fulfillment and reversal makes it possible for Luke to account for the exclusion of disobedient Jews as well as for the inclusion of believing Gentiles (cf. e.g. Acts 3:23; 28:25-28). But from his perspective, the basis for the faith of Gentile Christians would have been insecure if no significant part of Israel had accepted the promised salvation realized in Jesus, or if Paul had violated the law and taught apostasy from Moses.

The general scope, however, does not adequately explain all the problematic data in Luke-Acts. We must also reckon with more specific factors, especially with accusations against Paul, which were operative in Luke's environment and which to some extent conditioned the shape of his work. Jervell has argued that Luke-Acts presupposes "a milieu of a preponderant Jewish-Christian stamp."[23] Yet, he agrees with the majority of scholars that "at the time of Luke there was no longer a mission to Jews."[24] Apparently, he has taken the movement towards mission to the Gentiles to be too obvious to be in need of renewed elaboration. As a result, Jervell has in his essays made a number of excellent observations, raised provocative questions, and successfully challenged common opinions, but he has not yet integrated all the data into a clear and convincing synthesis.

The theory that Luke-Acts presupposes Jewish-Christian readers is not the only possible hypothesis. Until the time of Constantine, Christianity and Judaism remained competing minority religions. Both of them attracted converts from paganism and, to some extent, from one another.[25] From Acts, probably more than from any other source, we learn that a number of "God-fearing" Gentiles at the fringe of the synagogue were attracted by Christianity, a version of biblical monotheism that did not require

---

[22]Cf. by contrast, not only Justin but also Matthew, John, Hebrews, or Barnabas. See also my article on "Abraham in Luke-Acts," in this volume.

[23]Jervell, 175-177, 199 etc.

[24]*Ibid.* 68.

[25]Cf. M. Simon, *Verus Israel*,(Paris: E. de Boccard, 1948), and P. Donahue, *Jewish-Christian Controversy in the Second Century: A Study in the Dialogue of Justin Martyr* (Unpubl. diss., Yale 1973).

circumcision.[26] Even if obliged to observe the rules of the Apostolic Decree, Christians could also retain their social relations to pagan family and friends to a much higher degree than Jewish proselytes who were obliged to keep the whole Mosaic law.[27] At the same time, the "God-fearers" -- and others -- may have been impressed by the argument that Judaism and not Christianity (as represented by Paul) was the ancient and authentic form of biblical religion. If Luke-Acts, as a published literary work, was ever intended for a general reading public, we should certainly seek the prospective readers among the God-fearers rather than among Roman officials. Luke's special interest in the God-fearers is unmistakeable, but it remains questionable if it explains all the data. The strongest argument for Jervell's conjectured Jewish-Christian audience would seem to be the way in which James, the brother of the Lord, is introduced as a well known authoritative figure and acts as a "defender of Paul."[28]

The deliberations in the last part of this essay have yielded mainly negative results: The question of the purpose of Luke-Acts is interdependent with the question of the setting of the work in social and religious history, but we do not know exactly when and where, under what circumstances and in which milieu the work was written. I have no specific hypothesis to propose and prefer to conclude by mentioning some areas in which further research might bring us closer to a solution.

Luke's understanding of salvation for Israel and for the "associate people" from the Gentiles should be compared with other approaches which do not conform to the simplistic notion of the Christian church as the new people of God. Christian reworking of and interpolations in Old Testament pseudepigrapha seem to be the most promising field. Jervell's study of the Testaments of the Twelve Patriarchs, "Ein Interpolator Interpretiert," is so far the only published result of his extensive studies in this all too neglected area.[29] The question, in which areas and to what degree were the regulations of the Apostolic Decree ever enforced in its original (not Western) form, may also need to be re-examined. A complete collection and

---

[26]Cf. Acts 10:2, 22; 13:16, 2, 43, 50; 16:14; 17:4, 17; 18:7.

[27]As A.J. Malherbe reminds me, Luke makes this very clear to his readers, cf. Acts 10:16-29; 11:2-12; 16:15, 34; 18:7; 28:7, 10.

[28]Jervell, 185-207, "James: The Defender of Paul."

[29]In *Studien zu den Testamenten der zwölf Patriarchen*, ed. W. Eltester (Berlin: Töpelmann, 1969).

critical examination of the scattered evidence for later Jewish and Jewish-Christian polemics against Paul is an urgent task whose solution might also contribute to a better understanding of the setting of Luke-Acts.

The general notion of a progressive development from Palestinian Jewish Christianity by way of Hellenistic-Jewish Christianity, pre-pauline Gentile Christianity, Paul and Gentile Christianity besides and after him, to Early Catholicism is not likely to provide any natural setting for the composition of Luke-Acts. Both the continued interrelations between Jews and Christians and the history of Jewish Christianity have to be taken into account. Possibly, the whole history of early Christianity has to be re-written. Some of my younger colleagues are beginning to work in that direction, and I am happy to leave the task to them.

CHAPTER 7

THE JOHANNINE CHURCH AND HISTORY

The Problem

In his *Theology of the New Testament* Rudolf Bultmann discussed the theology of the Fourth Gospel without dealing with its attitude to Old Testament scripture and the history of salvation.[1] This does not mean that Bultmann considers all quotations and allusions to the Old Testament secondary--only a minority of them are attributed to the ecclesiastical editor[2]--but he thinks that they are of no serious theological importance. Eduard Schweizer, in an essay entitled "The Concept of the Church in the Gospel and Epistle of St. John,"[3] takes more seriously the Old Testament background of Johannine concepts. According to Schweizer, John has solved the difficult problem of how the church here and now can live by what happened in Jesus of Nazareth at another time and in another place: "There is no longer any problem about bridging the distance in time and

---

[1]The "Jewish religion" is merely discussed as an illustration of the perverted state of creation in his *Theology of the New Testament* (tr. K. Grobel; New York: Scribner's, 1955), II, 27-30.

[2]In Bultmann's commentary on John (*The Gospel of John* [tr. G.R. Beasley-Murray et. al.; Philadelphia: Westminster, 1971]), only the quotations in 1:22-23; 7:38 and 10:34 are attributed to the ecclesiastical editor. Those in 2:17; 6:31, 45; 12:39-40; 13:18; and 15:25 are attributed to the Evangelist; 12:38 derives from the Semeia-source; and 12:15; 19:24, 28-29, 36-37 derive from a tradition akin to that of the Synoptics. Only the revelatory discourses contain no quotations.

[3]In *New Testament Essays, Studies in Memory of T.W. Manson* (Manchester: Manchester University Press, 1959), 230-245.

space between the events of salvation and the contemporary church. For the church is not a people based on an act of God in history... It is the church only in so far as it lives 'in' the Son and he in it. The Son is present in the church today just as he was then, through the message..." "Here Church is placed in the present time and is proof against all forms of historicism and of millenarianism." But Schweizer sees one danger, "that the church may become detached from history."[4]

Bultmann would possibly see an advantage where Schweizer sees a danger. The first question to be asked, however, is whether the church, as conceived by John, is really detached from history or bound more closely to it than both Bultmann and Schweizer suppose. Obviously, their views are not without some basis. The usual ecclesiological terminology of the New Testament is not found in the Fourth Gospel; words like *hē ekklēsia, hoi hagioi, ho laos tou theou* are lacking, and so is the opposite term *ta ethnē*. The church is conceived as the community of the believers in contrast to the world, rather than as the people of God in contrast to the Gentile nations. We do not find any specific command concerning Gentile missions (cf. 20:21);[5] from the beginning it is made clear that the mission of Jesus is a mission to the world (1:9-10; 3:16-17); the existence of the disciples in the world is in itself a mission to the world (17:18). Schweizer himself points to the Old Testament background of the imagery of the true vine (15:1ff., cf. esp. Ps. 80:14-16) and of the good shepherd and his flock (10, cf. Ezek. 34). But such images are no longer employed in order to depict the way of God's dealing with his people in the course of history; they represent the actual relation between Christ and those who belong to him.

Not even Bultmann would pretend that Johannine theology is completely detached from history. The word became flesh; the concrete, historical man Jesus of Nazareth is proclaimed as the revelation of God. Schweizer stresses that John wrote a Gospel, not a dogmatic treatise. Further, the allusions to persons and events of the Old Testament do not look like merely traditional features. To be sure, in the Fourth Gospel, more often than in the rest of the New Testament, the significance of Christ is expressed by means of nouns or by sentences in the present tense.

---

[4] *Ibid.*, 240-241.

[5] Cf. my "Kristus, jödene og verden etter Johannesevangeliet," *NTT* 60 (1959), 189-203, an article that deals with much the same material as the present essay but with special emphasis on the conception of missions.

But this does not mean that the past and the future have simply been absorbed into the present. The Evangelist makes use of a number of temporal nouns and adverbs; he distinguishes between tenses, and between "now" and "afterward" (13:7, 36), "hitherto" (16:24) and "henceforth" (14:7), "not yet" (2:4; 7:6; 8:20) and "now" (12:23, 27; 17:1), "before" and "when" (14:29).

Some features of the Gospel seem to favor an existential interpretation; others seem more easily to lend themselves to an interpretation in terms of *Heilsgeschichte*. This may indicate that these alternatives within the modern approach to biblical theology do not do justice to the originality and complexity of the Fourth Gospel and of its conception of church and history.

The Time of the Church and the Time of Jesus

In his testimony (*martyria*) to the earthly ministry of Jesus, John at the same time bears witness to his presence in the church. Jesus of Nazareth, as John sees him, is "the Christ of faith;" to that extent Schweizer is right: there is no distance in time and space to be bridged. Yet that is not the whole truth. The Evangelist is fully aware of a distinction between the time of Jesus and the situation of the post-resurrection church. The Johannine Christ is looking forward - not so much to an eschatological consummation on the last day as to the day of his glorification and of his renewed presence among the disciples. Before his glorification the Spirit was not yet given (7:39); not until after his departure could the Paraclete be sent (16:7). Until "that day" the disciples were not praying in his name (16:26; cf. 16:23). "That day," the post-resurrection time, brings a deeper understanding (14:20; cf. 2:22; 12:16; 13:7) and greater deeds (5:20; 14:12). Then the disciples shall follow Jesus as they were not able to do at the time of his life on earth (13:36; cf. 12:26; 14:4-6).

The difference of time has also a spatial aspect. The earthly ministry of Jesus was restricted to Israel. This fact is not so strongly emphasized in the Fourth Gospel as in the First; but John does not say that Jesus moved outside the Holy Land, nor does he report that he had contacts with individual Gentiles. The miracle of 4:46-53 might be an exception, but it is - in contrast to Matthew 8:5-13 and Luke 7:1-10 - not directly said that the "official" was not a Jew. This cannot mean that the question of nationality was no longer relevant; other texts prove that John does reflect upon the position of the Greeks with regard to Jesus. We hear that the Jews misunderstand the saying of Jesus concerning his departure (7:33-36). They supposed that he intended to go to the dispersion among the Greeks and to teach the Greeks. As often in the Fourth Gospel, the misunderstanding conveys the truth: Jesus was, indeed, going to the Father, and thus also going to the Greeks - through the word of his missionary witnesses (cf. 10:16 and 11:52).[6]

The coming of Greeks, who wish to see Jesus, is the sign "that the hour has come for the Son of man to be glorified" (12:20ff.). His earthly ministry in Israel has come to an end; the universal mission is to be inaugurated by the death of Jesus. The grain of wheat has to die in order to bear much fruit (12:24). Lifted up from the earth, Jesus will draw all men to himself (12:32). The Greeks are to see him - as the glorified one. The great missionary text, John 12:20-33, shows why John does not need to make the Risen Christ give any specific commandment concerning Gentile missions. The historical and geographical limitations of the ministry of Jesus are dissolved by the very fact of his death, which in its unity with the resurrection is also his ascension to the Father. This finds its symbolic expression in the inscription which Pilate put on the cross, "Jesus of Nazareth, the King of the Jews." It was written in Hebrew, in Latin, and in Greek (19:19-22). The kingship of Jesus is not of this world. Bearing witness to the truth, he already exercised it during his ministry among the Jews (18:36-37); but not until he was crucified as "the king of the Jews" was he proclaimed even to Greeks and Romans, and his voice heard by "every one who is of the truth."

As there is a clear distinction between the time before the departure of Jesus and the time after his ascension, so there are in the Fourth Gospel also two stages within the earthly ministry of Jesus, the time *before* his hour had come and the time *after* it had come. By and large, these two stages correspond to the two main literary sections of the Gospel; chapters 1-12 deal with the public ministry of Jesus; and chapters 13-20 (21) deal

---

[6]J.A.T. Robinson ("Destination and Purpose of St. John's Gospel," *NTS* 6 [1959-60], 117-131) takes "the Greeks" of the Fourth Gospel to be Diaspora Jews. I am unconvinced. The meaning of the statement in 12:20 that the Greeks have gone up to worship at the feast might be that the Jewish Diaspora has had a preparatory mission, part of the means by which men are drawn by the Father to the Son (cf. 4:38; 6:45).

with the departure of the ascending Savior.[7] The coming of the Greeks, the missionary outlook and the final verdict on the unbelieving Jews in 12:20-50 mark the conclusion of the first section and provide a transition to the second. The farewell discourses center around the departure of Christ and its consequences for the disciples in the time to come, whereas the conflict with the Jews is a main theme in chapters 1-12. Even in the first part, however, many sayings point forward to that which is to come (e.g. 3:11-15; 6:61-62). The situation of the post-resurrection church is pre-figured and anticipated during the earthly ministry of Jesus in Israel.

The visit of Jesus to Samaria may here be taken as an important and illustrative example (4:1-42). The account of the dialog between Jesus and the Samaritan woman allows the Evangelist to show that the contrast between Jews and non-Jews is transcended by the coming of Christ - without letting the earthly Jesus move outside the Holy Land and the sphere of the Old Testament revelation. The Samaritan woman rightly recognizes Jesus to be a Jew (4:9) - salvation is from the Jews (4:22); but in the end he is hailed, not only as the Christ (4:25-26, 29), but as the Savior of the world (4:42). Jesus is greater than the father Jacob, as much as the "water" given by him is of a higher quality than that of Jacob's well (4:12-15). The coming of the Samaritans illustrates the missionary situation: "The fields are already white for harvest" (4:30-38). After two days, however, Jesus departed to Galilee; that means the work in Samaria had the character of an anticipation, the earthly ministry of Jesus being characterized by the saying about the prophet who has no honor in his own country (4:43-44).

Within this context we find the Johannine formula "the hour is coming and now is" (4:23). It is a formula of eschatological anticipation (5:25), but the coming day of fulfillment is that which is inaugurated by the ascension of Jesus, the "hour" in which the church is living. The "hour," when the Father will be worshipped neither on Gerizim nor in Jerusalem, but in spirit and truth, is identical with "that day," in which the disciples will pray in the name of Jesus (16:26), when the Spirit of truth will have been sent by the Father. This coming hour is already

---

[7]The interrelation between the farewell discourses and the earlier portions of the Gospel is a special problem the importance of which has been pointed out in articles by Alv Kragerud ("Kjaerlighetsbudet i Johannesevangeliet," *NTT* 57 [1956], 137-149, and "Jesu åpenbaring av de jorkiske og de himmelske ting," *NTT* 58 [1957], 17-53).

present, as Jesus during his earthly ministry is already the Savior of the world. But the point of the formula is not simply to state the eschatological character of the present hour; it serves, rather, to illuminate the relation between the "time" of the earthly ministry and the "time" of the church: in spite of the temporal distance, there is an essential identity. What is present in the time after the ascension was anticipated in the life of Jesus, and the witness borne to his historical ministry is, therefore, at the same time a testimony to his presence here and now. It would be as false to stress only the identity of the qualified time and dehistoricize the Gospel as it would be to stress only the diversity of the chronological time and give a historicizing, biographical interpretation to the Gospel.

The Jews and the Messiah

The relationship of the church to the Jews is of fundamental importance for the New Testament understanding of the church and of the history of salvation. In the Fourth Gospel the Jews appear as a rather homogeneous mass, hostile to Christ; this hostility often seems to be implied in the term *hoi Ioudaioi* itself. This way of speaking must date from a time when the cleavage between Jews and Christians had become definite; John carries the cleavage back to the days of Jesus himself (9:22; 12:42). The Johannine attitude should, of course, not be confused with any form of modern anti-Semitism. It differs also from the anti-Judaism of the "Epistle to Barnabas," to name but one extreme example from the ancient church. The Jews of the Fourth Gospel are representatives of the world in its hostility to God. That has been well established by Bultmann.[8] It is, however, equally important that those who represent the world are the Jews.

John does not make use of the traditional distinction between the people of God and the Gentile nations. But his point of view is based upon the Jewish idea that Israel is the center of the world.[9] This conception is interpreted in a new and revolutionary way in the Fourth Gospel. Positively, it implies that the mission of Jesus in Israel is a mission to the world

---

[8]In his commentary on John, 86-87, etc.

[9]Cf. A. Fridrichsen, "Missionstanken i Fjärde Evangeliet," *SEA* 2 (1937), 137-148, or "La pensée missionaire dans le quatrième Évangile," *Arbeiten und Mitteilungen aus dem neutestamentlichen Seminar zu Uppsala* 6 (1937), 39-45.

and that he fulfilled his ministry to the world within Israel. Negatively, it means that the world's enmity and opposition to God become most intense among the Jews.

In the Fourth Gospel, discussions concerning matters of the law and Sabbath observances (5:9-18; 7:21-24; 9:13-16) are but the starting point for debates on the real issue, the question of Jesus' authority. In the Synoptics, this question is latent in the background; in the Fourth Gospel it has become the manifest center of all discussions. Chapter 5 is especially instructive: Jesus defends his Sabbath healing by pointing to the activity of the Father, who is still working after the completion of the six days' work of creation - even on the Sabbath (5:17). What makes the opposition of the Jews so violent is this answer, by which Jesus makes himself equal with God. The basic conflict is throughout a christological one, not in the sense that matters of christological dogmatics are debated, but in the sense that the opposition is caused by the witness which Jesus bears to himself.

The Johannine Christ is much more than the "Messiah" in the Jewish sense of this word. But it is a remarkable fact, often overlooked, that the title *Christos* in the Fourth Gospel has not been made obsolete by predicates like "Logos," "Son of God," "Savior of the world."[10] John alone in the New Testament uses the title in its original form, the Messiah (1:41; 4:25). He is also aware of its meaning as a synonym for "king of Israel" (1:50). Moreover, John is familiar with the vagueness of Jewish messianic expectations, in which the Messiah was but one of several figures, like Elijah and "the prophet" (1:20-21) - a fact which has only recently been clearly observed by scholars.

For the Evangelist, Jesus is the Messiah in the sense that of him "Moses in the law and also the prophets wrote" (1:45). He also employs a number of formula quotations and allusions in order to show that the prophecies are fulfilled in Jesus. But at the same time in a most remarkable way he makes it clear that the term "Christ" means something very different in the Christian confession to Jesus (9:22; 20:31) and in the mouth of the Jews who discuss whether or not he could possibly be the Christ (7:26-27, 41-42; 10:24; 12:34). To the Jews, the Messiah is a political king (6:15; 11:48; 19:12). Jesus is king, but in

[10]Cf. B. Noack, "Johannesevangeliets messiasbillede og dets kristologi," *DTT* 19 (1956), 129-185; and W.C. van Unnik, "The Purpose of St. John's Gospel," *Studia Evangelica* (*TU* 73; Berlin: Akademie Verlag), 382-411.

quite another sense (18:33-37). When the Jews find a lack of conformity between the appearance of Jesus and messianic dogmatics, they are at fault because they understand everything in a this-worldly manner. The origin of Christ is hidden to men, as the Jews say; but this is true because he comes from above (7:26-29). Christ is to remain forever - as the ascended one (12:34).

John does not try explicitly to refute Jewish doubts as to the messiahship of Jesus; obviously, he has no hope that they would be convinced by exegetical arguments. In this he differs from Luke (e.g. Acts 17:2-3) and Justin, who hope to win Jews over by showing that 1. properly interpreted, the messianic prophecies conform to the portrait of Jesus; and 2. because Jesus fulfills these prophecies, he is the Christ.[11] As John sees it, a teacher of Israel is not in need of exegetical explanations, but of a new birth (3:1ff.). What matters is the witness which the Scriptures in their totality bear to Christ (5:39, 46), and this testimony cannot be understood by men who judge according to the flesh (cf. 8:15). The Scriptures, as understood by John, bear witness to Christ in the present, rather than to a history of a salvation in the past with an importance of its own. And yet, it is not ignored that there was a history even before Christ.

Witnesses Before Christ

Like the earlier evangelists and the tradition before them, John begins the Gospel story with John the Baptist. But in the Fourth Gospel the point is not that a new epoch within a continuous history of salvation begins. The Baptist is nothing but the voice of one crying in the wilderness; he is misunderstood if he is taken to have any greatness of his own (1:19-27; 3:25-30). His only function is to bear witness to Christ (1:6-8, etc.). In the Fourth Gospel a witness is conceived as one who tells what he has seen and heard (e.g., 3:11, 32; 19:35). This pattern is applied also to John the Baptist; what happened at the baptism of Jesus is understood as a revelation given to the Baptist, who can, therefore, say: "I have seen and have borne witness that this is the Son of God" (1:32-34). John came before Jesus, but his priority in time is only a this-worldly one: "He who came after me ranks before me, for he was before me" (1:15,

---

[11]Cf. Van Unnik, 395f. To me the distance between John and Justin appears greater than van Unnik assumes.

30).

The old Testament history is interpreted in a similar way. The historical persons and events are not spiritualized by means of allegorical interpretation in the way of Philo. The Evangelist rather insists upon their inner-worldly nature; in themselves, isolated from Christ, they are of no redemptive value. Whoever drinks of the well, which Jacob gave to his descendants, will thirst again (4:10-14). Moses did not give the true bread from heaven; the fathers ate manna in the wilderness, and they died (6:32, 49). Abraham died too, and so did the prophets (8:52). Like John the Baptist, the Old Testment fathers and prophets are, in the Fourth Gospel, witnesses to Christ, and that is their only true greatness.

As a witness, Isaiah "saw his glory and spoke about him" (12:41). The vision of Isaiah 6 is thus interpreted as a vision of Christ; the Lord, sitting upon a throne, is identified with the Lord Jesus. A christological interpretation of the *kyrios* of the Septuagint is frequently found in the New Testament, and the Old Testament theophanies are in the ancient church understood as revelations of the pre-existent Christ. According to Philo it was the divine Logos who revealed himself. But the Johannine interpretation of Isaiah 6 does not seem to be derived from a Logos doctrine of the Philonic type. The wording of John 12:41 comes very close to that of the Targum of Isaiah, which speaks of "the glory of YHWH" (6:1) and "the glory of the Skekinah of YHWH" (6:5). Within Jewish "Merkabah mysticism" the vision of the prophet must have been thought to imply a visionary ascent to heaven.[12] Traditions of this type are taken over by the Christian apocryphon "The Ascension of Isaiah," where they are combined with specifically Christian elements: in his heavenly vision Isaiah also saw the hidden descent and the triumphant ascent of the Savior. In the Fourth Gospel there is no mythological imagery of this type, but the basic idea in 12:41 is akin to that of "The Ascension of Isaiah." The prophet is supposed to have seen not simply the glory of the pre-existent

---

[12]This may be inferred from the central importance of Isa. 6:3 (often combined with Dan. 7:10) in accounts of mystical ascents; cf. G. Scholem, *Major Trends in Jewish Mysticism* (New York: Schocken Books, 1954), 40-79. Only scanty references to Isaiah's vision are found in Jewish sources known to me, but cf. Sir. 48:22-25; bHagiga 13b (Raba) and bYebamoth 49b, and the Hebrew apocalypse translated by M. Gaster in *Studies and Texts* (London: Maggs Bros., 1925-28), I, 156-158. Cf. also F.W. Young, "A Study of the Relation of Isaiah to the Fourth Gospel," *ZNW* 44 (1955), 215-232.

Logos asarkos, but the glory of Christ incarnate and crucified. In the context of John 12 there can be no doubt that this is the meaning.

The reference to Isaiah's vision is preceded by two quotations from the prophet (12:37-40). The first is taken from Isaiah 53:1, the first verse in the chapter on the suffering servant. In John, the verse refers to Jesus' rejection despite his many signs. The second quotation is based upon the Hebrew text of Isaiah 6:9-10. The verb *hšmn* and *hšʿ*, normally understood as imperatives are read as perfects (*hišmin* and *hešaʿ*). Christ, the object of Isaiah's vision, is also the speaking subject in the words reported by the prophet; he could not heal the Jews, because God had blinded their eyes and hardened their hearts. The meaning is clear; Isaiah could report on Christ's saying concerning the predestined unbelief of the Jews because he had in his vision seen the glory of the crucified Son of God.

This interpretation is confirmed by the correspondence between 12:41, "He saw his glory," and 1:14, "We saw his glory." That this correspondence is intentional is confirmed by the observation that the latter part of the Prologue alludes to another Old Testament theophany, the vision of Moses (Exod. 33:17-34:9).[13] Moses was not allowed to see the face of God, whom no one has ever seen (Exod. 33:20; John 1:18). And yet, God in another way made him see his glory and revealed himself as a God merciful, "abounding in steadfast love and faithfulness" (*rab chesed wʾemēth*, Exod. 33:18, 22; 34:5-6). The disciples saw the glory of the Logos incarnate, who was "full of grace and truth" (*plērēs charitos kai aletheias*). The Evangelist probably assumes that Moses too, like Isaiah, saw *his* glory. In any case, Moses is conceived as a witness of Christ, who wrote about him (5:46). In its Johannine context, the statement in 1:17 can hardly be taken to imply the Pauline contrast between law and grace and between works and faith. The Johannine contrast is that between the law given through Moses, which is a testimony, and the reality to which Moses bore witness, the true grace and gracious truth, which came through Jesus Christ. The Jews are at fault when they appeal to Moses in order to oppose Christ (9:28).

---

[13]Cf. e.g. M.-E. Boismard, *Le Prologue de saint Jean* (Paris: Editions du Cerf, 1953). On the vision(s) and the ascent of Moses, cf. Sir. 45:2-5; Jubilees 1; Biblical Antiquities of Ps. Philo 12:1; 4 Ezra 14:5; Syr. Baruch 59. In rabbinic traditions, Ps. 68:19 and Ps. 8 are related to Moses' ascent to God (bShabbath 88b-89a etc.); cf. Bill. III, 596-598; M. Abraham, *Légendes juives apocryphes sur la Vie de Moise*(Paris, 1925). Further literature in *TDNT*, IV, 848f.

They search the Scriptures because they think they have eternal life in them; but the Scriptures bear witness to Christ - and to believe this testimony is the only way to have life through them (5:39). Because the Jews do not see this, Moses, who is a witness to Christ, will become their accuser and not their advocate and defender as they believed he would be (5:45).[14]

The witness which the Father is bearing to the Son (5:37a) must be identical with the witness of the Scriptures. This becomes evident as soon as it is seen that 5:37b alludes to the revelation at Sinai. There the Israelites heard the voice of God, and - in spite of Deuteronomy 4:12 - according to some texts and traditions they also saw his "form" (shape, image, or glory).[15] Midrash Mekilta comments on Exodus 19:11 thus: "This teaches that at that moment they saw what Isaiah and Ezekiel never saw." The saying in John 5:37-38, "His voice you have never heard and his form you have never seen; and you do not have his word abiding in you," must be understood against this background. The meaning is that the Jews, refusing to believe in Jesus, prove that they have no share in the revelation given to Israel at Mount Sinai.[16]

A further reference to the giving of the law, as understood in the Haggadah, is found in Jesus' answer to the accusation of blasphemy, John 10:34-36: "Is it not written in your law, 'I said you are gods'? If he called them gods to whom the word of God came (and Scripture cannot be broken), do you say of him whom the Father consecrated and sent into the world, 'You are blaspheming,' because I said, 'I am the Son of God'?" The quotation here is taken from Psalm 82; in rabbinic interpretation it was applied to the restitution of the original, glorious state of mankind by the giving of the law. Receiving it, the Israelites became like angels, "gods." And yet, they had to die like men (Ps. 82:6), because of their sin with the golden calf.[17] Those

---

[14]On Moses as Israel's advocate, cf. N. Johansson, *Parakletoi* (Lund: Gleerup, 1940), 67, 124-125, and 162-166; J. Jeremias, *TDNT*, IV, 852-855.

[15]According to Exod. 20:18, the Israelites "saw" the voice; cf. further Exod. 24:10-11, 17; Deut. 5:24; 18:16; Sir. 17:6. Some of the rabbinic material is cited by J. Jervell, *Imago Dei* (Göttingen: Vandenhoeck und Ruprecht, 1960), 115. For combinations of Exod. 19 (and 24) with Ezek. 1, see also G. Kretschmar, "Himmelfahrt und Pfingsten," *Zeitschrift für Kirchengeschichte* 66 (1954-55), 209-253.

[16]Cf. J. Giblet, "Le Témoignage du Père (Jn. 5:31-47)," *BVC* 12 (1955), 49-59.

[17]Cf. C.K. Barrett, *The Gospel According to St. John* (London: SPCK, 1955), 319-20; Bill., II, 543.

"to whom the word of God came" are, thus, the Israelites at Sinai. They are called "gods"; should not then Christ, whom the Father sent into the world, and to whom the word of God, revealed at Sinai, bears witness, have a right to the name "Son of God"?

The reasons for the Jewish opposition to Jesus are most clearly stated in 8:30-59. The Jews will not let the Son make them free because they claim to be free already, being descendants of Abraham and having God as their Father. Jesus gives the answer: "If you were Abraham's children, you would do what Abraham did, but now you seek to kill me...; this is not what Abraham did." To do what Abraham did would have meant to believe in Jesus (8:45). This is also made clear at the end of the discussion: "Your father Abraham rejoiced that he was to see my day; he saw it and was glad" (8:56). As it is Christ who is contemporaneous with Abraham, and not vice versa (8:57-58), the reference here must be to an experience of Abraham during his life on earth. According to Jewish lore, mainly based upon Genesis 15:7-21 (the text following immediately after the words about Abraham's faith, Gen. 15:6), Abraham - like other fathers and prophets - had a vision of heaven and hell, of the time to come and the end of the world.[18] In the Fourth Gospel this vision is taken to have been a vision of Christ's day, analogous to Isaiah's vision of his glory. The joy of Abraham may be compared to that of John the Baptist (3:29). The Jews, who were not glad, but tried to kill Jesus, thereby proved that they were not Abraham's children, and that not God but the devil was their father (8:41-47). They claim that the Father is their God, but they do not know him (8:55).

The Jews, according to the Fourth Gospel, take the law and Moses, the Scriptures and the fathers, even God himself, as a religious possession of their own. Thinking that they already have life and freedom, they use their religious possessions as means of self-defense when they are confronted with the true God, revealed in Christ. That is what makes the contrast so radical. John does not think that Jews and Christians are standing on a common ground, faith in God and reverence for the Scriptures, diverging only on the question of the messiahship of Jesus. That is the opinion of Luke and of Justin. To John, "no

---

[18] 4 Ezra 3:14; Syr. Baruch 4:4; Apocalypse of Abraham 9-32 (!); Mekilta Ex. 20:18; Palestinian Targums and Genesis Rabbah on Gen. 15:7-13; Targum Isa. 43:12; cf. Bill., III, 525-526. Most interesting allusions to Gen. 15:7ff. are also to be found in the Apostolic Constitutions VII, 33 and Ps. Clem. Recognitions I, 32.

one who denies the Son has the Father" (1 John 2:23); "he who does not honor the Son does not honor (= dishonors) the Father who sent him" (John 5:23). Man's relation to the Father and to his revelation in the Old Testament depends upon the attitude which he takes to the Son. By their opposition to Christ and their appeal to Abraham, Moses, the Scriptures, and God himself, the Jews prove that they are not children of Abraham, that the word of God, revealed at Sinai, does not abide in them, and that God is not their father.

In all this, the Jews represent the world in its opposition to God. The essential nature of this world is self-assertion over against God, the vanity to assume that life and liberty are man's own possessions, so that he does not need the gift of God in Christ. The world's opposition to God is most intense among the Jews because it is to them alone that God has been revealed. They alone can use the name and the word of God as means of their own religious self-assertion and, thus, as means of the world's opposition to God. Only those who knew God and the law could find it blasphemous that Jesus pretended to be the Son of God; the Jews alone could demand that Jesus be crucified.

There is an element of irony in the Johannine account of the Jewish opposition to Jesus; its climax appears in the proceedings which led to his crucifixion.[19] The high priest's reason, based on political opportunism, proved to be prophetic; "Jesus should die for the nation - and not for the nation only..." (11:47-53). In their blind zeal for God and the law, the Jews conclude by saying, "We have no king but Caesar" (19:15). Thus, they end up representing the world by putting Caesar in God's place, whereby they deny the fundamentals of their own faith and forfeit the history of Israel.

The Fourth Gospel sees the importance of the Scriptures in the witness they bear to Christ. What matters in the history of Israel is the existence of witnesses to Christ before the coming of Christ. When Jesus in 4:36-38 speaks about "others" who have labored and sown, and into whose labor the disciples have entered, this is possibly to be understood as a reference to these witnesses of Christ before Christ. In any case, the fathers, the prophets, and the Scriptures point to something beyond themselves; whoever heard the word of God in their testimony

---

[19]Cf. H. Clavier, "L'ironie dans le quatrième Evangile," *Studia Evangelica* (TU 73), 261-276.

would be open to hear and see, to believe and rejoice, when he met the revelation of God in Christ, full of grace and truth.

The True Israelites

The continuity between Israel and the church is not only to be seen in that Jesus was a Jew and that the Scriptures were taken over by the church. In Israel Jesus also finds his first, prototypical disciples, those who come, see, and confess, "We have found the Messiah," "him of whom Moses and the prophets wrote." (1:41, 45). In a special way, Nathanael is the type of those within Israel whom the Father gives to the Son (cf. 6:37; 17:2-3), as his name indicates. As "an Israelite indeed, in whom there is no guile," Nathanael recognizes Jesus as the Son of God, the king of Israel (1:47-49).

To Nathanael and his fellow disciples is given the promise "You will see heaven opened, and the angels of God ascending and descending upon the Son of man" (1:51). This is another example of Johannine allusions to Old Testament visionary experiences, in this case to the dream of Jacob at Bethel. The true Israelite is to see what his ancestor saw. The angels are said to ascend and descend "upon the Son of man;" this does not mean that Jesus is identified with the ladder. The Johannine version has, rather, its analogy in rabbinic traditions, where "on it" can be taken to mean "upon him," that is, "over Jacob." Further, in the Haggadah, Genesis 28:12, like other visionary texts, is often combined with Daniel 7 and Ezekiel 1; the ascending and descending angels can be taken to refer to the worldly empires and to Israel.[20] In this context appears also the notion of the heavenly image (or model) of Jacob, an idea which must have had its scriptural base in the "human form" seated above the throne (Ezek. 1:26).[21] The Johannine idea of

---

[20]Genesis Rabbah 68-69, esp. 68:12 and 69:3; Lev Rabbah 29:2; Tanhuma Wayyese 38a; cf. Bill., III, 49-50; H. Odeberg, *The Fourth Gospel* (Uppsala: Almqvist and Wiksells, 1929), 32-42. An eschatological or mystical interpretation of Gen. 28:12 is pre-supposed in Wisdom 10:10: "She (Wisdom) showed him God's kingdom."

[21]Genesis Rabbah 58:12; Palestinian Targums on Gen. 28:12; Pirqe de Rabbi Eliezer 35, 82a; cf. Bill., I, 976-977. According to Hekaloth Rabbathi 9 (*Beth ha-Midrasch* [ed. A. Jellinek; 2nd ed.; Jerusalem: Bamberger and Wahrmann, 1938], III, 90), God embraces the image of Jacob whenever the Israelites say the "Holy." In "normative" Judaism the image is identified with the human face of the four living creatures in Ezek. 1:10. But as Jervell has noted (117), the original reference must have been to Ezek. 1:26. This seems to be confirmed by one of the Gnostic texts from Nag Hammadi (no. 40), in which themes from Jewish Merkabah mysticism have been incorporated. Cf. J. Doresse, *Les livres*

the Son of man may also connect with this notion; this could explain the longer text in 3:13: "The Son of man who is in heaven" (cf. also 1:18b). Whatever connections may be found here, the main point of the Johannine text seems to be clear. Nathanael is to see "greater things;" in analogy with 5:20 and 14:21 this promise refers to the ascension of Jesus. Even the ascending and descending angels must in some way represent his glory, or his glorification (cf. Mark 8:38; 13:26-27!).[22] The principal meaning of the promise given to Nathanael and his fellows is that they shall see the glory of the Son of man; they shall see the Son of man glorified.

The true Israelites, of whom Nathanael is the type, are the "sheep" who belong to "this fold," the fold of Israel, in chapter 10. They know the voice of the shepherd and follow him. The "Jews" do not believe, because they do not belong to the sheep of Jesus (10:26); but there are some in Israel who do believe. Jesus has also "other sheep, that are not of this fold" (10:16). In order to "bring them also," Jesus as the good shepherd has to lay down his life (10:15, 17). These "other sheep" are identical with the "children of God who are scattered abroad;" Jesus had to die, in order to gather them into one (11:52). In other words, they are those outside Israel who are "of the truth," who hear - or heed - the voice of Jesus (18:37). That they are drawn to Jesus (12:32) and, thus, gathered into one implies that they are united with those within Israel who are

---

secrets des gnostiques d'Egypte (Paris: Plon, 1958), 189: "Aupres de Sabaoth se tient un premier-né que l'on nomme Israël: 'L'homme qui voit dieu.'" The heavenly "image" was perhaps not originally conceived as a statue but as identical with the archangel "Israel," a version of the divine vice-regent elsewhere called Yaoel, Metatron, the "lesser YHWH," with whom Philo's Logos has some connection (cf. *de conf. ling.* 146). For further material and hypothetical reconstructions cf. J. Daniélou, *The Theology of Jewish Christianity* (tr. and ed. by J.A. Baker; London: Darton, Longman and Todd, 1964), 132-134; P. Winter, "MONOGENES PARA PATROS," *ZRGG* 5 (1953), 335-365, and "Zum Verständnis des Johannes-Evangeliums," *TLZ* 80 (1955), 142-150; G. Quispel, "Het Johannes-evangelie en de Gnosis," *NedTT* 11 (1957), 173-203; J.Z. Smith, "The Prayer of Joseph," *Religions in Antiquity* (ed. J. Neusner; Leiden: Brill, 1968), 253-294.

[22]On John 1:51, cf. further E. Eidem, "Natanaels kallelse," *Till ärkebiskop Söderbloms sextioårsdag* (Stockholm: 1926), 131-140; H. Windisch, "Angelophanien um den Menschensohn auf Erden," *ZNW* 30 (1931), 215-233, and "Joh. 1:51 und die Auferstehung Jesu," *ZNW* 31 (1932), 199-204; G. Quispel, "Nathanael und der Menschensohn," *ZNW* 47 (1956), 281-283; S. Schulz, *Untersuchungen zur Menschensohn-Christologie im Johannesevangelium* (Göttingen: Vandenhoeck und Ruprecht, 1957), 97-103.

"of the truth." "So there shall be one flock, one shepherd." In its Johannine context this saying neither states a program for ecumenical action nor refers to a purely "eschatological" unity of an invisible church; it looks forward to the unity which is to be realized after the ascension of Jesus, the unity of the "children of God scattered abroad" with those within the Jewish nation who hear the voice of Jesus and follow him.

In some respects this Johannine conception comes rather close to the Pauline one (Rom. 11:16-22; Eph. 2:11-22): the nucleus of the church is those Israelites who believe in Christ. To John, the most important point in this connection is that the disciples in Israel are the primary witnesses to Jesus (17:20-21). Only in communion with them can the believers outside Israel see what they saw: the glory of Christ incarnate. Continuity within the history of the church is the continuity of the witness borne to Christ (cf. 1 John 1:1-4; and also John 1:14; 19:35; and 21:24).

A Christocentric and Forensic Conception of History

The Fourth Gospel distinguishes between two classes of men, those who are of the world (from below, of the devil) and those who are of the truth, belong to the Father and are "sheep" of Christ (8:23, 44, 47; 10:26-27; 17:6, 9, 14; 18:37). As the origin betrays itself in the deeds, the distinction is at the same time one between those who "do evil" and those who "do the truth" (3:20-21; cf. 5:29). I need not discuss here how far the idea is that of a divine predestination or, rather, that of a human predisposition for faith or for unbelief. We should certainly not think that John would say that people of high moral standards are more inclined to believe than others, nor that he holds to the doctrine of a fixed number of the predestined. Only when a man is confronted with Christ does it appear what kind of man he is and to which category he belongs. He can come to Christ only through a decision of faith; if he comes, this fact proves that he is one of those who are drawn by the Father and given to the Son (6:37, 39, 44, 65).

In accordance with this view, John does not speak about a "change of peoples" by which the Jews are rejected and a new covenant people created.[23] The Jews who do not believe because

---

[23]The expression "change of people" was coined by A.V. Ström (*Vetekornet* [Stockholm: Diakonistyrelsen, 1944], 269 etc.). Ström sees this idea also in the Fourth Gospel, esp. in 12:34 (394-403); but cf. my critical review in *SEA* 11 (1946), 130-135.

they are "of the world" have never been true children of Abraham; those who do believe were always potential members of the church, whether they are true Israelites or "dispersed children of God." Before the coming of Christ both categories had been mixed, within the Jewish nation and also outside it. The case has been suspended - if that word be allowed. The word of Christ is the judgment by which the sentence is passed and the two groups are separated. Those who do evil prefer to remain in darkness; those who do the truth come to the light of Christ and receive the gift of life from him (3:19-21; 5:21-24).

The two categories are not distinguished by metaphysical qualities, as in Gnosticism. What John sees already latent in pre-Christian mankind is simply the duality which appears in the attitude taken to Christ. The whole outlook of the Fourth Gospel is characterized by its consistent christocentricity. The sin of the world is its self-assertion against the Word by which it was created, the Word who was in the beginning with God and who became flesh and dwelt among us. The conflict between light and darkness, between Christ and the world, is the one essential theme of history. The incarnation of Christ brought the conflict into the open; by his revelation of the Father, and of himself as the revealer, the darkness of the world also became manifest, as did the distinction between those who were of the world and those who were of the truth. The church, as understood in the Fourth Gospel, can be said to be the totality of those who are of the truth - insofar as they have already heard the voice of Jesus.[24]

John is a witness to Christ; he is not concerned with a philosophy of history. But the Johannine concepts of "witness" and "testimony" have juridical connotations; thus they are linked up with something which might be called a Johannine conception of history. The conflict between God and the world is conceived in forensic terms.[25] In this cosmic lawsuit Christ is the representative of God, and the Jews are representatives of the world. In their pleading, the Jews base their arguments upon the law, and Jesus appeals to the witness borne to him by John the Baptist, by his own works, and by the Scriptures, and refers also to precedents in Old Testament history. In the proceedings before Pilate the lawsuit reaches its climax. By his apparent defeat, Jesus won the case. By his ascension he was vindicated

[24]Cf. Bultmann, *Theology*, II, 92.

[25]Théo Preiss, "Justification in Johannine Thought," *Life in Christ* (tr. H. Knight; SBT 13; Chicago: Allenson, 1954), 9-31.

and proved right in his claim to be the Son of God, with authority to act and speak as the delegate of the Father and to give eternal life to those who believe in him. This vindication of Jesus implies legal defeat of the world and of the Jews as its representatives. The prince of this world has been cast out from the heavenly court, so that he can no longer plead the cause of the world and oppose those who belong to Jesus (12:31; cf. Rev. 12:9-12). The claims of the world and of the Jews have been proved untrue; vindicated through his ascension, Jesus will draw all men to himself (12:32). The ministry of Jesus in Israel, his voluntary death as "king of the Jews," and his glorification by God are, thus, the historical and juridical bases for the life of the church and for the witness which it brings to all men.

In the time of the church, the world is still opposing God, but as a world already legally defeated; in their tribulations the disciples know that Christ has overcome the world (16:33). After the departure of Jesus, the Paraclete is pleading his case, assisting the disciples and convincing the world of sin (its lack of faith), of righteousness (the vindication of Jesus by his ascension), and of judgment (the sentence passed upon the prince of this world, 16:7-11). As the fathers and the prophets were witnesses to Christ before his coming, so the disciples have to bear testimony to him after his departure, and thus to play their role in the lawsuit of history. By their word the verdict which was pronounced when Jesus was glorified is applied to individuals: those who believe receive the gift of eternal life; those who do not are already judged and remain in darkness. This, however, does not mean that the believers within the church are safe. Even the Jews to whom Jesus is speaking in John 8 are said to have believed; only those who remain in the word of Jesus are true disciples (8:31). Judas was one of the Twelve; in the Fourth Gospel he typifies those who belong to the church but who are not of the truth and do not remain in Jesus (6:64-65, 70-71; 13:10-11; cf. 15:6; 1 John 2:19). Thus the members of the church are constantly on trial as to whether they really are of the truth or not.

The coming of a last day is presupposed, but it is not thought to bring a new and independent act of judgment. It will, rather, reveal the final outcome of the lawsuit which is in progress. Even on the last day the word of Jesus will be the judge of those who did not believe (12:46-50; cf. 5:25-29).

John is not a historian telling about the past and trying to find causes and effects. Neither is he a theologian of *Heilsgeschichte*, seeing a series of redemptive acts of God in history. His attitude to history is more like that of an advocate, who appeals to prior testimony and to precedents and judicial decisions of the past. The situation of the church, as it is conceived in the Fourth Gospel, is hardly to be compared to the military situation between "D-Day" and V-Day." We should rather use forensic similes: The Supreme Court has already rendered its verdict, but its decision has still to be applied to individual cases. Trials are still going on; those who do not fulfill the conditions for acquittal are already judged by the sentence passed. Before local courts, which do not recognize the authority of the Supreme Court, the case must still be pleaded, but the final outcome is only the consequence of the legal victory already won.

Thus the historical and "legal" basis for the existence of the church is the glorification of Jesus through death and resurrection. The consistent christocentricity of the Fourth Gospel does not exclude a sense of historical continuity, going backwards from the Church Universal to the first disciples and eyewitnesses of Jesus in Israel and farther back to those who believed and bore witness to him before his incarnation. In this sense, even John is aware of a "history of salvation" and sees the church as the "true Israel" to which the "children of God scattered abroad" have been added. The church has also a historical task in the present, through its existence and through its preaching to bear testimony to Christ in a world which is still hostile to him, even if it has already been legally defeated.

It is obvious that John's conceptions of the past are rather different from those of modern historical criticism. The problem of the relation between the "Johannine Christ" and the "Jesus of history" is not the only one; we could also ask how the figures of Abraham, Moses, Isaiah, and John the Baptist in the Fourth Gospel are related to the historical persons with the same names. But that would be an anachronistic way of putting the question. With regard to the Old Testament history, the Evangelist uses not only exegetical methods of his own time but also haggadic traditions, taken over from Judaism. With much of the freedom of the Haggadah, John may have used also the Gospel traditions at his disposal, traditions which are mostly independent of the Synoptics.[26] All his material the author interprets in order to make it serve his one purpose, to bear witness to Christ.

As the Gnostics often made use of the Old Testament and of the Gospel traditions to illustrate the one theme of the saving knowledge, the Old Testament background of the Fourth Gospel does not disprove its affinity to Gnosticism. One example of this affinity may be seen in the conception of the church as the community of those who are of the truth and have heard the voice of the Savior. But it is not necessary to assume that the Gospel presupposes any fully developed gnostic system; pre-gnostic trends within Judaism and early Christianity are more likely to have been part of the environment of the Evangelist. The Qumran idea of the elect "children of light" who are gathered into a community of the true Israel in some respects comes rather close to the Johannine conception of the church. And very remarkable indeed is the attention which the Gospel pays to texts of importance for Jewish Merkabah mysticism.[27] But John stresses that no one has ever seen God, and no one has ascended into heaven (1:18; 3:13; 6:46). The christological interpretation of Old Testament visions and theophanies, therefore, seems to have a polemical note directed against a type of piety which made the patriarchs and prophets heroes of mystical visions of the heavenly world. Even a Docetic christology may have been supported by allegorical interpretations of the Old Testament.[28]

---

[26]Cf. esp. B. Noack, *Zur johanneischen Tradition* (Copenhagen: Rosenkilde and Bagger, 1954). K. Stendahl (*The School of St. Matthew*, 31 and 163) assumes the existence of a "school of St. John," and I think that my observations lend new support to his thesis. A. Kragerud (*Der Lieblingsjünger im Johannesevangelium* [Oslo: Oslo University Press, 1959]) would rather picture the Johannine circle as a body of wandering prophets, symbolized by the beloved disciple. Even if this hypothesis is unconvincing, it does draw attention to the inspired nature of John's handling of texts and traditions. As as analogy, cf. 1QpHab. 2:5-10.

[27]The standard texts of the Merkabah mysticism (Exod. 19; Isa. 6; Ezek. 1; Dan. 7; etc.), which in Jewish tradition were combined with one another and with Gen. 15:7-13; 28:12, etc., reappear in a remarkable way in the Revelation of St. John. John's vision (Rev. 4-5) may help us to understand how the Old Testament witnesses' visions of Christ were viewed by the author of the Fourth Gospel.

[28]The heretics combatted by John (cf. also John 2:18-27; 4:1-6; 5:5-8; 2 John 7) seem to have been of much the same type as those in the Ignatian letters; cf. E. Molland, "The Heretics Combatted by Ignatius of Antioch," *Journal of Ecclesiastical History* 5 (1954), 1-6. E. Schweizer ("Das johanneische Zeugnis vom Herrenmahl," *EvT* 12 [1952-53], 341-363) also recognizes an anti-Docetic tendency in the Fourth Gospel. I do not suggest that the antiheretic purpose be viewed as the major one; the aim

Over against such tendencies, John bears witness to the true humanity of Jesus and to the reality of his death (6:41-42, 61; 19:35). Facing the danger that the church might become detached from history, he counters it at the essential point and insists that those who see Jesus see the Father (14:9), and that God is to be seen in no other way. The question may remain as to whether or not the Old Testament is deprived of a historical meaning of its own when Moses and the prophets are simply made supporters of John's own testimony to Christ. But basically John shares the Old Testament faith in God, the Creator, who acts in history and is, accordingly, not an unknown God to be reached by a mystical escape from history. The continuity between Israel and the church is understood in a peculiar way, but it is not dissolved.[29]

---

is certainly also missionary, apologetic, and devotional. We should not, I think, expect a precise answer to the question whether the Gospel is intended for Christian, Jewish or Gentile readers. According to the Johannine conception, all the answers that might be given are aspects of the one purpose of the Gospel, to bear witness to Christ in the "lawsuit" between God and the world.

[29] I have not taken account of questions of literary criticism in this essay, not because I doubt that a complicated history of tradition preceded the present literary form of the Gospel, but because I am inclined to think that the Evangelist himself was the "ecclesiastical editor" of the traditions of the Johannine "school."

CHAPTER 8

CHRIST, CREATION, AND THE CHURCH

The rediscovery of the importance of eschatology within the New Testament has been one of the most outstanding achievements of historical theology. It is also one of the factors which has led to a new understanding of the New Testament church; we have learned to see the church as an eschatological community. This does not only mean that the church has an eschatological hope for the future, but also that the very existence of the church is due to what Professor Dodd has called "Realized Eschatology". The church exists in the interval between Christ's death, resurrection and heavenly enthronement and his final revelation as Lord, Judge and Savior; not only his *parousia* but also his birth, death and resurrection are seen as messianic, "eschatological" events, happening "when the fullness of time was come", "in these last days".

According to this view the church is something new; it is seen not simply as a new religious society but rather as a new creation: "the old has passed away, behold, the new has come" (2 Cor. 5:17). This complete, eschatological newness does not mean, however, that the church stands without positive relations to the times before Christ. The "new things" are the fulfillment of prophecy; the new covenant is bound up with the old one, and what happened in the Old Testament is a "type" and prefiguration of the events of the last days. The church is the eschatological community as the "people of God", redeemed by Christ; Gentiles are included, but the continuity with the old Israel is not broken. But the realized eschatology of the New Testament shares a more universal outlook with eschatology in general. What is given in Christ is not only a new covenant, but a new creation. Not only have the first covenant, the "letter", the external descent from Abraham and the circumcision of the flesh grown old, but also the whole of the present age, from which Christ delivers those who believe in him. This fact does not exclude the existence of a positive connection between salvation and creation, corresponding to the continuity between the old covenant and the new. The New Testament conception of the church as the eschatological community has in this way a double consequence for its relation to the world: a contrast between the church and "this world" and a positive attitude to all things which God has created.

It is important that neither of these two aspect be neglected. As far as I see, both supporters and opponents of consistent eschatology have in general stressed the negative aspect too exclusively.[1] But already in Jewish eschatology the correlation of first and last things is hardly less emphasized than the contrast between this aeon and the coming one.[2] It is also worth while to observe that the positive correlation of "eschatology" and "protology" held a very firm position within the ancient church.[3] This was partly due to anti-gnostic tendencies; Irenaeus developed his theory of "recapitulation" and Origen taught the *apokatastasis* of all things. But the idea is not only a favorite theme of the anti-gnostic fathers; it belongs to the common tradition of the church. The renewal at baptism is seen as a new creation, conforming to the patterns of the first creation.[4] At the eucharist the fruits of the earth

---

[1]Among scholars who have paid some attention to the positive correlation I would include: J. Jeremias, *Jesus als Weltvollender* (BFTh 30; Gütersloh: Bertelsmann, 1930), 4; L. Goppelt, *Typos* (BFTh series II, 43; Gütersloh: Bertelsmann, 1939); J. Hering, "Les bases bibliques de l'humanisme chretien," *RHPR* 25 (1945), 17-40; W.D. Davies, *Paul and Rabbinic Judaism* (London: SPCK 1948), 36-57, 147-176; G. Lindeskog, *Studien zum neutestamentlichen Schöpfungsgedanken* (UUA 9; Uppsala, 1952).

[2]Cf. H. Gunkel, *Schöpfung und Chaos in Urzeit und Endzeit* (Göttingen: Vandenhoeck und Ruprecht, 1895). B. Murmelstein, "Adam. Ein Beitrag zur Messiaslehre," *WZKM* (1928), 242-275 and (1929), 51-86. A wealth of material is found throughout the four volumes of Billerbeck's *Kommentar*. Cf. also W. Staerk, *Die Erlösererwartung in den östlichen Religionen, Soter II* (Gütersloh: Bertelsmann, 1938); P. Volz, *Die Eschatologie der jüdischen Gemeinde* (2nd ed.; Tübingen: Mohr, 1934).

[3]Cf. e.g. J. Daniélou, *From Shadows to Reality. Studies in the Biblical Typology* (tr. W. Hibberd; London: Burns and Oates, 1960).

[4]Daniélou, *op.cit.*, 22; cf. my "La terre ou coulent le lait et le miel, selon Barnabé 6:8-19," *Aux sources de la tradition chrétienne* (Paris: Delachaux et Niestle, 1950), 61-70.

mediate the heavenly gifts, and God is praised for his creation through Christ as well as for salvation in him.[5] The idea that God will make "the last things like the first things" (Barn. 6:13) is used as a hermeneutical principle for the interpretation of Genesis.[6] In legendary traditions, especially popular in the East and partly bound up with local traditions of Jerusalem, the parallelism between Adam and Christ is carried through even in details.[7]

The purpose of the present article is to give a short survey of similar ideas in the New Testament, especially in the Epistles of Paul. I find it most convenient to start with the general patterns of eschatology, then to proceed to Christology, and finally to point out the consequences for the doctrine of the church and for the church's relation to the created world. This last topic will also have an indirect bearing on the present-day discussion about the relevance of Christian ethics for the orders of society, an ecumenical discussion in which Professor Dodd has taken a very prominent part.

When Gunkel in 1895 wrote his book *Schöpfung und Chaos in Urzeit und Endzeit*, he assumed that the myth of creation had been transposed into an eschatology that had already been accepted by the Babylonians. Later research has not, as far as I know, corroborated this hypothesis. The correlation of eschatology and protology in Israel has turned out to be at the same time more organic and more complex. Most important has been the discovery of the significance of temple worship, especially the great festivals. The cult was not only a common point of departure but also a point of coincidence between eschatology and protology. In common worship the creation was commemorated and re-enacted, and the future renewal for which Israel hoped was prefigured.[8]

Salvation is conceived not only as a counterpart to the beginnings of the world, but still more as a parallel to the

---

[5]Cf. the anaphora in Hippolytus' *Apostolic Tradition* or in the *Apostolic Constitutions* 8:12. Further: Jus. *Dial*. XLI, i CXVII, 3; Iren. *Adv. Haer*. IV, 17-18 and V, 2.

[6]Cf. my study of Barn. 6:8-19 noted above, esp. 69.

[7]Most interesting are the legends in the Syriac "Cave of Treasures," *Die Schatzhöhle* (ed. B. Bezold; 2 vols.; Leipzig: 1883-88). Cf. J. Jeremias, *Golgotha und der heilige Felsen* (Leipzig: Pfeiffer, 1926).

[8]Cf. S. Mowinckel, *Psalmenstudien II. Das Thronbesteigungsfest Jahväs und der Ursprung der Eschatologie* (Kristiana, 1922); and *He that Cometh* (tr. G.W. Anderson; Nashville: Abingdon, 1954), esp. 142ff., and *The Psalms in Israel's Worship* (tr. D.R. Ap-Thomas; Nashville: Abingdon, 1962) 140ff., 186ff.

primeval times of the people, as a new Exodus. But as the first Exodus is already depicted as a divine act of creation, conforming to the creation of the world, eschatology and creation can be connected also in this way (e.g. Isa. 43:16ff.). At an early stage the narratives about Paradise can also more directly influence the prophecies concerning coming, happy days (e.g. Isa. 11:6-8; Ezek. 34:25-27). In the learned theology of the Scribes the conceptions of Paradise, of the Mosaic times, and of the days of the Messiah still mutually influence one another.[9]

The hope for a return of "the golden age" seems to be widespread, and can perhaps be found in every religion which has developed an eschatology. Both among the Greeks and the Babylonians we find the theory of a periodic return of the end to the beginning in a cycle of successive world-ages. This idea may to a certain extent have influenced the more systematic elaboration of the correspondence between protology and eschatology in the Judaism of the Hellenistic and Roman age; but this does not justify the view that this doctrine of a cyclic return should be the root of the whole conception that the last things will be like the first.[10]

It is further necessary to observe that the correlation between the first and the last things can be elaborated in several forms, between which we must differentiate, even if in practice they are often combined in various ways. The main types may be summarized in the following way:

First, we find *analogy* or parallelism; here we may mention the ideas of a new creation, a new heaven and a new earth.[11] This pattern is especially applied to the acts of God at the beginning and the end of the world; they are to conform to one another. But the doctrine of the Savior can also follow the same pattern. According to the Similitudes of Enoch, the name of the Son of Man is named on the day of judgment as it was

---

[9]Cf. e.g. Wisd. 19:6, and Bill. I, 69f., 594-96; Murmelstein, *WZKM* (1929), 51-64.

[10]This view is held by Staerk, *op. cit.*. Cf. also R. Bultmann, "Ursprung und Sinn der Typologie als hermeneutischer Methode," *Pro Regno pro Sanctuario* (ed. W.J. Kooiman; Nijerk: Callenbach, 1950), 89-100. For criticism of Staerk, cf. Mowinckel, *He that Cometh*, 158-159, 460-461. The influence of Greek terminology is evident in places like Rom. 11:36, 1 Cor. 8:6, Col. 1:15-20.

[11]Isa. 65:17; 66:22; Jub. 1:29; 1 Enoch 91:16; 4 Ezra 7:30ff.; Targ.Jer. 23:23 etc.; Rev. 21:1, 5; 2 Peter 3:12f.; James 1:18 (?). Cf. Volz, *Eschatologie*, 338f., 361; Bill. III, 840-847; E. Sjöberg, "Wiedergeburt und Neuschöpfung im palästinischen Judentum," *ST* 4 (1950), 44-85. C.-M. Edsman, "Schöpfung und Wiedergeburt," *Spiritus et Veritas* (Auseklis, 1953), 43-55.

named before the creation (1 Enoch 47:2-3).[12] The Pauline typology Adam-Christ also comes in here (Rom. 5:12-19; 1 Cor. 15:22).[13]

Where the sin of Adam and its effects stand in the foreground, we find instead the idea of *contrast* (e.g. Rom. 5:18-19, disobedience-obedience).[14] The contrast is in general bound up with the idea of a *restitution* of creation, which has been under a curse. Rabbinic theologians speak about the glory and other things which were lost through the fall of Adam, but shall be brought back when the Messiah comes,[15] and Paul thinks in similar categories.[16]

The ideas of "typological" analogy and of restitution may easily be combined. But the *superiority* of the new creation can also be stressed; it brings not only a restitution but also a *transformation* of the first one. The light of the heavenly bodies will be much stronger (Isa. 30:26) -- or, there will be no need for them, as God himself (and the Lamb) will be the light (Isa. 40:19f.; Rev. 21:23). The righteous ones will be transformed into glory and brightness at the resurrection (Dan. 12:3).[17]

---

[12]Cf. E. Sjöberg, *Der Menschensohn im äthiopischen Henochbuch* (Lund: Gleerup, 1946), 87ff.

[13]In Jewish Lore there are many similarities between Adam and the Messiah (Murmelstein, *WZKM* [1928]; Staerk, *Erlösererwartung*, 7-40). To a great extent, however, these are due to a general phenomenological kinship and a common origin in the ideology of "divine kingship" and not to any scheme of correspondence between "Urzeit und Endzeit." The relation between king, "Urmensch", first created man, and Messiah is discussed by Mowinckel ("Urmensch und 'Königsideologie', *ST* 2 [1948], 71-89) and Bentzen ("King Ideology -- 'Urmensch' -- 'Throonsbestijgingsfeest',"*ST* 3 [1949], 143-157). Cf. further E. Sjöberg, "Uttrycket 'Männeskoson' i gamle testamentet," *STK* (1950), 35-44, and I. Engnell, "Människosonen," *Svenskt bibliskt Uppslagsverk* (ed. Engnell and Fridrichsen; 2 vols; Uppsala, 1948-52), II, 399-403, and the review of Sjöberg, *Der Menschensohn*, *BO* 8 (1951), 187-192.

[14]Some scholars view this contrast as the background for Phil. 2:5ff. Cf. esp. J. Hering, "Kyrios Anthropos," *RHPR* 16 (1936), 196-209.

[15]Gen. R. 12:6 and par.; cf. T. Levi 18:10f.; Bill. I, 19, IV, 886ff. Murmelstein, *WZKM* (1928), 254-57. For the general idea of restitution, cf. e.g. Jub. 23:26ff., 1 Enoch 90:37f.; further Bill. III, 247-255; Volz. *Eschatologie*, 359ff., 383, 398; Staerk, *Erlösererwartung*, 23f., 166, 178.

[16]Cf. the "glory of God" in Rom. 3:24 and 5:2; C.H. Dodd, *The Epistle to the Romans* (London: Harper and Bros., 1932), 50f., 73. For the idea of restitution, cf. Rom. 8:19ff.; Col. 1:15-20 etc.; Rev. 20:13; 21:4. (Matt. 19:28?).

[17]Cf. 1 Enoch 45:4-5; 2 Bar. 51, etc.; Bill. IV, 891 and 958ff., 887 and 941f.; Volz, *Eschatologie*, 339f., 396-401. In later Judaism, especially among the Rabbis, there is a tendency to subordinate the idea of transformation to the idea of restitution; cf. Sv. Aalen, *Die Begriffe "Licht" und "Finsternis" im Alten Testament, im Spätjudentum und im Rabbinismus* (Oslo: J. Dybwad, 195), 25ff., 162f., 181f., 261f., 319f.

Paul emphasized the superiority of the coming glorious and incorruptible state of things.[18]

The idea of restitution can also be combined with the other idea, that the very things which existed at the beginning will return: Paradise, the tree of life, etc.[19] In this case we have an *identity* between the first and the last things. In certain Jewish-Christian circles even Adam and Christ are identified; this view is perhaps influenced by gnostic ideas, which, however, in general distinguish between the primordial (heavenly) Man -- sometimes identified with the Savior -- and the first created man.[20]

Another idea, which is less familiar to us, is that of a *reservation* of some of the first things for the end of the world. Thus, the light of the first day (Gen. 1:3) is said to be reserved for the righteous in the age to come,[21] and similar statements are made concerning Leviathan and Behemoth.[22] These ideas are not found in the New Testament, but the conception of the sabbatical rest in the Epistle to the Hebrews belongs to the same type of thought. The "works were finished from the creation of the world", but it still "remains for some to enter into it" (4:3-6); the "rest" is reserved for the people of God in the last days. According to this view, Christ is not thought to bring a new creation, restoring and transforming the first one, but to open the free entrance to that "sabbatical rest", the world to come, which since creation exists as a heavenly reality.[23]

The idea of reservation can be said to be based on the *inclusiveness* of creation; it includes also the world to come. In Rabbinic writings the proof of this is found in prepositions, conjunctions and the like in Genesis 1, which are taken to signify that also the new heaven and the new earth are included.[24] A

---

[18]1 Cor. 15:35ff.; cf. Mark 12:25.

[19]1 Enoch 24-25; Bill. IV, 1144ff.; Rev. 2:7; 21:1, 14, 17, 19.

[20]Cf. e.g. H.J. Schoeps, *Theologie und Geschichte des Juden-christentums* (Tübingen: Mohr, 1949), 100ff.; Staerk, *Erlösererwartung*, 125ff.

[21]Gen. R. 3:6; bHagiga 12a, etc.; Bill. IV, 961f.; Aalen, *Licht und Finsternis*, 265f.

[22]4 Ezra 6:49f.; 2 Bar. 29:4; Bill. IV, 1147, 1159ff.

[23]For Jewish speculation, cf. E. Käsemann, *Das wandernde Gottesvolk im Hebräerbrief* (FRLANT; Göttingen: Vandenhoeck und Ruprecht, 1939), 40-45; H. Riesenfeld, *Jesus transfiguré* (ASNU 16; Copenhagen: E. Munksgaard, 1947), 206-216; Bill. II, 77, III, 687; Volz, *Eschatologie*, 384.

[24]Gen. R. 1:10 (the world created with ב); 9:3 (*and behold* -- Gen. 1:31; R. Simeon B. Lakish); 1:13 (*the* new heavens -- Isa. 66:22; R. Eliezer b. R. Jose).

similar view is again found in Hebrews: "the aeons" which are created in Christ seem to include the world to come (1:3; cf. 4:3); in Chapter 2 it is quite clear that "all things" in Psalm 8 is taken to include also the world to come (cf. vv. 5, 8 and 10).

This synthetic view is, in somewhat divergent forms, characteristic of the more speculative trends in Judaism. The "new creation" is seen as the final establishment and perfection of the first one, rather than as an independent, parallel act. "This world" is marked by the duality of light and darkness, and of good and evil powers; even the darkness is created by God and has a necessary function in this present, preparatory world. What the new creation will bring is the *elimination* of the powers of darkness. This view is most clearly stated in the Qumran Community Rule (1 QS 3:13-4:26), but it seems to be predominant in Rabbinic sources too, even if the dualism is here still more modified.[25] In a somewhat similar way, the putting away of sin and the removal of the present earth and heaven is stressed in Hebrews (9:26; 1:11f. and 12:27); but here there is a sharper contrast between this visible world and "that which cannot be shaken", and we find no trace of the rationalizing view that the potentiality of sin is implied in creation.

Two other themes have still to be mentioned, the ideas of *preexistence* and of *predestination*; the things which are to appear at the end of the world are thought to have existed since the beginning as heavenly realities or in the mind and purpose of God.[26] The whole conception of the last things as mysteries which are to be revealed comes in here.[27] The distinction between "real" and "ideal" preexistence is often fluid, as is the distinction among existence from the foundation of the world, pre-creational, and eternal existence.

---

[25]Cf. Aalen, *Licht und Finsternis*, esp. 170-75, 269-71, 306-14; for criticisms of some exaggerations in Aalen's book, cf. my remarks in *NTT* (1952), 61-84.

[26]Matt. 25:34; Eph. 1:3ff.; 1 Peter 1:2, 20; Rev. 13:8; 21:2; etc. Cf. IC, Ezra 4:36f.; 7:70; Gen. R. 1:4; bPesahim 54a; etc.; Bill. I, 974f., 981f.; II, 334f., 353. In Judaism, present things of central religious significance may also be thought to be preexistent. The Christian concept of preexistence seems to have its roots in eschatology, but it soon gained independent significance; the christology of "realized eschatology" was superseded by a christology of preexistence. The whole theme requires a new, thorough investigation.

[27]Matt. 13:35; 1 Cor. 2:6ff., etc. For Jewish conceptions, cf. G. Bornkamm, *TDNT*, IV, 815ff.; E. Sjöberg, *Der Menschensohn im äth. Henoch*, 102-115.

In general, these various themes and patterns are combined; a systematic and consistent elaboration of one of them seems rather to be an exception. The main idea, common to the different forms of combining the last things with that which was at the beginning, is that the end will bring the final realization of what was from the beginning the will of God the Creator, who is himself the first and the last (Isa. 44:6; 48:12; Rev. 1:8; 21:6). Most of the themes and patterns can be found in Christian as well as in Jewish eschatology. But there is a rather clear difference of emphasis: the antithetic parallelism between creation and salvation is more marked in Christianity, whereas a synthetic view is more characteristic of Jewish cosmology and eschatology.

The difference can most clearly be illustrated by the interpretation of the first two chapters of Genesis. Paul, and the Fathers after him, give the words in Genesis an eschatological application according to the principle of analogy (typology), often combined with the idea of the superiority of the new creation. The statement in Genesis 2:7 that (the first) man (Adam) was made a living soul is thus taken to imply that "the last Adam"was made "a life-giving spirit" (1 Cor. 15:45).[28] In Rabbinic writings too, the story of creation can be used to illustrate eschatology. But the fundamental idea is not the conformity of the eschatological salvation with the original creation, but the idea that creation, as described in Genesis, prefigures the whole history of the world, including its eschatological fulfillment. This is the meaning when, for example, the Spirit of God moving upon the face of the waters is said to be the Messiah, or when the evening and the morning of the first day are taken to signify the evening for the godless and the morning (of salvation) for the righteous, and so on.[29] In this

---

[28]Cf. 1 Cor. 15:47-49; 6:16; Eph. 5:31f.; 2 Cor. 4:6; cf. also note 4 above.

[29]Gen. R. 2:3-5 (R. Judah, R. Simeon b. Lakish, and R. Abbahu and R. Hiyya) and 3:8 (R. Yannai). Murmelstein (*WZKM* [1928], 245, note 2) and Staerk (*Erlösererwartung*, 21) seem to think that Pesikta Rabbati 33 (ed. Friedmann 152b) applies Gen. 1:1f. to the new creation. Even here, the idea is that already when God created the world, he had the slavery of Israel to the four kingdoms and its redemption through the King Messiah in mind. Rabbinic interpreters were less interested in the analogy between the first and the last things than in the correspondence between the creation of the world and the giving of the Law (cf. e.g. Gen. R. 4:2, R. Abba b. Kahana). R. Tanhum b. Hanilai finds the hermeneutical warrant for this correlation in Isa. 46:10: "Declaring the end from the beginning." (Gen. R. 4:6). The analogy with, and the difference from Barn. 6:13 is most remarkable.

connection it may also be mentioned as highly symbolic that Jews celebrate the Sabbath, pointing to the fulfillment of creation, whereas Christians celebrate the first day of the week, pointing to the beginning of the new creation by the resurrection of our Lord.[30]

This difference of emphasis corresponds to a different doctrine of sin; as the corruption of man and the world is thought to be more total, the newness of the new creation is stressed in the New Testament, and especially by Paul, much more than is usual in Judaism. The deeper consciousness of sin is again bound up with faith in Jesus as the crucified Christ, in whose name forgiveness of sins is offered; Christ, the Messiah, has already risen from the dead and is enthroned in heaven. This Christian faith, and not a divergence into eschatological themes and patterns, is the essential fact which also gives the correlation of the first and the last things a new meaning and significance in Christianity. Eschatology is thought to be "in process of realization"; the last things which correspond to the first are no longer merely future; they are also present, actual realities.

At this point it is important to remember that, even for Judaism, it is both an eschatological hope and an actual experience that God the Creator deals with the world, man, and Israel in a way similar to his activity at the creation of the world. We can here apply the notion of *creatio continua*, but can also speak of a *creatio actualis:* by liberating a man from disasters and bringing him into a new positive relation to himself, God makes him "a new creation". This actual experience does not need to have any relation to eschatology, but eschatological connotations easily come in.[31]

Even in post-biblical Judaism the cult is related both to "protology" and to "eschatology"; this is true not only of the great festivals and the days of the New Year and Atonement,[32] but also of the Sabbath, which corresponds both to the Sabbath of the creation week and to the final Sabbath in the world to come.[33] In the daily liturgy God is praised for renewing the

---

[30]Cf. esp. Ign. *Magn.* 9; Barn. 15; and Jus. *Dial.* 138.

[31]Cf. the perceptive investigation of Sjöberg, *ST* 4 (1950), noted above.

[32]For the interrelation of eschatology and cultus in Judaism, cf. Riesenfeld, *Jésus transfiguré;* Sjöberg, *ST* 4 (1950), 56ff., 66ff.; Aalen, *Licht und Finsternis*, 255-258.

[33]Cf. Gen. R. 17:5 (R. Hanina b. Isaac); bBerakoth 57b; Bill. III, 672; IV, 839f.; cf. note 23 above.

work of creation every morning.[34]

In a more speculative way Zion, the temple and the "stone of foundation" are thought to be the cosmic center, from which the world was created and at which the glory of God shall be revealed at the end of the world.[35] From a more historical point of view, Israel is seen as the center; this world has come into being on account of the righteous, and it is only on their account that that which is to come shall come (2 Baruch 15:7).[36] The first and the last things are also, to an increasing degree, bound together by the Torah, which as the expression of God's will contains not only his commands, but also his entire plan for the world, from its beginning to its end.[37]

In the New Testament, Christ has a central significance, which corresponds not only to that of the Jewish Messiah, but also to that of the temple and cultus and of the Torah and Wisdom. The Christian correlation of salvation and creation is not merely derived from the eschatological idea that the end shall be like the beginning; it also has antecedents in applications of the creation-pattern to historic and actual experience, where eschatology is "realized", and where "reality", as given in Christ, is eschatologically interpreted. As in Judaism, both the actual facts of central religious significance and the last things are related to creation, or thought to be predestined or preexistent; but in the New Testament these two lines of though coincide, since that which is already given in Christ is thought to be part of the last things.

We must now proceed from the survey of general motifs to sketch their more concrete application in the doctrine of Christ and the church. I shall draw attention especially to some texts in which the analogy between the beginning of the world and the beginning of the church is made manifest. I mention first the application of predicates of divine eternity to Christ: as God

---

[34]Esp. in the benediction *yoser 'or;* cf. Aalen, 248-254.

[35]Cf. e.g. Jub. 1:27-29; 8:19; bYoma 54b; Aalen, 263f., 290, 299, Jeremias, *Golgotha*, 94f.

[36]Cf. Gen. R. 66:2; and my *Das Volk Gottes* (repr. Darmstadt: Wissenschaftliche Buchgesellschaft, 1963), 77f., 88.

[37]Cf. e.g. Gen. R. 1:1; Aboth 3:19; Bill. II, 174-176, 356f.; I, 245f.

he is the first and the last.[38] Further, as Christ is pre-existent and elected from eternity and is revealed in the last days, in him also the mystery of the whole divine plan of salvation is revealed.[39]

The accord between the work of salvation and the eternal purpose of God is made especially clear in Ephesians 1:3-14.[40] To the actual "blessing" in Christ, 1:3, corresponds the election in him before the foundation of the world, 1:4. The whole "eulogy" develops this theme, showing how the eternal universal purpose of God is realized in Christ. That also Gentiles are given a share in Christ is part of the "recapitulation of all things" in him.

In other texts it is directly said that Christ is the mediator of creation as well as of salvation; this corresponds to Jewish ideas about Wisdom and the Torah. In John 1 it is not quite clear how far the *Urzeit-Endzeit* - scheme has influenced the composition; but both in Hebrews 1 and in 1 Corinthians 8:6 and Colossians 1 it is evident. In Hebrews 1 the scheme seems to me to have an even greater importance for the whole structure than has been generally recognized. Clauses speaking about the eschatological appointment or enthronement of Christ alternate with predictions of his eternal status, in a series of introverted parallelisms according to the scheme *a b b a ab (ba):*

...by (his) Son
a whom he hath appointed heir of all things
b by whom also he made the worlds;
b who being the brightness of his glory...
and upholding all things by the rod of his power
a when he had...purged (our) sins
sat down on the right hand of the Majesty on high;
a being made so much better than the angels
b as he hath...obtained a more excellent name
than they
(b For unto which...Ps. 2:7 + 2 Sam. 7:14
a) And again...Deut. 32:43 (LXX).

The recognition of this formal structure[41] renders

---

[38]Rev. 1:17; 2:8; 22:13; Heb. 13:8.

[39]Col. 1:26f.; Eph. 1:9f.; 3:4ff.; 2 Tim. 1:9f.; Titus 1:2f.; 1 Peter 1:20. Cf. note 27 above.

[40]For a more thorough analysis of this passage, cf. my "Adresse und Proömium des Epheserbriefes," *TZ* 7 (1951), 241-264.

[41]The same formal structure, a threefold introverted parallelism according to the scheme ab ba ab, is found in the hymn 1 Tim. 3:16.

superfluous and unlikely the assumption that the name-giving, vv. 4-5, should be thought to take place at the enthronement of Christ, a view which can hardly be harmonized with the use of the title "Son" already in v. 2. Rather, a reference to primeval time is an ancient feature of enthronement hymns (cf. Ps. 109:3 LXX; 1 Enoch 47:3).[42]

As the aeons were created through Christ, all things, and especially the world to come, are also put in subjection to him (Heb. 1:2; cf. 2:5ff.). Not only his enthronement is set in relation to the creation; also his identification with his "brethren" through incarnation and passion is brought into correspondence with their common origin in God, "for whom and by whom all things exist" (2:10-11). Through the sacerdotal purification which Christ has accomplished, the people of God is given access to the heavenly world, which is also the world to come (1:3; cf. 10:19ff., etc.). But in accordance with the whole eschatological outlook of Hebrews, the church itself is not directly said to be a new creation.

At this point the Pauline idea is different. In 1 Corinthians 8:6 the creation of all things through Christ and the creation of the church through him are mentioned side by side. In Colossians 1:15-20 this parallelism is worked out in detail: Christ is the "firstborn of all creation" and the "first-born from the dead"; all things are created "in him...through him and to him," and "in him" the fullness was pleased to dwell, and "through him" to reconcile all things "to him." In a very impressive way, the idea of universal restitution is here combined with the conception that the reconciliation is a parallel to the creation. Here also the church is included in the protological-eschatological parallelism; it is the body of which Christ is the head, just as all things, the universe, are held together in him (cf. 2:10, 19; Eph. 1:22f.). We have the right to say that in the church the reconciliation and re-creation of the universe are already realized.

Parallels to the Christological hymn in Colossians 1 can be found in Gnosticism and in Hellenism in general, but it can hardly be denied that the Jewish ideas of the law, Israel,

---

[42]References are given by the authors referred to in notes 12 and 13 above.

the temple, etc., must also be taken into account.[43] It is at least possible also to find an allusion to Gen. 1:1; "In the beginning..." seems here to be interpreted as meaning "in Christ", as in Rabbinic interpretation it is taken to mean "by the Torah" (= Wisdom, Prov. 8:22) or "on account of Israel" (the beginning = the first fruits, Jer. 2:3).[44] More indisputable is the allusion to Gen. 1:26f. when in Col. 1:15 Christ is said to be "the image of the invisible God." As the "image of God" Christ is the representation and manifestation of God, both as the mediator of creation and in his work of atonement, when "the fullness was pleased to dwell" in him. We may therefore safely assume that we have here traces of a "christological" interpretation of Genesis 1, with a double reference both to creation and to salvation.

In 2 Corinthians 4:4 the idea is simply that Christ, as proclaimed in the gospel, is the "image of God", in whom God is revealed; the glory of Christ is, accordingly, "the glory of God in the face of Christ." But the allusion to Genesis 1:3 in 4:6 makes it probably that here too we have a vestige of an identification of the image of God in Genesis with Christ. Here, in 2 Corinthians 4 the two notions "image" and "glory" are closely associated with one another. This combination reappears in 1 Corinthians 11:7 and also in some passages in which Paul speaks of the "image" of Christ as the archetype, to which the faithful are to be made to conform in glory (Rom. 8:29; 1 Cor. 15:49; cf. Phil. 3:21).[45]

In 1 Corinthians 15:44-49 the allusions to Genesis are clear. The point is the difference between the "psychic body"

---

[43]Cf. Dibelius' commentary *An die Kolosser/Epheser/an Philemon* (ed. H. Lietzmann; HNT 12; Tübingen: Mohr, 1927), and E. Käsemann, *Leib und Leib Christi* (Tübingen: Mohr, 1933); for a different view, cf. the commentary of E. Lohmeyer, *Die Briefe an die Kolosser und an Philemon* (Meyer 9; 13th ed.; Göttingen: Vandenhoeck und Ruprecht, 1964), and S. Aalen, "Begrepet πλήρωμα i Kolosser - og Efeserbrevet," *Tidsskrift for Teologi og Kirke* (1952), 49-67. In such cases we should not assume that only the Jewish or only the Hellenistic parallels are relevant.

[44]Cf. W.D. Davies, *Paul and Rabbinic Judaism*, 150ff., and C.F. Burney, "Christ as the APXH of Creation," *JTS* 27 (1926), 160-177; Bill. IV, 852.

[45]On Christ as "Image," cf. G. Kittel, *TDNT*, II, 383-388; H. Willms, *Eikon* (Münster i. W., 1935). It is worthwhile to remember the sage remark of Ad. Schlatter: "The concept 'image of God' might easily be employed as a fundament underlying all of Paul's christological statements. But in interpreting Paul's thought we may not impose systems" (*Die Theologie der Apostle* [Stuttgart: Calwer Verlag, 1922], 338 note 1).

of created man and the "pneumatic body" of the resurrected. The archetypes are respectively the first man, Adam, who is a man of dust, and the "second man", the resurrected Christ, who is from heaven: as we have borne the image of the man of dust (cf. Gen. 5:3), we shall also bear the image of the man from heaven. The superiority of the "image of Christ" over that of Adam marks the superiority of resurrection over creation. It is quite clear that Christ as the "last Adam" is here thought to bring something more than what was lost through the Fall. Yet Paul has probably found in Genesis 1:26f. the intention of the Creator to make man conform to Christ as the archetype. We may here compare Romans 3:23 and 8:29f.: "All have sinned and come short of the glory of God" -- but justification leads to conformity with the image of Christ and thus to glory, in accordance with the predestination of God.

Without direct use of the noun "image", the idea of Christ as Adam's antitype is also found in 1 Corinthians 15:22 and Romans 5:12ff. Here the point is not correspondence on a higher level, as in 1 Corinthians 15:44ff., but analogy in contrast.[46] Resurrection and life stand against death, but the relation of the one and the many is the same in the realm of life as in the realm of death. In the fuller development of the theme in Romans 5, the point is that the trespass of Adam, which brought sin into the world, also caused the death of all men; accordingly, the obedience of Christ and the grace of God in him, which has brought justification, will also bring life to all men without distinction. Salvation is as universal as sin; the Law has come in as an intermediate ordinance, which neither belongs to the first nor to the last things.[47]

A similar, yet different, conception is that of the "new man" (Col. 3:10; Eph. 4:24; cf. 2:15). Here the contrasting element is not Adam as the prototype of humanity, but "the old man", man under the domination of sin, conceived as a kind of

---

[46]Regarding analogy in contrast, cf. 4 Ezra 4:30-32 and also the citation from Sifra on Leviticus by Raymundus Martini given by Jeremias in *TDNT* V, 696. That the conception of Christ as the antitype of Adam is particularly associated with his resurrection may be explained by the widespread view that resurrection is a new act of creation (Rom. 4:17; Sjöberg, *ST* 4, 60, 76f.). Since Adam is the father of mankind, his resurrection has a special importance (Apoc. Moses 28 and 41; cf. the late *Pirke Mashiah*, Bill. III, 10).

[47]Cf. my "Two Notes on Rom. 5," *ST* (1951), 37-48; M. Black, "The Pauline Doctrine of the Second Adam," *SJT* 8 (1954), 170-179.

"corporate personality", and at the same time the individual, sinful self, mankind, and the totality of vices, the "members which are upon the earth" (cf. especially Col. 3:5ff., and also Rom. 6:6). In a similar way, "the new man" is not simply the converted individual, but an eschatological entity, personal, corporate and pneumatic, nearly identical with Christ himself, whom the baptized have put on and ever again are to put on (Gal. 3:27; Rom. 13:14). By putting on this "new man", men become what God at the creation intended that men should be; the new man is created "after God" (Eph. 4:24) and is "renewed in knowledge after the image of him that created him" (Col. 3:10).[48]

The corporate aspect, which is quite clear in Colossians 3:10f., is the main theme in Ephesians 2:15. The passage Ephesians 2:11-22 draws upon the terminology of Jewish proselytism. According to Jewish doctrine individual Gentiles were "brought near", incorporated into Israel and given access to the holy sphere of worship, through (a) the "blood of the covenant" at circumcision, (b) proselyte baptism and (c) the expiating blood of the proselyte sacrifice. In analogy to this, in Ephesians 2 the Gentiles are said to have been brought near by the blood of Christ, and made not merely strangers and sojourners (*gerim*), but real fellow citizens, members of the household of God.[49] Ephesians 2:13-18 is a kind of midrash on Isaiah 57:19, a passage which in Judaism referred to those Gentiles "far off" who had become proselytes -- or to penitents -- and to the Israelites who were near; it is here applied to Gentiles and Jews in the church, to whom Christ has brought peace through his work of reconciliation.[50] It was said that if anyone brought a Gentile near and made him a proselyte it was as if he had created

---

[48]Cf. Davies, *Paul and Rabbinic Judaism*, 120ff., and P.V. Hansen "Det nye Menneske," *DTT* (1950), 193-202; cf. also my "Gamla Människan," *Svenskt bibliskt Uppslagsverk*, I, 644f.

[49]H. Sahlin (*Die Beschneidung Christi* [*SBU* 12; Lund: Gleerup, 1950] has given a stimulating interpretation of this passage even if it is somewhat fantastic in details. He assumes that the "blood of Christ" is to be contrasted with the blood of circumcision. The conclusion that an analogy to the proselyte sacrifice may be intended can be drawn from the study of W.C. van Unnik, "De Verlossing I Petrus 1:18-19 en het Problem van van den Eersten Petrusbrief," *Mededeelingen der Nederlandsche Akademie van Wetenschappen, Afdeeling Letterkunde* V, 1 (1942), esp. 51-57, 69-87.

[50]Cf. Num. R. 8:4 (149d): the proselytes; Targ. Isa. 57:19; S. Num. 6:26, par 42; bBerakoth 34b; bSanhedrin 99a: the penitents. Bill. I, 167, 216, 603; III, 586.

him;[51] but here Christ is said to create "in himself one new man", reconciling Jew and Gentile to God in one body, his church, and giving both access to the Father in one Spirit. The "dividing wall" of enmity, which was caused by the Law but has been broken down by Christ, not only alienated the Gentiles from Israel, but also separated Gentiles and Israelites from God, in the time when both of them were "in the flesh".[52] The creation of the church as "one new man" in Christ means at the same time the incorporation of Gentiles into the people of God and the coming of the new age of the Spirit. Reconciliation brings a new creation in the double sense of the conversion of the Gentiles and the realization of eschatology (cf. also Gal. 6:15 and 2 Cor. 5:17).[53]

The unity of Jews and Gentiles is to Paul an essential sign of the new creation or the "new man". This unity is of an eschatological character, but it is already a sacramental and social reality in the church. In this world the differences between circumcised and uncircumcised, slave and free, remain, and are to remain, even if they are no longer of any essential relevance (1 Cor. 7:17-24). But none the less, the unity within the church is thought to be a restoration of the original unity of mankind and of creation. Through the very existence of the church, in which Jews and Gentiles are united, "the manifold wisdom of God" is made known to the principalities and powers which constitute the universe, and the dispensation of the Creator to re-unify all things begins to be realized (Eph. 3:10). And to the soteriological arguments for the equality of Jew and Greek in justification, Paul can also add the more "rational" argument that God is not the God of Jews only, but also the God of Gentiles (Rom. 3:29).[54]

---

[51]Gen. R. 39:14; Sjöberg, *ST* 4, 53f.

[52]The main theme of the passage is that the Gentiles are rendered in Christ free access to God, on equal terms with the Israelites; cf. Percy, "Zu den Problemen des Kol. - und Epheserbriefes," *ZNW* 43 (1950/51) 187f. This access to God is understood as access to God in the temple (of the church) (2:20-22). Thus I believe that the "middle wall of partition" alludes to the wall in the temple, dividing the court of the Gentiles from the inner yards, into which Gentiles were not allowed to enter under penalty of death. But this does not exclude the possibility that the passage also contains vestiges of cosmic symbolism according to which the wall is the boundary separating the divine world from this world. Cf. the notion of the veil in Heb. 6:19; 9:3ff.; 10:20; Num. R. 12:13.

[53]Cf. Davies, *Paul and Rabbinic Judaism*, 119ff.

[54]Cf. also the summary of the history of salvation in Rom. 9:32-36. Stig Hansson (*The Unity of the Church in the N.T.* [ASNU 14; Uppsala: Almqvist & Wiksells, 1946]) has, with good reason, made the restoration of the original unity a main theme in his book.

The unity in Christ is also a unity of male and female (Gal. 3:27f.). To Paul, this unity does not imply any social equality; the wife has to be subject to her husband. In this case the difference is not caused by the Law, but belongs to the original order of creation (1 Cor. 11:2ff.). But none the less, the Apostle finds that the equal dignity and interdependence "in the Lord" is foreshadowed in the order of creation and procreation. The eschatological unity corresponds to the common origin.[55] The subordination of women, of which their hair style and their silence is to be a sign, belongs to the order of creation, not to the order of salvation. But decent order is to be respected also in the church. This, and not any incapacity in women to represent Christ as his messengers, is the motivation for the Pauline ordinances in 1 Corinthians 11:2ff. and 14:34ff.[56] (The problem is whether or not the conception of what is decent according to the order of creation should be regarded as binding for the church today.)

The idea of Christian marriage is a characteristic proof of the practical consequences of the correspondence between the first and the last things. In Ephesians 5:21-33 the theme is the relation between husband and wife, which has its model in the relation of Christ to the church. The exhortation is strengthened by a reference to Genesis 2:24. According to the hermeneutical principle that the last things shall be like the first, this text is taken to point to Christ as the "Man" and the church as his wife. But this "mysterious" interpretation does not exclude the literal one; it gives it a definite validity. The marriage which reflects the relation between Christ and the church is at the same time the marriage which corresponds to the will of the Creator.

In 1 Corinthians 6:16f. we find a similar application of Genesis 2:24 in a more individualized form: "He who is joined to the Lord becomes one spirit (with him)." The introduction of the word "spirit" is due to the superiority of the eschatological antitype, as in 1 Corinthians 15:45. The idea is here that the union with Christ, which is the eschatological fulfillment of Genesis 2:24, should make fornication impossible, while at the

---

[55]1 Cor. 11:11-12; cf. the similar saying in Gen. R. 22:2 (R. Akiba) and 8:9 (R. Simlai): "Neither man without woman nor woman without man nor both of them without Shekinah."

[56]In contrast to H. Riesenfeld in *En bok om kyrkans ämbete* (ed. Hj. Lindroth; Uppsala, 1951), 64ff. Some valuable observations on the passage are made by R. Gyllenberg, "Den välklädda kvinnan," *Acta Acad. Aboensis, Humaniora* 18 (1949), 143-155.

same time sanctifying marriage (cf. 1 Cor. 7:14). Marriage belongs to "the form of this world" which is passing away (1 Cor. 7:25-31); and yet, the order of creation is not to be destroyed but rather to be restored in the "eschatological community" of the church.

We may at this point add some general remarks on Pauline ethics. Its basis can be said to be eschatological, christological and sacramental. But the concrete content of the exhortations is to a considerable extent ethical commonplace, well known also to Judaism and Hellenism. The "great mystery" of Ephesians 5, for example, leads to the rather traditional moral commands of a *Haustafel*. The somewhat sublime arguments of 1 Corinthians 11:2ff. are corroborated by a reference to what is decent and proper, according to common opinion and the teaching of nature (11:13-14). This and similar appeals to "natural law" are not due to any lack of consistency; they are in full harmony with the Apostle's fundamental conviction that what is realized in the church, the new creation, is in harmony with the original will of God the Creator. Sin corrupts creation; deification of the creature in the end leads to unnaturalness (Rom. 1). But in the church all natural, human virtues should be held in high esteem (Phil. 4:8).[57]

Not only the personal relation between men is restored in Christ, but also the right relation to material things. The great christological hymn in Colossians 1 implies an indirect polemic against the asceticism of the false teachers. Later in the epistle Paul goes on to say that Christians, who are dead with Christ to the cosmic powers, are therefore free to use what God has created, the things which "perish when they are used" (Col. 2:20-23; cf. Rom. 14:6, 14; 1 Tim. 4:4). The paradoxical situation of the church here becomes very clear; Christians are no longer living "in the world", but precisely for this reason they are free from "ordinances" and free to make use of material things, without discrimination. In a similar way, there is a clear inner unity between the theological statement in 1 Corinthians 8:6 and the practical rules given in 10:23ff., to eat whatever is sold in the meat market. "The earth and its fullness" belongs to the Lord, and in Christ men are made free to make the right use of it.

The doctrine of correspondence between the first and the

---

[57]Cf. C.H. Dodd, "Natural Law in the Bible," *Theology* (1946), 130-133, 161-167.

last things has in this way very practical consequences. Christian ethics are more other-worldly than Jewish, but are at the same time characterized by a free and thankful acceptance of all gifts of the Creator, without any legal restrictions. The inner unity between these two apparently divergent tendencies is given by the fundamental, eschatological conception. Where this has been lost, the other-worldliness has deviated into a dualistic asceticism or a pietistic introversion, and the positive attitude to the world has resulted in tendencies towards an ecclesiastical world-domination, or in a cultural optimism and evolutionism on a religious basis.

Against such deviations, it is important to reconsider the biblical, and especially Pauline, doctrine that the purpose of the Creator is realized in the new creation, that is in Christ, who is both the mediator of creation and the first-born from the dead, the head of the church. In the church men are included in this new creation in Christ. The gospel is itself a divine word of creation, like the first "let light shine out of darkness" (2 Cor. 4:6). In baptism the "old man" is put off and the "new man" is put on.[58] The gospel and the sacraments are the means by which the church on earth is called into existence as the eschatological community, in which the will of the Creator is brought to realization.

The restoration of creation in Christ is not simply an empirical, visible fact; like the life of the Christians it can rather be said to be hidden with Christ in God (Col. 3:3). Creation is in the present time not yet delivered from the futility to which it was subjected. It is still "groaning", and even those who are in Christ, and have received the Spirit as first fruits, are groaning and waiting with patience. Until the day of redemption they have to endure sufferings; their relation to the course of events in the world is restored only in so far as they know that "everything works for good with those who love God" (Rom. 8:18-28).

Christians have to face sufferings, and they have also to

---

[58]Nearly all the texts about the new creation seem in some way to have the renewal at baptism in view, however the relation between the creative act of God in Christ and the baptismal rite is to be defined. Cf. the studies of Hansen (note 48 above) and Sahlin (note 49 above); Lindeskog, 252ff.; and my article "Dobet i Efesierbrevet," *STK* (1945), 85-103. The hymnic texts, praising Christ as the mediator of creation and of salvation, like Col. 1:15-20 and Heb. 1:2ff., probably also have a liturgical background, perhaps especially in the eucharistic thanksgiving. Cf. note 5 above and my article "Anamnesis" in this volume.

face temptations. There exists a real danger that a church might be seduced as Eve was, a satanic travesty between the first and the last things (2 Cor. 11:3). But sufferings and temptations are not the only actual experiences of Christians; the renewal of the "new man" in a life of Christian virtues is also part of their experience (Col. 3:10ff.). The Spirit makes the transformation into the likeness of Christ, "from glory to glory", beginning already here and now (2 Cor. 3:18). The church is growing towards its eschatological perfection (Eph. 4:13ff.).

That the life of the church is, at the same time, marked by sufferings and temptations, and by renewal and growth, may seem to be paradoxical. But this paradox is only the reflection of the faith that it is the crucified and risen Lord who is the beginning and archetype of the new creation. The growth of the church is growth towards him (Eph. 4:15). The identifying mark of the new creation is therefore conformity with Christ in sufferings and future glory (Rom. 8:17ff.; Phil. 3:8ff.), a glory which is already partly anticipated by the activity of the Spirit.

The Pauline idea of a restoration of creation in the church is rightly understood only if the main emphasis is laid, not upon any moral and social ameliorations, but upon participation in Christ through the gospel and the sacraments, leading to conformity with him in life. Accordingly, the church's conformity with creation is dependent upon its conformity with Christ.

Outside the Pauline corpus, the idea of correspondence between the first and the last things is not in the same direct way applied to the doctrine of Christ and the church. The fundamental idea can, however, be expressed in a different terminology, where the eschatological conception differs from the Pauline pattern. The incidental remarks on the Epistle to the Hebrews ought to have made this clear. In still another way the Fourth Gospel stresses the intimate connection between the work of God in creation and in salvation: "The gospel is a record of a life which expresses the eternal thought of God, the meaning of the universe," to put it in the words of C.H. Dodd.[59]

I would now only like to add a few remarks on the interpretation of the Synoptic Gospels. Here, too, we must take care not to operate with a false antithesis between eschatology and the work and will of God the Creator. The miracles of Jesus

---

[59]Cf. C.H. Dodd, *The Interpretation of the Fourth Gospel* (Cambridge: Cambridge University Press, 1953), 284.

should, for instance, hardly be understood as *either* eschatological signs *or* deeds of mercy; as deeds of mercy which restore the fullness of human life, they are eschatological signs. In a similar way, the moral teaching of Jesus insists upon the original will of the Creator, and in this way it is the revelation of the will of God for the last days in which the kingdom of God is proclaimed on earth.[60] The freedom of Jesus with regard to Sabbath laws is derived from his messianic authority and at the same time brings the purpose of the Creator to realization: "The sabbath was made for man, not man for the sabbath" (Mark 2:23-28).

Still other points might be mentioned. But it is impossible to pursue here the investigation any further. The intention of my article has not been to exhaust the material, but to draw attention to an important aspect of the "realized eschatology" of the New Testament.

---

[60]Cf. Jeremias, *Jesus als Weltvollender*, 68; H.J. Schoeps, "*Restitutio principii* as the basis of the *Nova Lex Jesu*," *JBL* (1947), 453-464.

CHAPTER 9

The Parables of Growth

After the lively discussion prompted by the publication of Jülicher's standard work on the parables of Jesus,[1] a period followed of relatively little progress in the field of parable research. In recent years the discussion has been revived. The most stimulating new approach was that of C.H. Dodd;[2] the most successful study was the brief but compact monograph by Joachim Jeremias.[3] Methodologically Jeremias follows Dodd. If he often reaches different results it is principally because he is not able to agree with Dodd's conception of "realized eschatology." Jeremias himself would prefer to speak of an "eschatology in process of realization" (*eine sich realisierende Eschatologie*).

Different conceptions of Jesus' eschatology produce different interpretations, especially with respect to the parables of growth. According to Dodd, their message is that the harvest has come, the crisis is here, the kingdom of God is already present. According to Jeremias these parables are, on the contrary, expressions of great confidence "that the hour of God is coming." Compared with the interpretation of Dodd, this means

---

[1] *Die Gleichnisreden Jesu* (2 vols.; Freiburg i.B.: Mohr, 1886-1899).

[2] *The Parables of the Kingdom* (London: Nisbet, 1935).

[3] *Die Gleichnisse Jesu* (Zürich: Zwingli Verlag, 1947). References in this essay will be to the English translation of the considerably revised and expanded 6th edition: *The Parables of Jesus* (tr. S.H. Hooke; New York: Scribner's 1963). In view of the good bibliography contained in this work, it has been considered unnecessary to reproduce all bibliographical references contained in the first publication of the present essay.

a renewal of an older, futurist eschatological interpretation in new form. Parable research today has to face the following questions: Should the interpretation of Dodd or that of Jeremias be given preference? Is there another option? If so, does that mean that we should abandon the methodological principles common to Dodd and Jeremias, or does it mean that we should make a better and more consistent use of them? The intention of the following article is to show that the latter alternative should be chosen. Before we turn to the individual parables it will be useful to clarify the methodological principles and the idea of growth common to these parables.

Methodological Principles

A discussion of the method of parable interpretation must still begin with Jülicher. His work is well known for its penetrating criticism of allegorical interpretation and its consistent application of the principle that the parables of Jesus are to be interpreted as "pure" parables with one single point of comparison. It should not be overlooked, however, that this main idea is intimately connected with two other principles: the necessity of literary criticism, and of what was later called form criticism, and the idea that the parables of Jesus were intended to serve as arguments. The methodological problem of parable interpretation can still be stated as the problem of the validity of these three principles on which the work of Jülicher was based. To put it briefly, it can be said that not one of these principles has been invalidated by later research. But all of them have to be modified, and to be understood and applied in somewhat different ways than in the work of Jülicher.

1. It should not be necessary to stress the necessity of higher criticism with regard to the Gospel parables. Certainly it is an important, indeed the primary, task of the New Testament scholar to interpret the Gospels in their present form as literary and theological documents. The urgency of this task has often been neglected by biblical critics and it is important that in our generation scholars have called it to our attention. But this does not mean that critical work is made superfluous. We cannot be satisfied with asking: How did the evangelists understand the parables? We must also ask: What did Jesus intend to say when he spoke them? An answer to this latter question can only be found by way of systematic study. The answer may be hypothetical, but it is neither necessary nor justifiable to

abandon the quest.

The systematic application of form criticism to the study of the Gospels has proved the necessity of isolating the small units, stories and pronouncements in the Gospels, and of studying them in isolation, as Jülicher did with the parables. The framework of the Gospels is to a large extent secondary, and so also are the interpretations of the parables found in the Gospels.[4] If we ask how Jesus intended the parables to be understood, we cannot depend upon the Gospels' context or their interpretations. On the other hand, we have every reason to assume that the content and to a great extent also the wording of the parables themselves have in general been transmitted with great fidelity. Only where synoptic variants or other special reasons make it necessary are we justified in assuming that the similitudes or parabolic stories have undergone any considerable change during the process of transmission.

Quite as much as their predecessors, Dodd and Jeremias have emphasized the necessity of critical work. The greater part of Jeremias' monograph has the provocative title "The Return to Jesus from the Primitive Church" (23-114). It is not necessary here to review or to discuss the different "laws" which according to Jeremias have determined the transformation of the parables in the history of tradition. The most significant shift has been that whereas Jülicher laid the main emphasis on the evangelists' theory that the parables were to be understood as allegories, more recent research explains the transformation as due to a shift in audience: parables which Jesus addressed to his contemporaries are understood as sayings of the Lord meant for his church. The tendency toward allegorical interpretation is largely the consequence of this shift. When we preach, we apply the sayings of the Lord to our contemporary situation, a process which parallels the gospel tradition's transformation of the parables. We can therefore evaluate positively such a transformation from a theological perspective, even if the evaluation must be negative from a historical-critical point of view. In this article I must presuppose the critical work. With regard to the parables of growth it implies that the interpretation can be based neither on the interpretations given by the evangelists (Mark 4:14-20, Matt. 13:37-43) nor on the sayings concerning the

---

[4]Cf. the fundamental work of R. Bultmann, *History of the Synoptic Tradition* (tr. J. Marsh; New York: Harper and Row, 1963), esp. 166-205.

secret of the kingdom of God (Mark 4:11f.).

In Jülicher's work, the isolation of the parables from their context in the Gospels resulted in a modernized European interpretation of their message. At this point later research has taken a decisive step forward by stressing the background of the parables in the Old Testament and in first century Palestine. The parables are related to typical situations in the life of Jesus. The attempt is made to understand them in light of his eschatological message and of the problems and conflicts which he had to face: they functioned as apologetic and polemic. It is maintained that Jülicher did only half the work in liberating the parables from the dust of allegorical interpretation: instead of setting the parables in their original situations he was content to give them the broadest possible application.[5]

2. The main thesis of Jülicher was that the parables of Jesus are not allegories, but similitudes or parables in the narrower sense of this word. They contain concrete pictures expressing a moral which should be applied, not metaphoric, cryptic language which should be deciphered. This principle too is generally sound. Different attempts have been made to rehabilitate allegorical interpretation, but the real progress in the field of parable research has been made by scholars like Dodd and Jeremias, who are almost as hostile to the allegorical method as Jülicher was.

Later research has departed from the rigidity with which Jülicher pursued his method. The breadth of the Hebrew word *māšal* and the corresponding Greek *parabolē* warns us not to stress

---

[5]Dodd, 24-27; Jeremias, 18-22. Even if the criticism of Jülicher at this point is justified, it should not be exaggerated. Jülicher did not mean to deny that the parables might have been spoken in concrete historical situations and were to be applied to them. His principle was that the point of comparison, the *tertium comparationis*, should have the character of an, often subconscious, general truth; he did not argue that the application should have this character (cf. e.g. vol. II, 535). But Jülicher fails to draw a clear distinction at this point, since he was mainly concerned with the destruction of the allegorical method. In practice he tends to prefer the "broadest possible application" (II, 481; cf. the citation from B. Weiss in I, 105: "The interpretation of the parable can only lie in a common truth.") The lack of methodological clarity at this point is related to Jülicher's own theological position which made him view Jesus as a teacher of general religious truths. The essential criticism was already voiced by E. Billing, *De etiska tankarna i urkristendomen* (2nd ed.; Stockholm: Studentrörelsens Bokförlag, 1936; first published in 1907), esp. 336.

the contrast between "parable" and "allegory" too strongly. The present texts in the Gospels are sufficient proofs that intermediate forms really exist. In many cases these forms are probably due to secondary allegorizing, but it cannot be stated as a principle that this must always be the case. The classification of the material in different forms of figurative speech is a necessary tool, but it does not create absolute norms to which the concrete material can always be made to conform.

Jülicher said that "Halb Allegorie, halb Fabel sind nur mythologische Wesen."[6] The answer to this is that "allegory" and "parable" (or "fable") may indeed have common mythological ancestors. The clear distinction between picture and reality seems to be a relatively late product in human history, as is the clear differentiation between the pure forms of "allegory" and "parable". This might be verified by a study of the use of figurative speech within the Old Testament. At the time of Jesus, a rather clear differentiation has been reached, but we still find intermediate forms.[7] Where such "irregular" forms are found, we can only decide in each individual case whether they are due to later adaptations or to mixture of style or to survival of a more primitive type of figurative speech.

It is more important to recognize that a number of parables are not simply pictures derived from the processes of nature and the life of common men, but are modelled upon traditional metaphors (God as King, Judge, Father, Lord, salvation as a feast, wedding, etc.).[8] This use of traditional metaphors does not make a parable into an allegory. The point is, as in many Jewish parables, that a conclusion should be drawn from the conduct of an earthly king as to the conduct of the heavenly King and so on. At least in principle it is also possible that a parable can make use of several traditional metaphors and thus approximate allegory without ceasing to be a "real" parable which is to be "applied", not an allegory which is to be "interpreted" (= deciphered).

---

[6] I, 107.

[7] In the Apocalypse of Ezra (4 Ezra) there is a clear difference between the visionary allegories found in chapters 10-13 and argumentative similitudes such as 4:13-21, 40-43; 5:46-49, 51-55; 7:51-61; 8:2-3, 41. There are, however, some forms not so easily classified: 4:44-50; 7:3-14; 4:28-32; 9:21-22.

[8] Cf. Jeremias, 115ff.; E.C. Hoskyns and F.N. Davey, *The Riddle of the New Testament* (London: Faber and Faber, 1931), 177-191.

The emphasis on a single point in a parable does not exclude the possibility that there may be several points of deliberate correspondence between the image and the reality which is compared to it. The decisive thing is that the parable is built upon comparison of two realities, its aim is to illustrate and to argue, and so it is used in popular speech, preaching and discussion. The allegory is composed of metaphorical "cryptograms" and is used for the purpose of secrecy or poetry; it is used in Jewish apocalyptic to endue the revelations with a mysterious form. If a parable is meant to illustrate several aspects of a reality, it does not therefore become an allegory. In principle my compatriot Chr. A. Bugge was correct when he differentiated between "argumentative parables" which could have only one point of application, and "illustrative parables" which could have several points.[9] The question is whether or not the parables of growth -- or any of Jesus' parables -- can be classified as purely illustrative. But it is worth-while to notice that the assumption that the parables of Jesus have only one salient point depends upon the theory that the intention of the parables is to make the hearers draw a conclusion, or agree in a conclusion drawn by Jesus, hence that they have an argumentative force. The idea that the parables are meant to serve as "proofs" is thus a constitutive element in Jülicher's theory of the parables.

3. The character of the parables as "proofs" or arguments has not been universally recognized. In opposition to Jülicher, A. Nygren for one, tried to show that the parables are not to be understood as "proofs", but as means of revelation.[10] It is not difficult to understand the reason for this criticism, and it contains an element of truth. The parables of Jesus are not rational proofs, based on the *analogia entis*, and it cannot be denied that there is a certain tendency in Jülicher's work to understand the parables as proofs of this kind which demonstrate the validity of general religious truths. And yet the parables *are* proofs, but in another and more popular sense; they are proofs in the sense of convincing arguments. This corresponds to the Hebrew mode of thought, which is not interested in the ideal of mathematical demonstration. The use of parables is a popular and effective way of convincing one's hearers or of

---

[9]Chr. A. Bugge, *Die Hauptparabeln Jesu* (2 vols.; Giessen: J. Rieker, 1903), esp. I, 55ff.

[10]A. Nygren, *Agape and Eros* (tr. A.G. Hebert; London: SPCK, 1932), 56-65. Cf. *STK* (1928), 217-236, and the counter-criticism of A. Fridrichsen, *STK* (1929), 34ff.

refuting one's opponents. The parable provokes a judgment, and intends to make the hearer assent. We can think of the way in which parabolic narratives are used in the Old Testament, e.g. how the prophet Nathan convinces David of his sin by means of a parable (2 Sam. 12:1-14).[11]

That the parables of Jesus are meant as "proofs" in this sense is a hypothesis which in the most recent period of parable research has been worked out with much vigor and consistency. Dodd and Jeremias, and their predecessors and followers, seek to understand the parables in light of the situations which Jesus had to face, and to show how they served as arguments in controversy and in preaching. The parables neither prove nor reveal general religious truths; their point is to clarify the significance of what was happening: the kingdom of God had drawn near, it was time to repent. There is no real contrast between the argumentative and the revelatory character of the parables; they argue in order to bring revelation near to man, in order to convince or to refute.

It cannot be claimed that all the parables of Jesus *must* have been meant as arguments, but it is likely that they were. In some cases we know the situations in which they were spoken, in others we can only guess the specific problems to which they give answers. In the case of the parables of growth it is not immediately clear that they confront some specific question, opposition or doubt. But as this assumption has proved to be successful with regard to other parables, it is a reasonable working hypothesis to assume that these parables also are addressed to specific problems and have an argumentative character. But neither Dodd nor Jeremias has interpreted these parables in a way fully consistent with his own methodological principles. Dodd's interpretation made clear the relation to the situation of Jesus but not the argumentative force: Jeremias' interpretation -- especially in its early form -- restored the argumentative force but disregarded Jesus' specific situation.

Jülicher has something to say here that is still worthy of note: "In our parables Jesus is seeking a comparison between the Kingdom of God, an ideal inherited from the fathers, for whose realization he himself longed, and the presence of this Kingdom he experienced; he found it, without compromising in the least his conviction or common hopes, by assigning to the Kingdom

---

[11]But cf. Jeremias' reference to my article in the later editions of his work (*Parables*, 149 and 151).

of God a history, by maintaining a period of its existence in this age, with its attendent woes, preceeding the glorious days for which everyone hoped. He did not differentiate between the establishment and the subsequent development of the Kingdom of Heaven; he was satisfied if his followers no longer sought in this age what only the Kingdom of Heaven could bring at the time of consummation: untarnished glory."[12] The words are spoken about the parables of the Drag-net and of the Tares, but they seem to be applicable to all the parables of growth and to provide a key to the interpretation which can be better used than it was by Jülicher himself.

Later disregard for Jülicher's insight is probably due to the reaction against his modernizing, "liberal" interpretation of the idea of the kingdom of God. It is possible, however, to interpret the parables of growth in light of the contrast between messianic, eschatological expectations and the actual process of the coming of the kingdom of God into the present time, without falling back into an immanent-evolutionary interpretation of the kingdom. Of the greatest importance in this connection is the proper understanding of the idea of growth.

The Idea of Growth

The interpretation of the kingdom of God in liberal Protestantism, which understood the kingdom as a purely spiritual, religio-ethical reality, growing and successively developing towards its perfection, found a scriptural basis in the parables of growth. The "eschatological school" proved that this modernizing interpretation was untenable, but the protagonists of the school had considerable difficulties in finding a satisfactory interpretation to replace it. We must agree with Dodd when he says: "At no point does the eschatological interpretation of the Gospels appear more strained and artificial."[13]

Dodd himself reckons with a real process of growth, but thinks that this has taken place in the history of Israel before Jesus. The crisis occasioned by the ministry of Jesus is the eschatological "harvest" (cf. Matt. 9:37f.). It is thus supposed

---

[12] *Die Gleichnisreden Jesu*, II, 569. On the same page Jülicher stresses the dualistic element in Jesus' world view, which "was much too strong for him to have reckoned with a gradual diminishing and an eventual disappearance of evil by means of the development of good."

[13] *The Parables of the Kingdom*, 176.

that Jesus has made a radical reinterpretation of the traditional eschatological metaphors. Dodd's interpretation of the parables of growth will be accepted only by those who have, on other grounds, accepted his thesis that Jesus preached "realized eschatology" in a way which left no room for a future coming of the kingdom in glory. With Jeremias and the majority of continental scholars, I consider this view a false "abbreviation" of Jesus' eschatology.[14]

To banish the idea of an inner-worldly evolution of the kingdom of God, other scholars have argued that "the idea of organic growth is totally foreign to the man of antiquity."[15] A somewhat more prudent formulation of the same idea is given by Jeremias: "The modern man, passing through the plowed field, thinks of what is going on beneath the soil, and envisages a biological development. The people of the Bible, passing through the same plough-land, look up and see miracle upon miracle, nothing less than resurrection from the dead."[16] I have to confess a certain skepticism about such references to the ancient, oriental mode of thought, by which the most incredible things are claimed to be made credible. In this case the fault is to be found in the lack of differentiation between the idea of growth in itself and the biological-scientific explanation of it.

It is quite right that the modern, evolutionary idea of biological growth lies totally outside the horizon of the Bible. But this does not imply that the idea of organic growth was in itself unknown to the biblical authors or to Jesus himself. The growth of seed and the regularity of life in nature have been known to peasants as long as the earth has been cultivated. The demythologizing of nature in biblical religion opened new possibilities for appreciating the order in nature. Several decades ago the Swedish theologian and bishop Einar Billing called attention to the place that the biblical idea of God's ordinances for the life-processes of nature have in the prehistory of the concept of physical law.[17]

Natural law is foreshadowed in the Bible, especially in its recognition of the regular change of day and night and, to an increasing degree, of the fixed movements of the heavenly bodies. But order is also found in the periodic course of the seasons and in the processes of organic life. The classical

---

[14] *Parables*, 21.

[15] Cf. Ch. Masson, *Les Paraboles de Marc IV* (Paris: Delachaux & Niestlé, 1943), 46.

[16] *Parables*, 149.

[17] "Ett bidrag till naturlagbegreppets förhistoria," 253-290 (originally appeared in 1911).

statement is Genesis 8:22: "While the earth remains, seedtime and harvest, cold and heat, summer and winter, day and night, shall not cease." A very clear expression of the idea from a later time is found in 1 Enoch 2-5: the stars do not transgress their appointed order, the seasons follow each other regularly, the trees wither and shed their leaves in winter, and cover themselves with green leaves and bear fruit in summer. "And all his works go on thus from year to year for ever, and all the tasks which they accomplish for Him, and their tasks change not, but according as God has ordained so it is done." Only men transgress the law of God: "But ye -- ye have not been steadfast, nor done the commandments of the Lord."[18]

That the idea of organic growth is neither unknown nor irrelevant can also be seen from the parables of growth themselves, cf. esp. Mark 4:8: the seeds brought forth grain, "growing up and increasing and yielding thirtyfold" etc., and Mark 4:28: "The earth produces of itself, first the blade, then the ear, then the full grain in the ear." The idea that it is the earth itself which brings forth its crops is familiar from the Old Testament. At the same time, the fruit of the earth is a blessing of God. The biblical authors do not feel a contrast: the processes of nature are due to the wonderful work of the Creator.[19] "God gave the growth," says the Apostle Paul, expressing in these words the view of the whole Bible about natural as well as about spiritual growth (1 Cor. 3:7).

The idea of unbroken order in organic life is also present in metaphoric language: "Every sound tree bears good fruit, but the bad tree bears evil fruit." "Whatever a man sows, that he will also reap."[20] Certainly, the growth of seed is not a progressive evolution; it includes catastrophes and wonders, death and resurrection. But in all this there is order, according to the commandments of God. God gives the grain "a body as he has chosen, and to each kind of seed its own body" (1 Cor. 15:38). Thus we should bear in mind that the idea of organic growth was far from foreign to men of antiquity; to Jews and Christians organic growth was but the other side of the creative work of God who alone gives growth.

Against the background of this conception of nature, we

---

[18]The same topic is found in Jer. 5:22ff.; T Napht. 3. Regarding the general idea of God's order in nature, cf. e.g. Ps. 104 and 148; Jer. 31:35f.; Ps. Sol. 18.

[19]Cf. Gen. 1:11; 2:9; Lev. 26:4; Deut. 11:11-17; Ps. 65, 67, etc.

[20]Matt. 7:16-20; 12:23; Gal. 6:7.

can understand the application to human history of images and terms from organic life. History is not understood as an inner-worldly evolution; at all stages it is determined by God, or by the struggle between God and evil forces. But history also follows a pre-ordained order, where one period follows another according to the ordinance of God. This conception lies at the bottom of the apocalyptic conception of periodicity in history. It is made explicit in the Apocalypse of Ezra, cf. e.g. 7:74: "For how long a time hath the Most High been longsuffering with the inhabitants of the world -- not for their sake, indeed, but for the sake of the times which he has ordained."

The seer of 4 Ezra is troubled by the prospect of a long interval before the judgment comes; why couldn't all generations be created at once? He is answered by a parable: "Ask the womb of a woman, and say unto it: If thou bringest forth ten children, why (dost thou bring them forth) each in his own time? Demand, therefore, that it produce ten all at once. And I said: It cannot possibly, but (only each) in its own time. Then said he unto me: Thus have I also made the earth the womb for those who in their own time are conceived by it. For just as the young child does not bring forth, nor she that is aged any more, so have I also disposed the world which I have created by defined periods of time" (4 Ezra 5:46-49).

In another passage the process leading from seed to harvest furnishes the image: "For the evil concerning which thou askest me is sown, but the ingathering of it is not yet come. Unless, therefore, that which is sown be reaped, and unless the place where the evil is sown (= this world) shall have passed away, the field where the good is sown cannot come." The souls of the righteous "in their chambers" ask: "How long are we (to remain) here? When cometh the fruit upon the threshing-floor of our reward?" And to them the answer was given: "Even when the number of those like yourself is fulfilled! For he has weighed the age in the balance and with measure has measured the times, and by number numbered the seasons: Neither will he move nor stir things, till the measure appointed be fulfilled". A parable makes clear that the sin of the godless will not delay the end: "Go and ask the woman who is pregnant, when she has completed her nine months, if her womb can keep the birth any longer within her?" (4 Ezra 4:28-89. 35-40). The pictures from organic life and from childbirth illustrate the idea that the process of world history has to follow its predetermined order and will not end till the time is ripe: then the new age will come. In accordance with this view, the Syriac Apocalypse of Baruch speaks of the coming days, "when the time of the age has ripened and the harvest(s) of its evil and good seed has come" (2 Apoc. Baruch 70:2).

In the Epistle of James, the patient farmer who waits for the harvest until the earth has received the early and the late rain, serves as an illustration for Christians, who are to be patient in their waiting for the coming of the Lord (James 5:7-8).

Most interesting is a citation of unknown, but probably Jewish, origin which is found both in 1 and 2 Clement: "Wretched are the double minded who doubt in their soul and say: 'We have heard these things even in the days of our fathers, and behold we have grown old, and none of these things has happened to us.' Oh, foolish men, compare yourself to a tree: take a vine, first it sheds its leaves, then there comes a bud, then a leaf, then a flower, and after this the unripe grape, then the full bunch." In 2 Clement the text goes on: "So also my people has had tumults and afflictions; afterward it shall receive good things."[21] The idea is clear: as the ripe grape cannot appear until the whole process of growth has come to its end, so the future glory cannot come until everything has happened which according to the will of God must precede it. Whereas the author of 2 Clement adds an exhortation to endurance in hope, the author of 1 Clement, rather interestingly, stresses "how in a little time the fruit of the tree comes to ripeness," and concludes: "Truly his will shall be quickly and suddenly accomplished."

With such applications of the idea of growth in mind, we can now turn to the synoptic parable, or rather similitude, of the fig-tree: "From the fig tree learn its lesson (the parable): as soon as its branch becomes tender and puts forth its leaves, you know that summer is near. So also, when you see these things taking place, you know that he is near, at the very gates."[22] The regular order is here too the basis for the application: when the process of growth has reached a certain point it is possible to conclude that summer is at hand. In the same way the eschatological events follow each other according to a fixed scheme: from the occuring of the "signs" it is possible to know

---

[21]1 Clem. 23:2; 2 Clem. 11, from translations of K. Lake, The Apostolic Fathers I (LCL 24; Cambridge, Mass.: Harvard University Press, 1914).

[22]Mark 13:28-29, cf. Matt. 24:32-33; Luke 21:29-30.

that the kingdom of God has drawn near (so Luke).

The parable of the fig-tree has found its place in the synoptic "Apocalypse," which described the tribulations and catastrophes which are to precede the end and the coming of the Son of man. This fundamental idea is characteristic for the eschatological way of thinking in Primitive Christianity as well as in Jewish apocalyptic. There is a fixed plan and order for the eschatological series of events, which can be illustrated by the process of growth. But what happens is not due to a historic development following an immanent necessity, but to the creative activity of God, who, according to his own plan, leads history towards its goal. God sends his kingdom and the Messiah on the day he alone has fixed and which he alone knows. To men the end comes suddenly, like a thief in the night; but it does not come unprepared. There is a series of events leading up to it, including wonders and catastrophes. The pictures taken from organic growth illustrate the divine predetermination and eschatological necessity of what is happening.[23]

We do not know to what extent the apocalyptic picture in Mark 13 par. goes back to Jesus himself. It's present form certainly does not go back to Jesus. It is unlikely that the parable of the fig-tree originally had its place within an apocalyptic context of this kind, and it is quite possible that it was first spoken about what was already happening in Jesus' ministry: the signs of the coming of the kingdom were already to be seen by those who had eyes to see.[24] But even if this is so, the presupposition of the parable is an eschatological process corresponding to the growth of the tree in spring: the coming of the kingdom is preceded by events which indicate its nearness.

The modernization of the kingdom of God is not overcome simply by exchanging a modernistic conception of its immanence in favor of a transcendentalism which may be just as modern and unbiblical. To Jewish and ancient Christian thought the kingdom of God comes neither through an inner-worldly evolution nor through an unprepared catastrophe by which the transcendent breaks in. Even if the day itself comes suddenly and unexpectedly, there are certain events which have to precede it, by which God

---

[23]A similar eschatological way of thinking provides the background for Paul's thought. Cf. A. Fridrichsen, *The Apostle and His Message* (Uppsala: Lundequistska Bokhandeln, 1947).

[24]Cf. Matt. 11:2-6; Luke 12:54-56; Dodd, 137, note 1; Jeremias, *Parables*, 118f.; B.T.D. Smith, *The Parables of the Synoptic Gospels* (Cambridge: Cambridge University Press, 1937), 89-91.

according to his plan leads the course of history toward its end and its goal, the destruction of the old aeon and the inauguration of the new. In the Gospels we find a series of sayings speaking of what must happen: a divine *dei* expresses the eschatological necessity of what must take place before the establishment of the kingdom of god in glory.

Elijah must first come to restore all things; indeed, he has already come. It is necessary that offences come - woe to the man by whom they come. The Son of man must suffer many things. Jesus has a baptism with which to be baptized and a cup to drink, an initiation to messianic work and power to which he must submit. The disciples must face suffering and persecution, and many will be led astray before the end comes. Judgment will come upon the temple and the Jewish leaders. And the gospel must first be preached to all nations.[25] Certainly, there may be good reasons to doubt the authenticity of one or more of these utterances. But there are so many of them, and their form and context are so divergent, that we are not justified in doubting that Jesus shared the fundamental idea of which they are expressions, an idea which we have found to be fundamental both to Jewish and to primitive Christian eschatology.

We have every reason to assume that in the parables of growth the concept of growth is used in a similar way. To the growth which God gives in the sphere of organic life, in accordance with his own established order, corresponds the series of events by which God leads history toward the end of the world and the beginning of the new aeon, in accordance with his plan of salvation. This should, however, not be taken to mean that we must seek the point of the parables in this concept of growth. Rather, it is presupposed as a matter of course.

The parables of growth in Mark 4 and Matt. 13 are at the same time parables of contrast. The interest is not concentrated upon the process of growth in itself, but upon two stages in it, which are contrasted with each other. This corresponds to Jesus' concern that men neither speculate nor calculate about the course of the eschatological events, but interpret the signs of the time which should lead to repentance and conversion. Exegesis of the individual parables will show how they are made to serve this purpose, and how far our assumptions prove to be justified.

---

[25]Mark 9:11; Matt. 18:7; Mark 8:31, etc.; Luke 12:50; Mark 10:38; 13:9-13, etc.; Mark 12:1-12; 13:2; 13:10.

The Individual Parables

1. *The parable of the mustard-seed* has been preserved both in Mark (4:30-32) and in Q (Luke 13:18-19); Matthew conflates the two versions (13:31-32). We do not need to deal with the variants here. The smallness of the mustard seed was proverbial, so that the contrast between the little seed and the great, tree-like plant is in any case an essential point in the parable.

A feature common to Mark and the Q version is the illustration of great size: the birds of the air can find shelter in the shade of the great shrub (Mark), or in the branches of the tree (Luke). This has often been considered an allegorizing addition, pointing to the ingathering of all peoples within the church. But the clause can perfectly well be understood in a Jewish environment with its Old Testament background. The figure of a great tree giving shelter to the birds of the air is a traditional picture of a great kingdom.[26] In the allegory of the cedar and the eagle of Ezekiel 17, the coming Davidic kingdom is depicted as a tender twig from the lofty cedar which, when it is planted upon the high mountains of Israel, will grow into a noble cedar. In the shade of its branches, birds of every kind shall dwell. The allusion to such Old Testament images should not be seen as an allegorical addition; it has rather furnished the metaphor which is the nucleus of the whole parable.

If this is correct, the message of Jesus' parable is not the greatness of the coming kingdom; that was described already in the Old Testament. Neither is the parable intended to convey certainty that the kingdom will come; no pious Israelite doubted that. And it is not said that the kingdom is to come in the immediate future. That may be so, but in this parable the duration of the time of growth has no importance. That the kingdom in its future glory is to be like a tree in whose shade the birds find shelter, is taken for granted. The point of the parable must be that even the mustard plant is a "tree" of this kind, and yet the seed from which it grows is minute. In the same way, the initial appearance of the coming, glorious kingdom of God might seem quite insignificant. But despite the disparity of size there is an essential identity. The lesson of the parable is, thus, not directed toward the final consumation but emphasizes the "organic unity" between Jesus' present ministry in Israel and

---

[26]Cf. Dan. 4:10ff.; Ezek. 31:6; Judg. 9:15; Lam. 4:20; 1 Bar. 1:12. Connections between the King and the "tree of Life" may be in the background.

the future kingdom of God.

The parable should not be understood as a promise of a general kind. It answers a question of paramount importance to Jesus' contemporaries. What Israel expected was a glorious kingdom of God, a universal kingdom, in which the heathen sought shelter with Israel, its God and its Messiah. Of all this nothing was to be seen in the ministry of Jesus. Could that which was happening really be the beginning of God's establishment of his kingdom? The Baptist and his disciples were probably not the only ones who asked: "Are you he who is to come or shall we look for another?" The parable gives the answer: Look at the mustard seed; in spite of its smallness, a great plant, providing shelter for the birds, grows out of it. The apparent insignificance of what is happening does not exclude the secret presence of the coming kingdom.[27]

2. In Matthew and Luke the parable of the mustard seed has a parallel in *the parable of the leaven*. Leaven was a traditional metaphor for an evil beginning having great effects.[28] If the parable is to be interpreted as analogous to the parable of the must seed, it does not refer to usual eschatological metaphors, but makes an unusual figurative use of "leaven". The point must in any case be sought in the contrast between the small amount of hidden leaven and the great mass of dough to be leavened by it. Perhaps we should also take into account Dodd's observation "that the working of leaven in dough is not a slow imperceptible process. At first, it is true, the leaven is hidden and nothing appears to happen; but soon the whole mass swells and bubbles, as fermentation rapidly advances."[29]

The kingdom of God was expected to bring a complete change of all conditions of life for Israel and the world. It was not at all apparent that Jesus' ministry inaugurated any such revolutionary change. No, answers the parable, but neither is anything to be seen when a woman has hidden leaven in three measures of meal, and yet the entity is present which will soon make the whole dough bubble until it is all leavened. In a similar way, the proclamation of the kingdom and the signs which are happening signify the hidden presence of the kingdom of God.

---

[27]For a similar interpretation cf. T.W. Manson, *The Sayings of Jesus*, 123: "The preaching and healing mission of the Carpenter of Nazareth hardly seems to usher in the new age. Yet it does."

[28]Cf. Matt. 16:6, 11f.; 1 Cor. 5:6; Gal. 5:9; and parallels cited in Billerbeck.

[29]*The Parables of the Kingdom*, 192.

God has already taken the decisive action which initiates the series of eschatological events which will lead up to the coming of his kingdom and to the total change of all things which it is to bring.

3. The parable of *the seed growing secretly* (Mark 4:26-29) should be called more correctly the parable of the patient husbandman.[30] The essential contrast is not between the passivity of the husbandman and the growth of the seed, but between his passivity during the time of growth and his hurry to harvest at the moment the grain is ripe. As in the parable of the mustard seed, the concluding phrase contains a direct allusion to the Old Testament, and we have no reason to assume that it is secondary. The putting in of the sickle to the ripened grain is a traditional metaphor for judgment at the end of the world.[31] This metaphor forms the nucleus of the parable. By pointing to the behavior of an ordinary farmer, Jesus illustrates the proper attitude toward the eschatological harvest: it will come when the time is ripe, when the eschatological process leading up to it has reached its climax. It will not come any earlier, but then it will come without delay; it would be useless and meaningless to try to hasten its coming.

It is not difficult to determine the problem this parable solves. Unlike the Zealots, Jesus did not attempt to establish the kingdom by revolutionary activity. How could he be the Coming One? How could the kingdom be breaking in? The parable says that between the coming of the kingdom and the ministry of Jesus in Israel there is a relation similar to that between the harvest and the time of sowing and growth which has to precede it. Jesus does not need to try to establish the kingdom of God by any messianic activity. The events of the final era have already begun to take place, the forces of the kingdom are at work; when the time is ripe, at the end of the world, God will certainly intervene without delay, bring judgment and establish his kingdom in glory. To urge that Jesus, if he was the Coming One, should engage in messianic activity would be as foolish as to press the husbandman to be active in order to make the grain grow or to urge him to reap it before harvest-time.

---

[30]B.T.D. Smith, *The Parables of the Synoptic Gospels*, 129ff.

[31]Joel 4:13; Rev. 14:15.

4. The *parable of the drag-net* (Matt. 13:47-50) does not properly belong to the parables of growth, but its connection with the parables of tares makes it natural to treat it in this connection. The interpretation given in vv. 49-50 is strongly influenced by the specific terminology of the first evangelist,[32] but its main point is probably correct: the separation of good and bad fish alludes to the final judgment. The figurative language is, as Dodd has stated, to be seen in relation to the metaphor "fishers of men" (Mark 1:17 par.).[33]

Even in this parable a contrast is pointed out: When the net is thrown into the sea, it gathers fish of every kind. Only afterwards, when the net is drawn ashore, do the fishermen sit down to sort the fish, putting the good into vessels and throwing away the bad. This parable, like several others, answers those who criticized Jesus because he called "tax collectors and sinners" and associated with them.[34] Like the parables of growth, it has special reference to the contrast between the messianic expectations and the actual facts of Jesus' ministry. The purification of the people and the exclusion of all sinners was a common feature of eschatology. The Messiah himself could, as in Psalms of Solomon 17, be expected to drive out the sinners and gather the holy people. Jesus, on the contrary, gathered sinners around him. How could this have anything to do with the coming of the kingdom of God? Jesus answers by pointing to what fishermen do: first they throw their net into the sea and gather all kinds of fish; only afterwards do they separate the good from the bad. This is what fishers of men must do: Jesus calls all kinds of people and gathers them around him. On the day of judgment the unworthy will certainly be culled out.[35]

5. The *parable of the tares* (Matt. 13:24-30) may be seen as a parallel both to the parable of the seed growing secretly and to the parable of the drag-net. It differs from the other parables of growth in its novelistic form. In this case not a typical, but a singular incident is narrated, and the greater part of the story is told in dialog form. Some details are a bit embarrassing, especially the questions of the servants, vv. 27 and 28; but they may be due to the technique of story-telling.

---

[32]Jeremias, *Parables*, 85.
[33]Dodd, 188.
[34]Cf. Luke 15; Matt. 20:1-15; 22:1ff., etc.
[35]This interpretation is similar to that of Jeremias (*Parables*, 225-226), but it places more stress upon the secret presence of the kingdom in Jesus' ministry.

It is not necessary to assume that the story itself has suffered secondary allegorizing.

In this parable the essential contrast is between the time when grain and weeds grow together and the time of harvest, when weeds and wheat are separated, the weeds to be burned, the wheat to be gathered into the barn. When the harvest comes, and not before, will it be time for separation. The novelistic introduction to the story, in which an enemy sows the weeds, is only intended to make it quite clear that the husbandman sowed good seed free from weeds. He was not at all to be blamed either for the weeds in his field or because he allowed them to grow until the harvest.

The nucleus of this parable, too, is the traditional metaphor of the harvest, denoting the eschatological crisis at the end of the world. But the harvest is seen from another perspective than in the parable of the seed growing secretly. There it was the time for beginning the work of reaping, here it is the time for separating wheat from weeds. The allusion to the Old Testament is not so direct as in the parables of the mustard seed and the seed growing secretly. The final words of the parable, however, call to mind the words of the Baptist, which depict the Coming One as he who should stand with the winnowing fork in his hand: "He will clear his threshing floor and gather his wheat into the granary, but the chaff he will burn with unquenchable fire."[36] It does not seem unlikely that this parable, and perhaps also the other parables of growth, are spoken with special regard for expectations present in circles influenced by the preaching of John the Baptist.

The problem to which the parable of tares is directed is Jesus' failure to purify Israel of sinners and to create the pure community of the eschatological future. Such an attempt characterized various sectarian movements within Judaism.[37] The parable of the drag-net focuses on the scandal occasioned by Jesus' gathering sinners around him, while this parable focuses on his failure to gather a holy community of the pure. The answer is, however, analogous: it is as foolish to demand that Jesus weed out the sinners before the day of judgment as it would be to demand that the man in the story ask his servants to go and gather the weeds before the harvest time. Even if Jesus did not create the pure community, the powers of the age to come

[36]Matt. 3:12; cf. 4 Ezra 4:30, 35; 2 Bar. 70:2.
[37]Cf. Jeremias, *Parables*, 226f.

were already at work and the events of the final age already occurring, just as in the story good seed had been sown and the wheat was growing, even though there were weeds in the field.

6. The *parable of the Sower* is interpreted in the Gospels as a parable about the word and its effects. But it is likely, as many scholars have suggested, that it was originally intended as a parable of the kingdom, like the other parables of growth. The form makes it most natural to see the first three examples of what happened to the seed as variants of one and the same theme: much of the seed brought no fruit. To this threefold picture of failure the fruitfulness of the fourth portion of seed is to be contrasted.[38] The general sense of the parable is, accordingly, not that the fate of the seed depends on the nature of the soil but that the sower can get an extremely rich harvest even though much of the seed has been lost.

The question is how the parable should be more concretely applied. By Jeremias, and independently by Noack, the parable is understood as proclaiming: The kingdom of God will come, in spite of all failures, without anything being able to hinder it. Against this interpretation two objections can be raised: 1. It hardly takes sufficient account of the allusion to traditional eschatological ideas. 2. Interpreted in this way, the parable does not solve a real problem. Jesus' contemporaries did not doubt that the kingdom of God would come; but it was hard to believe that the words and deeds of Jesus were in an essential way linked up with the coming of the kingdom.

In the parable of the Sower the traditional metaphor of the eschatological harvest is again seen from another perspective, that of the richness of crops. Behind the figurative language lie very ancient fertility beliefs. Genesis 26:12 mentions that Isaac received one year a crop of one hundred fold to show that he was a tribal leader blessed by God. The widespread idea that the fertility of the land depends on the king has in the Old Testament found its classical expression in a royal psalm (Ps. 72:16). Later this is transposed into a hope for the future: during the reign of the Messiah, or more generally, in the coming happy days, the people will live in safety and the earth will give its fruits.[39] The pseudepigrapha and rabbinic sources give quite fantastic descriptions of the fertility of the messianic

---

[38]Jeremias, ibid., 150. Cf. B. Noack, "Om Sædemands-parabelen," *Festskrift til Jens Nørregaard* (Copenhagen: Gad, 1947), 203-213.

[39]Cf. e.g. Amos 9:13; Joel 2:19ff.; 4:18; Isa. 4:2; Jer. 31:12; Ezek. 34:27; 36:29f.

age. Ideas of this kind were still alive in primitive Christianity.[40]

In Israel, as in all the ancient world, agricultural life was intimately associated with religion, especially at great festivals. As time went on, the ideas connected with them were more or less spiritualized, often without losing the connection with the cult and agriculture. That "they that sow in tears shall reap in joy" becomes the symbol of the turning of the whole course of life for Israel.[41] Eschatological metaphors and similes were derived from agricultural language. Salvation can be conceived as harvest time; Israel, or the remnant of Israel, is to bring forth rich fruits in the days to come.[42] The figurative language of the Ezra-Apocalypse stands especially close to that of our parable. The problem raised by the destiny of sinners to perdition is answered by a parable: "For just as the husbandman sows much seed upon the ground and plants a multitude of plants, and yet not all which were sown shall be saved in due season, nor shall all that were planted take root; so also they that are sown in the world shall not all be saved" (8:41-42). The rich "harvest" is contrasted in 4 Ezra, not directly with the great loss of seed, but with the consequences of Adam's sin: "Reckon up, now, in thine own mind: if a grain of evil seed has produced so much fruit of ungodliness, when once the ears of the good seed shall have been sown without number, how great a floor shall they be destined to fill" (4:34). In this passage not only the reaping but also the sowing of the good seed is seen as an event belonging to the coming aeon; elsewhere too the saving act of God can be seen as a "sowing", not only as a harvest.[43]

As the other parables of growth, the parable of the Sower should be interpreted in the light of traditional figurative language. The rich harvest which the farmer in the story received symbolizes the greatness and glory of the assembly of the saved

---

[40]A wealth of material is given in Bill., IV 888-890, 948ff.; R. Patai, *Man and Temple* (London: T. Nelson, 1947), esp. 202ff. Cf. the citation from Papias, Irenaeus, *Adv. Haer*. V, 33:3-4.

[41]Ps. 126. Cf. S. Mowinckel, *Psalmenstudien II: Das Thronbesteigungsfest Jahväs und der Ursprung der Eschatologie* (Oslo: Videnskapsakademiet, 1922), 133-135; F.F. Hvidberg, *Weeping and Laughter in the Old Testament* (tr. N. Haislund; Leiden: Brill, 1962), 132-134.

[42]Cf. e.g. Hos. 6:11; Isa. 27:6, 12; 37:31.

[43]Cf. e.g. Hos. 2:21; Jer. 31:27f.; 1 Enoch 62:8. It may also be said that the Law has been sowed in men's hearts, 4 Ezra 9:31.

in the kingdom of God, or more generally, the coming blessings. The story contrasts this rich harvest to the things happening at the time of sowing and growth, when much of the seed was lost. This corresponds to the contrast between eschatological expectations and the ministry of Jesus: in many ways his work might seem to be a failure without result, or at least without enduring result.

The problem to which the parable of the Sower is directed is a special aspect of the problem with which all the parables of growth deal: Could Jesus be the Coming One, when in many respects it was quite apparent that he did not succeed in his work? Could this be the way in which the kingdom of God was to be inaugurated? The answer is: Look at the sower, who received an immensely rich harvest even though much of the seed was uselessly scattered. Though the ministry of Jesus in Israel often did not lead to anything, yet it was the condition for and the initial realization of the coming of the kingdom of God. The kingdom of God has not yet come in glory, but its powers are at work, its seed has been sown. The interpretation given in the Gospels is not entirely wrong when it says: "The Sower sows the word."

7. The Johannine saying about *the grain of wheat* (John 12:24) may also be mentioned in this connection. In the Fourth Gospel it stands in a typically Johannine context. But the logion itself is most certainly independent of this framework. It is probably derived from an old pre-Johannine tradition and may be a genuine saying of Jesus. The fate of the grain of wheat is here not simply a symbol for the resurrection -- life through death -- as e.g. 1 Corinthians 15:36f. The Johannine idea is "fruit through death," the rich fruit being the symbol for all men who are drawn to the exalted Christ (12:32).[44] We should, however, not fail to note that the idea of fruit also has eschatological connotations which are not entirely lost in the Gospel of John (cf. 4:35!). Is it too hazardous to assume that originally the idea was more consistently eschatological? To the audience of Jesus the words about the rich fruit, like the parable of the Sower, probably called to mind the coming eschatological fulfillment.

Like the synoptic parables of growth, the Johannine

---

[44]Cf. A.V. Ström, *Vetekornet* (ASNU; Stockholm: Diakonistyrelsen, 1944), 416-423.

simile alludes to two stages in organic life which stand in contrast to each other and yet are inseparably bound together. In this case the contrast is between the perishing of the old grain and the bearing of rich fruit. Once again we stand before the contrast between messianic expectations and the actual course of Jesus' life. No prophetic foreknowledge was necessary to see that Jesus, and perhaps also his followers, had to face the possibility of suffering and death. We know that this was a great offence: How could he be the Coming One, if his way led not to triumph but to death? Our simile gives the answer: "Unless a grain of wheat falls into the earth and dies, it remains alone; but if it dies, it bears much fruit." According to God's plan, the death of Jesus is the necessary precondition for the eschatological fulfillment (cf. Mark 10:37-40, Luke 12: 49-50). According to this interpretation the simile forms a close analogy to the parables of growth, the difference being that here not the present circumstances of Jesus' ministry but a future event, his death, is seen as the necessary precondition for the eschatological fulfillment.

The Eschatology of Jesus and the Church

If the message of the parables should be understood along the lines which I have sketched, Jeremias is wrong in saying that the presence of salvation is here being proclaimed, and only in short similitudes.[45] The parables of growth do proclaim the presence of salvation; but they do it in a special way, by preaching the presence of salvation and the activity of the powers of the kingdom in spite of all facts which seem to point to the contrary. So far, our investigation confirms the view that the parables in narrative form are used principally for apologetic or polemic purposes.

In the parables of growth Jesus faces problems which must have been acute in his surroundings, in narrower as well as in wider circles. The answer to the problem which arose from the contrast between messianic expectations and the actual facts of Jesus' ministry is given by references to similar contrasts in organic life and agriculture: a great tree, yielding shelter to the birds, can grow out of the smallest seed. Before harvest, a time passes in which the seed grows without any activity of the farmer. Before weeds and wheat are separated, they grow together in the field. Before the sower gets his rich harvest, much of

---

[45]*Parables*, 123-124.

his seed has been lost. In the same way, before the kingdom of God comes in glory, there must be a time in which its powers are at work, but in which what happens may seem insignificant, during which no zealot activity is undertaken to establish the kingdom. During this time the power of evil are still at work and the pure community is not yet created, and the activity of the power of the kingdom often has no enduring results.

The parables of growth presume that as the harvest cannot begin until the grain is ripe, so the eschatological consummation cannot come until the day which is ordained by God. But they show no interest in the process of growth and ripening for its own sake. If the Johannine similitude stating the necessity of Jesus' death is left aside, they say nothing about what has to happen before the end. All interest is concentrated upon an initial and a final stage in the process of growth, upon the ministry of Jesus in Israel and the coming of the kingdom in glory and power. No attempt is made to give a complete apocalyptic picture of the events leading up to the end.

Manifestly, it is the final stage in the process of growth that most directly corresponds to the kingdom of God as it was traditionally conceived: the full-grown "tree", the putting in of the sickle, the burning of the weeds and gathering of the wheat, the manifold fruit of the seed. Whether the coming of the kingdom corresponds only to the final stage of growth, or to the initial stage as well, or even to the whole process of growth, is a question of terminology to which we should not attach too great importance. Jesus usually speaks of the kingdom of God as still belonging to the future, but with regard to "proleptic realization" he can also say: "The kingdom of God has come upon you" (Matt. 12:28). Under certain circumstances he could also speak of the present situation not only as a time of sowing, but also as a harvest (Matt. 9:37, cf. John 4:35). He is not concerned with a terminological distinction between the coming of the kingdom in secrecy in the present time, and its future, manifest coming in glory.

We may say that the parables of growth teach that the kingdom has a "history", a period of its secret presence preceding its final revelation. But this does not mean that the kingdom is a spiritual or social entity, "growing" and developing. The kingdom is in itself always perfect; only the conditions of its presence change and are different in this world from what they shall be in the coming one. In this sense we may say that Jesus taught two stages in the coming of the kingdom, one corresponding to the time of sowing and growth, the other corresponding to the harvest. The parables do not, however, call for a theoretical insight into the nature of the kingdom and its history, but for a faith which is not offended by the humble appearance of the kingdom in the present time.

It therefore makes sense that the evangelist has related the parables of growth to the saying about "the mystery of the kingdom of God" given to the disciples (Mark 4:11-12 par.). The real message of these parables could, in fact, only be grasped by those who in faith had understood the mystery of the secret presence of the kingdom. This does not mean that we should accept the parable theory of Mark, with the stress it lays upon the enigmatic form of the parables, which were then interpreted to the disciples. But it is an advantage of the interpretation proposed here that it does not set the conjectured original meaning of the parables in too great contrast to the applications which are actually found in the Gospels.

The detailed interpretations of the parables of the Sower and of the Tares found in the Gospels are not entirely wrong. But they introduce a homiletical application of details, which leaves aside the central point and draws interest away from it. The parables are used for paraenetic purposes. The parable of the drag-net for example seems to be understood by Matthew as a warning to church members, that they should not believe themselves to have received a guarantee of final salvation; the end of the world is to bring a separation of the wicked from the just, even among those who have been gathered into the church.[46]

It is often rather difficult to say exactly how the evangelists wish the parables to be understood, and we need not go into detail here. It is sufficient to observe that the central message of these parables, the eschatological significance of the earthly ministry of Jesus, is no longer a matter of central importance. It is not difficult to understand why this should be so. In the early church, the inauguration of the eschatological era was proclaimed in the form of an explicit christology, with its center in the message of the death, resurrection, and heavenly enthronement of Christ. The germinal form of this message, implying the secret presence of the kingdom in the preaching and healing activity of the Son of man,

---

[46]According to Matt. 13:36ff., vs. 47-50 are part of esoteric teaching of the disciples; cf. Matt. 7:21-23; 22:11-13, 25.

was to a certain extent superseded and was no longer appropriate; the parables could find new applications. A very interesting result of our investigation is that, at least in the case of the parables of growth, the original meaning of the words of Jesus was more, and not less, "christological" than the interpretation given to them in the synoptic Gospels.[47] This is indeed a result which neither critics nor apologists in former generations foresaw.

The "christology" contained in these parables is, however, implicit and indirect. They can be said to contain the answer to the question: "Are you he who is to come?" But they no more contain a direct claim to messiahship than did the answer given to the disciples of John. They speak of what is happening as part of the events which have to precede the end of the world, as signs of the coming of the kingdom, and, indeed, of its secret, dynamic presence. The stories themselves do not even make it clear that they have Jesus' ministry in view. That may have been clear in the concrete situations in which they were originally spoken. If the questions to which they are directed were only latent, they must have had to some degree the character of riddles. But in their mysterious and indirect form the parables do make the claim that Jesus is the Coming One.

---

[47]Cf. R. Otto, *The Kingdom of God and the Son of Man* (tr. F.V. Filson and B.L. Woolf; London: Lutterworth Press, 1938), 141-146; Hoskyns and Davey, 190f. and 206f.

CONCLUSION

The Early Church and Jesus

To speak about the memory of Jesus is to speak simultaneously about the person remembered and about those who remembered him and who later passed the traditions on to others, some of whom incorporated them into literary works. For purposes of historical investigation it is necessary to approach the traditions with two distinct sets of questions, one pertaining to their historical accuracy, the other to the ways in which they were used. The two sets of questions are obviously interrelated, so much so that the distinction between them might be considered a scientific abstraction. It is helpful and necessary, but there is some risk that the questions asked may prejudge the answers given. A brief sketch of some tendencies in modern gospel criticism may illustrate this.

Recent studies have to a large extent been shaped by the form critical method which gained prominence around 1920. The early form critics classified small units of oral tradition and tried to relate the various forms to their *Sitz im Leben*, i.e. to recurring occasions on which they were used such as worship, preaching, controversies, etc. More recently, form criticism has been integrated with a broader sociological approach to religious history, including early Christianity. All texts, literary as well as oral, are addressed with questions about their social setting and function. An eventual consequence of this may be that the Jesus Christ of the early church is seen as a symbolic figure and his story as an etiological myth, whose function it was to warrant the existence and safeguard the identity of the community of believers. The same tendency can also be stated in more theological terms: What really matters is not the historical Jesus but rather the collective memory of the worshiping community and its continuous tradition.

The social setting of the Jesus tradition has usually been sought and found in the mission and/or the communal life of the church which proclaimed Jesus as the crucified and risen Christ. Only a minority of scholars have taken serious account of the possibility that the disciples quoted sayings of Jesus and told stories about him while he was still alive. As a consequence, the interest in the social function of the tradition has tended to result in a social isolation of Jesus himself. This tendency is further strengthened by the widely accepted principle that among sayings attributed to Jesus, those are most likely to be authentic which can not have originated either in contemporary Judaism or in the church after Easter ("the criterion of dissimilarity"). The irony of the matter is that the application of rigid critical principles opens the doors to new versions of a modernized Jesus who is separated both from the church and from his Jewish environment but relevant for our time.

This brief sketch is a caricature; all nuances have been left out. The oversimplification is permissable because neither of the tendencies is due to the arbitrariness of individual scholars or schools. As possibilities, both of them are inherent in the questions asked and the methods employed. In fact, both trends are modern variations of ancient themes. Throughout the centuries the memory of Jesus, contained in the New Testament, has been used to legitimize the existence, doctrine, practice, and even the power of the church. But the sayings and the story of Jesus have also inspired men and women to imitate his life in poverty, to call for reformation, or to pronounce judgment on church establishments. Thus, the history of Christianity shows what critical study can only confirm, that the problem of the relationship between the church and Jesus is given by the New Testament writings themselves. The treatment of these writings as sources of historical information, either about Jesus or about the early church, has not created the tension but has aggravated it.

The essays in this collection have in one way or another dealt with the relationship between Jesus and the church. Here I would like to add some more general reflections and begin with a brief survey of the New Testament evidence. Ancient summaries of the content of missionary preaching like Romans 1:2-5 and 1 Corinthians 15:3-8 center around the crucifixion and/or resurrection of Christ. The proclamation of the gospel is likely to have concluded with a call to repentance and baptism (cf. e.g. Acts 2:38), but there is no evidence that the kerygma included any direct reference to the church.[1] The gospel proclaimed Jesus Christ and in doing so it laid the foundation for the church.

Some texts, both within and outside the New Testament, explicitly relate Christ's redeeming work to the church. Titus 2:14 provides a good example: "...Jesus Christ, who gave himself for us to redeem us from all iniquity and to purify for himself a people of his own who are zealous for good deeds." Such formulations are commemorative rather than kerygmatic.[2] They speak of the creation of a new community as the purpose of Christ's ministry in order to remind persons who are already Christians of the privilege and the responsibility given to them. As evident from writings like Hebrews and Revelation, reminders of this type may very well be combined with stern warnings addressed to individuals or to churches which fail to live up to the grace bestowed upon them.[3]

In his letters, Paul interprets the significance of the gospel, relating it both to specific problems in local churches and to the universal unity of Jews and Gentiles in Christ. Occasionally, he refers to sayings of Jesus as norms of conduct and of church order, but he adapts them to the circumstances with a considerable amount of freedom (cf. 1 Cor. 7:12-17 and 9:14-15). It is therefore all the more important to observe that he qualifies the church's unity with Christ by insisting on two historical facts: Jesus was crucified, and he was a Jew. On this basis, Paul opposes Christians who boast of their power, wisdom, and righteousness or who in their self-sufficient triumphalism despise the Jews (cf. especially 1 Cor. 1-4 and Rom. 9-11).

As we can see from the letters of Paul, there is no direct correlation between the number and the accuracy of specific

---

[1]In *The Apostolic Preaching and its Developments*, (New York: Harper and Row, 1935, 41 [7 .ed., 1951, 23]), C.H. Dodd wrote that part of the earliest kerygma was "that by virtue of the resurrection, Jesus had been exalted at the right hand of God, as Messianic head of the new Israel," but the last clause is a free paraphrase without foundation in the texts.

[2]Cf. Eph. 1:22-23; 2:14-16; 5:25-27; Col. 1:18-20; Heb. 2:14-17; 13:12, 20; 1 Peter 2:4-10; Rev. 1:5; 5:9-1-; Acts 20:28; Barnabas 5:7; Irenaeus, Apostolic Preaching, 35-39; Hippolytus, Apostolic Tradition 4. Some of these texts are liturgical. Several of them represent the "teleological pattern" described above in Chapter 2, "Form-critical Observations."

[3]Cf. esp. Heb. 2:1-4; 6:4-8; 10:26-31; Rev. 2:5, 16, 20-25; 3:1-3, 15-19; and also 1 Peter 4:17.

memories and the degree to which early Christian writings make Jesus stand forth as a distinct person with a specific identity of his own, not merely the symbolic hero of the community that calls upon his name. Yet, the writings of the evangelists have a special importance. They do not follow any uniform pattern, but all of them relate the story of Jesus to Christian communities of their own time, reminding them that their Lord and savior is the Jesus who taught and healed the sick in Palestine, who was opposed by the religious leaders and finally executed by the Romans.[4]

Mark stresses the mystery that surrounded the earthly life of Jesus, and the inadequacy of his disciples. Thereby he warns the Christians of his day, to whom the mystery has been revealed, not to seek their own glory and power, lest they too should prove to be inadequate.

Matthew tells the story of Jesus in such a way that it warrants the emergence of a church of Christ, distinct from the Jewish nation. At the same time he represents Jesus as the teacher whose messianic interpretation of the will of God remains binding for the members of the church. As the coming judge, Jesus will only recognize those who have done what he said.[5]

John seems to have little interest in church order and organization. He makes the goal of Jesus' ministry the gathering of a group of disciples who are united to Jesus, to his Father, and to one another. After Jesus' ascension all those who heed his voice will be drawn into this fellowship. The sayings of Jesus are the words of eternal life, not simply rules of conduct. Yet, not all who believe are true disciples but only those who remain faithful to the words of Jesus.

Luke is too much of a historian and an apologist to use the memory of Jesus to warn or rebuke his own constituency. In his two volume work, a period in which the gospel was preached to the Jews intervenes between the time of Jesus and the time of the Gentile mission. There is a striking contrast between his representation of Jesus as the helper and savior of the poor, afflicted, and outcast within Israel and his emphasis on the piety and prominence of men and women who later became Christians. It

---

[4]This and the following paragraphs draw upon an essay on the theme "Kerygma and Church in the Four Gospels," published in Norwegian in *NTT* 60 (1959), 1-20. An English translation of the entire article has not been included because much of its content overlaps with the articles on the individual gospels.

[5]Cf. Matt. 7:13-27; 10:37-42; 13:36-50; 16:27; 18:23-35; 24:45-51, and see G. Bornkamm, "End-Expectation and Church in Matthew," in Bornkamm-Barth-Held, *Tradition and Interpretation in Matthew*, (Philadelphia: Westminster, 1963), 15-51.

is not clear to what extent the author was himself aware of this contrast, but he does limit the validity of some of Jesus' most radical injunctions to the period before his death (cf. Luke 22:35-38). It is easily understandable that existentialist interpreters have felt little or no sympathy for Luke's theology. But just because he has a sense of distance, Luke sets Jesus off from the later church as a historical person with a discrete identity of his own -- yet still alive. Regardless of the author's intention, features from the Lukan portrait of Jesus have time and again been used to call the churches of the satisfied and affluent to repentance.

In all New Testament writings there is a close relationship between the church and Jesus, but within this relationship Jesus retains priority and sovereignty. Without doubt, it has always been possible to use the sovereignty of the Lord to conceal his servants' will to power and to enforce conformity upon lax and dissident members of the church. But at least in the major writings of the New Testament, the memory of Jesus transcends ecclesiastical expediency and collective needs. For this reason, both loyal Christians and outside critics have been able to use the Jesus tradition to rebuke the state and the practices of the church at any given time and place. As we have seen, already some of the New Testament authors themselves have done this. In doing so, they did not follow any uniform pattern but drew upon various aspects of the tradition, using it for their own purposes. Just this diversity within the New Testament canon makes it impossible for a conservative or critical orthodoxy to resolve the problem of the relations between the church and Jesus once and for all times. It rather calls for spiritual discernment, and the answer depends upon the ability to distinguish between the spirits.

The quest for the historical Jesus has increased our awareness that before there was any Christian church Jesus lived and died within the social context of first century Palestinian Judaism. Yet, our knowledge of Jesus remains dependent upon the memory of his disciples. The traditions were shaped by the experiences, practices, and needs of the early church, but the memory of Jesus must also have been one of the contributing factors which shaped the life of the community that emerged after his death. An empty tomb, post-mortem appearances, and religious enthusiasm could not possibly have called the Jerusalem church into being unless the life and death of Jesus had already created the context within which the disciples interpreted their experiences. In order to gain historical probability, any reconstruction has to relate Jesus to his Jewish environment. It must also be able to explain why Jesus was crucified and why the conviction that God had vindicated him made the disciples think of themselves and their adherents as "the church of God," "the saints," who were, at the end of time, heirs of God's promises to his people. The "criterion of dissimilarity" should only be used in conjunction with historical considerations of synchronic similarity and diachronic continuity.

Any reconstruction of the life and message of Jesus is at best an approximation. My own essay on "The Parables of Growth" is more conjectural than I was aware of when I wrote it. Yet, I would like to think that it retains some value. The proposals are based upon the assumption that Jesus used metaphors and parables in a way that was understandable to his contemporaries. He even presupposed much of Jewish eschatology in order to explain what ran contrary to expectations: the apparently insignificant beginnings, the apparent failure that preceded the rich harvest, and so on.[6] If these parables, and other sayings as well, interpret what happened during the ministry of Jesus as a hidden, proleptic presence of the kingdom of God, this presence included his whole activity, not only preaching and healing but also gathering and sending out of disciples, and table fellowship with "sinners and tax collectors." This means that the religious attention and the eschatological hopes of the disciples were focused on Jesus already before his death, and just that is what we have to assume in order to explain, to some degree, what happened afterwards.

Already the eschatology of Jesus is likely to have had a communal aspect, related to his own disciples as well as to the

---

[6]This paragraph and the next summarize and modify suggestions that were originally made in the concluding part of "The Parables of Growth," on the pages which have been left out in this volume. The original conclusion may be one of the reasons that made some readers and critics think that I would attribute an independent, thematic significance to the idea of growth and the corresponding idea of an eschatological series of events. The real point of the essay was, however, that Jesus used the image of organic growth in order to make his hearers draw the concludion that apparent contrasts do not exclude close interconnections or even a kind of identity, and to apply this to the relationship between the ministry of Jesus and the coming of the kingdom of God. I willingly concede that all abstract formuations of the salient point of a parable and its application are wooden, and that formulations like "proleptic presence" and "eschatology in process of realisation" are less than adequate. But in spite of J.D. Crossan, *In Parables* (New York: Harper and Row, 1973) and other recent studies, I still think that Jesus used parables as rhetorical means of persuasion, that the parables had a salient point, and that we have to ask what reality they originally applied to. A comparison between his interpretation of the Parable of the Treasure and mine (see below) should make the basic contrast clear.

people of Israel and the future table fellowship in the kingdom of God. If historical, as I think it is, the symbolic number of "the Twelve" would confirm this. The famous saying "You are Peter, and on this rock I will build my church" can hardly be authentic. In its present form it is part of a secondary addition to the Caesarea Philippi pericope (contrast Matt. 16:13-23 and Mark 8:27-33). Yet, the midrashic interpretation, given in Matthew 16:17, could possibly be correct in that the symbolic name "rock" (*kēfe, petros*) suggested that a house, perhaps a temple, was to be built upon the rock. None of the contemporaries of Jesus would have thought of the church of Christ upon earth, as it later came into being. The symbolic name would rather have been associated with the "house" of the kingdom of God, the assembly into which the elect were to be gathered.[7] In that case, the name would be a prophetic sign, stating that the time for building God's eschatological house had come; the rock had already been found.

If Jesus in symbolic terms identified the Galilean fisherman Simon bar Jonah as the "rock" of the assembly that was to gather in the kingdom of God, he stated an offensive paradox. The analogy with the parable of the mustard seed proves that he could have done so, but the interpretation remains conjectural. The symbolic meaning of the name "Boanerges" or "sons of the thunder" given to the sons of Zebedee, has been lost in the process of tradition. Could it possibly have been that where the claps of thunder are heard, the eschatological thunderstorm which is to come upon the earth, is not far away? Whatever the exact meaning, the fact that Jesus gave symbolic names to some of his disciples indicates that he made them a part of his prophetic message.[8]

Many references to the disciples are likely to be secondary, but we should not overlook the other possibility, that some allusions to them were lost in the process of tradition. The parable of the hidden Treasure (Matt. 13:44) may be an example.

The story of a man who found a hidden treasure was a

---

[7]The possibility of this association is indicated by the alleged saying of Jesus, that he would destroy the temple and build another (Mark 14:58; 15:29; cf. John 2:19).

[8]For analogies, cf. the symbolic names which Hosea and Isaiah gave to their children (Hos. 1:4, 6, 8-9; Isa. 7:3 (,14); 8:3-4; further Gen. 17:5; 32:28, etc.), and from a later period, the name of "Bar Kochba" and the name "City of Refuge," which is given to Asenath, the symbol of conversion, in the Jewish-Hellenistic novel Joseph and Asenath (15:7). The pericope in Matthew 16:13ff. has some formal analogies to other stories about the giving of a symbolic name. It does also contain a paradox: Peter is both the rock of the church and a stumbling block.

popular tale used in some cases as a parable. The moral of the story may be that it was sheer luck or pure grace that the man found the treasure, but he would never have found it unless he had worked hard, digging the soil.[9] Jesus has given a new twist to the story, adding the feature that the man sold all that he had in order to purchase the field in which the treasure was hidden. A unique opportunity made him disregard ordinary standards of prudence and risk everything. Matthew seems to understand the parable as a call for radical obedience to the teaching of Jesus, addressed to the disciples and through them to all Christians. Many modern interpreters prefer to take it as a call to repentance, stressing either the sacrifice or the joy that makes it meaningful. Yet, the argumentative point would be much clearer if the parable was not originally meant as an exhortation but related to something that had occurred. Jesus and his disciples, and John the Baptist before them, had left home, family, and work. Thus, they had disregarded what was considered their religious duty, but -- the parable argues -- this kind of behavior is reasonable when the kingdom of heaven is at stake.

In social terms, the original disciples can best be described as a group of persons who followed an itinerant charismatic leader. We cannot separate the historical Jesus from his followers any more than we can separate the Christ of faith from the church. It would be misleading to think that during the lifetime of Jesus the presence of the kingdom was limited to the person of Jesus, whereas after Easter it was extended to include the church.[10] The emergence of a new, messianic community was correlative to faith in the vindication of the crucified Messiah. A new epoch had dawned, and the fellowship between disciples and Master was transformed into a communion between the church and the risen Lord. But neither had the relationship between the Master and his followers lacked intimacy, nor did the church gain a religious significance of its own, separable from its relation to Jesus. There was a danger that the tradition about Jesus would

---

[9]Philo, *On the Immutability of God*, presupposes that the tale was already current and open to various applications. For rabbinic parallels, see A. Marmorstein, *The Old Rabbinic Doctrine of God*, (II [1936], repr. New York: KTAV 1968), 13-16. In the Gospel of Thomas, Logion 109, the parable of Jesus has, apparently, been conflated with some other version of the tale.

[10]In *ST* 5, 1951, this point was elaborated at some length, in discussion with W.G. Kümmel and A. Oepke. Kümmel has later critized my position and modified his own in the article "Jesus und die Anfänge der Kirche," *ST* 7, 1953, 1-27, now in *Heilsgeschehen und Geschichte*, (Marburg: Elwert, 1965), 289-389, with an excellent survey of literature up to 1953.

be made subservient to church structures, or that it would vanish into myth and gnosis. But the composition and canonization of the gospels restored the importance of the memory of Jesus as basis of and criterion for the church.

It would have been a theological disaster if we had really been faced with a choice between an isolated, allegedly historical Jesus and a Christ-myth, or a collective memory of the church. The interrelation and the tension between the church and the crucified Jew, Jesus of Nazareth, to whom its confession and doctrines refer, remains essential for the vitality of Christianity. Historical criticism has sharpened the tension and thereby complicated the problems, but it can also contribute to their clarification, even if it does not solve them.